The Education of Anna

By the same author:

Chennault and the Flying Tigers
A Thousand Springs
Way of a Fighter

This is an anthorized Edition Reprinted in
TAIWAN by **IMPERIAL BOOK, SOUND & GIFT CO.**
615 Lin Shen North Road Taipei, Taiwan.
Republic of China

FOR SALE IN TAIWAN ONLY: NOT FOR EXPORT

Frist Printing ·················January 1980

作者： **Anna Chennault**

本書經作者　陳香梅授權皇家圖書有限公司
在台灣地區發售。

發 行 人：陳　　　　明　　　　輝
發 行 人：皇 家 圖 書 有 限 公 司
地　　址：台 北 市 林 森 北 路 615 號
電　　話：5 9 1 7 6 3 3 · 5 9 6 7 0 3 9
郵政劃撥：1 　 8 　 9 　 0 　 3 　 　 號
總 經 銷：林 口 圖 書 有 限 公 司
地　　址：台北市中山北路三段54之3號
電　　話：5 　9 　5 　1 　5 　6 　5
總 經 銷：嘉 新 圖 書 有 限 公 司
地　　址：台 北 市 中 山 北 路 二 段101號
電　　話：5 8 1 4 6 6 9 · 5 7 1 5 3 9 5
登 記 證：局 版 台 業 字 1 1 9 7 號
中 華 民 國 六 十 八 年 　 月 　 日 第 一 版
印 刷 廠：文 巧 印 刷 有 限 公 司
地　　址：板橋市中山路二段531巷17弄10號
電　　話：9 　5 　2 　4 　2 　1 　9

定　價：新 台 幣　　120　元

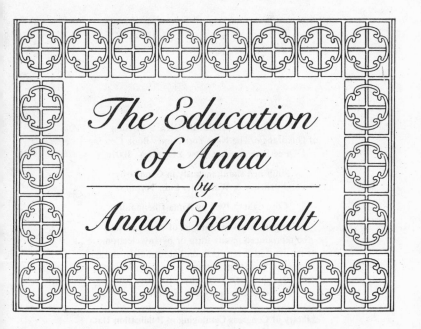

The Education of Anna

by

Anna Chennault

Times
BOOKS

Published by TIMES BOOKS, a division
of Quadrangle/The New York Times Book Co., Inc.
Three Park Avenue, New York, N.Y. 10016

Published simultaneously in Canada by
Fitzhenry & Whiteside, Ltd., Toronto.

Library of Congress Cataloging in Publication Data

Chennault, Anna.
The education of Anna.

1. Chennault, Anna. 2. Chennault, Claire Lee,
1890-1958. 3. China—Social life and customs.
4. China—Description and travel—1901-1948.
5. Politicians—United States—Biography.
I. Title. E748.C524A33   973'.04'951   79-51436
ISBN 0-8129-0844-9

Manufactured in the United States of America.

This book is dedicated to all my teachers,
and to the best teacher of them all,
Thomas G. Corcoran.

# *Acknowledgments*

would like to thank Wendy Law-Yone for editing this manuscript. I am also indebted to Jean Mesle and Joan Lee for their help in retyping. I would also like to thank Claire K. P. Lee for doing the proofreading with me.

Contents

(Illustrations follow page 86)

The Education of Anna

The Book of History

1

In Peking, where I was born, the new planting season began in early summer when willow catkins dropped like snow and paper kites with bells and wind chimes turned into musical butterflies in the sky.

It was during this season that I was born, but the occasion was not a joyful one for my parents, who were counting heavily on a boy. I learned this from servants and relatives over the years. "When your sister was born," they said, "she, too, was a disappointment. But because she was the first born, your grandparents sent pickled pigs' feet, red eggs, and sweetmeats to friends and relatives, and there was a big celebration. When you came along, there was nothing to celebrate. Another girl! What a shame! Your grandmother Chan even suggested to your father that he take a concubine."

But I was born during a season of festivals, and so it always seemed to me that my birthdays were great events. For I was a child of the Double Fifth—the fifth day of the fifth moon of the Chinese calendar—and on this day fell one of the grandest entertainments of the year.

I remember the ceremonial boom of the cannon. Even before its echoes were gone, the temple bells chimed in, the gongs sang in brassy voices, and the kettledrums rattled in the old Drum Tower. The servants would dress my sisters and me like dolls and take us to the ruins of the Summer Palace adjoining the old

3

Forbidden City. I have memories of a log bridge, an old water reservoir, and a winding pathway through a jumble of massive, broken-down pillars and arches where Emperors and Empresses had lived. At last we would come to the North Lake, not far from the dazzling marble houseboat which "The Old Buddha," the Empress Dowager Tz'u-hsi, had spent the money budgeted for a navy to build. There, at the lake, we cast offerings of sweet rice cakes wrapped in lotus leaves, and joined the crowd of spectators, tea and chestnut vendors, musicians, jugglers, and fortune-tellers, all waiting for the wild regatta to begin.

Soon the noisy crews would appear, heaving their dragon boats into the water. The boats were long and sleek, wide enough for only two abreast, and prone to tipping over easily at slow speeds. They held what seemed to me to be hundreds of rowers, though the actual number was more like fifty. At the prow of each boat was a glaring dragon; amidships, a huge drum to beat the rhythm for the oarsmen. Laughing and shouting, the crewmen would line up their unsteady craft to wait for the starting signal. Then off they went, thrashing through the water to the pounding of drums, the banks of oars sending out clouds of spray. On shore, we children would cheer them on with clenched fists, hoarse voices, and firecrackers that shattered the air long after the winners had collected their prize.

The Dragon Boat, or Fifth Moon Festival, marks the turn of a year, an excellent time to pray to the gods for a good harvest. Several different legends explain the origins of the dragon boat. One says it first appeared when the early boat people who lived along the coasts and waterways of China decided to honor the watergods as insurance for plentiful fish. To placate the hungry ghosts as well—so the legend goes—the fishermen tossed offerings of rice into the water.

Another version explains the dragon-boat race as a mock battle on earth, a contest between representative dragons designed to incite war among the dragon spirits in the sky. The clash then produces the thunder and rain necessary for a good harvest.

A third myth describes the efforts of a musician in the T'ang dynasty who played so sweetly that clouds stopped to listen and flower buds burst open with joy. So enchanting was his music that when a deadly epidemic ravaged the land, he lured the demons out of the city by building a gargantuan boat and directing a million spirits to beat drums on it.

But my favorite legend was the one I learned in my third year of school, at age seven. Our teacher, Li Chieh, was a young man with eyebrows like the brush strokes of an angry calligrapher, thick and black. When he found that I was born on the Double Fifth, he told me I was destined to be a writer, because the Dragon Boat Festival began as a tribute to one.

"About two thousand four hundred years ago," he said, "a son was born to wealthy parents related to the royal house of Ch'u. His name was Ch'u Yüan, and he grew up to be a brilliant student and a great leader. But he lived at a time when the country was divided among many kingdoms, all fighting and plotting against one another. It happened that in Ch'u Yüan's kingdom, some were jealous of him and went to the Emperor to tell evil lies about him. When the Emperor heard these stories, he believed them, and punished Ch'u Yüan by ordering him to leave his home and country and never come back.

"For years Ch'u Yüan wandered about in distant places like a restless ghost, writing poems so sorrowful that they drew 'tears of blood,' bitter tears. At last, unable to bear his loneliness, he wrote a final poem and drowned himself in Lake T'ung Ting.

"It is said that when the fishermen in the region found out about this, they formed large groups and spread out over the waters to search for the missing poet. They searched for days and days, but at last lost hope of ever finding the body. So they scattered bundles of cooked rice into the lake, to appease the ghosts that might be following Ch'u Yüan's restless soul, and to keep the fish from feeding on his body."

The story of Ch'u Yüan stayed with me, and years later, when I began to study his poetry, I came across his last poem and was struck by its brisk courage:

HUGGING SAND IN THE BOSOM

Safe in packs the city dogs bark
At anything they do not know.
To hate the great, distrust the good,
Of course, is only right.

With a strong heart and ready mind
What have I to fear?
Since I know there is no escape from death,
Let me not cling to a foolish love of life.

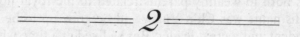

My paternal Grandfather Chan was a man of high expectations and precocious financial talent. The expectations had been shaped by the spirit of Sun Yat-sen's Republican movement, in which he had been active. The talent was apparent when, at age thirty, he became the first president of the China Merchant Steamship Company.

Emboldened by this success and impatient to set progress in motion, Grandfather Chan decided to gamble on public transportation. It was the turn of the century, when trolley cars were beginning to nudge the horses and carriages off the streets in the cities of the West. But in China public transportation was still muscle-powered, propelled by coolies who trotted in front of rickshas, and stooped under the burden of sedan chairs. Grandfather felt the moment had come to start the transition from muscle to machinery. He bought a streetcar company and began operating it on the streets of Hong Kong.

The streetcar was a miserable failure. The people refused to go anywhere near it. It was a mysterious contraption, and therefore to be distrusted. How could a car run of its own accord?

Where were the humans who propelled it? The devil had to be behind it—the devil of foreign gadgetry.

The miscarriage cost Grandfather his fortune. His wife implored him repeatedly to cut his losses and sell; his partners had long since pulled out. But with the tenacity of the desperate, he clung to his crumbling enterprise.

By New Year's Eve of the year 1910, he had exhausted all his credit and debtors were closing in. New Year's Eve was the beginning of both the lunar and fiscal year in China, a time when debts had to be liquidated and accounts begun on a clean slate. To carry debt and delinquency into the new year was considered bad luck, a superstition reinforced by the reality of the credit system.

Grandfather made a few last-ditch attempts to raise money—trying to mortgage some of his land, for instance—but it was too late. As the strictures of commerce and custom tightened, he lost both shirt and face.

The festivities, so the family story goes, were in full swing, noisy with banquets and firecrackers, and overflowing with food and drink and inflated purse-pride. Purse-pride meant that shipments of fruits, cakes, and sweets which arrived at each house had to be sampled, but then returned, the message being, *Thank you for your much too generous gift.* A chicken or duck or suckling pig had to be divided in half, one half kept, the other sent back with yet another gift to compliment the original donor's generosity.

The volume of gifts exchanged among the wealthy families in Grandfather's circle of friends was such that the bearers and runners hurrying from house to house, delivering and collecting, had to be rewarded, too.

In that ever-widening abyss between the wild prodigality of New Year's Eve and his own depleted means and spirits, Grandfather lost all hope.

He was standing in his library on the fourth floor of his mansion in Canton. His wife, dressed in ceremonial red, was flitting in and out of the room with last-minute preparations. His concubines, dressed in pink, were downstairs with the children. The servants were all occupied.

Suddenly, he picked up a bottle of brandy as though to quaff it, but splashed it instead into his eyes. It was a fumbling effort to blind himself just before leaping off the balcony.

It happened before his wife's very eyes. The moment she saw what was happening, or was about to happen, she rushed to him as fast as she could—not very fast since she had bound feet—and reached him, screaming, just in time to feel the tip of his silk mandarin gown slip through her delicate fingers. He fell and died without uttering a sound.

Besides his wife, Grandfather left behind five small children and two concubines. Grandmother Chan was still a young woman, but decorum prevented her from remarrying. She sold the valuables she had and managed somehow to maintain that large household of complicated relations. (One of the children was the son of the first concubine, the second concubine was childless, and the other four offspring were hers.)

They were housed in a rambling structure with multiple courtyards and entrances, a Cantonese-style mansion built to Grandfather's specifications in the old section of the city. Sedan chairs came through the first entrance, beyond which footmen and messengers were forbidden. The second entrance led to the living room, the study, and the dining room, where guests and callers were met and entertained. Beyond the third entrance resided the women and children.

It was this third entrance that I remember most vividly. It led to three separate wings, the middle one containing Grandmother's courtyard which opened onto her bedroom and her Buddhist temple. To the east and west were separate quarters for the concubines and children.

In 1937, when we were moving south to escape the Japanese invasion, our family stopped in Canton on our way to Hong Kong. There, I saw Grandmother Chan for the first time. By then she was in her early fifties, full of ancient anecdotes and family lore. I loved her at once. She was outspoken, stubborn, fanciful, warm, and generous—Cantonese, in other words, to the core.

I was only twelve at the time, but the month my sisters and I spent at her house stands out in my memory though we saw much more of her when, a year later, she came to join us in Hong Kong.

She was a religious woman, worshipping at her Buddhist altar twice daily at dawn and at dusk, burning joss sticks and *tan shun* wood incense, and rattling her prayer beads.

Father was thirteen at the time of Grandfather's suicide. Wanting to shelter him, her eldest son, from the cloud of bankruptcy and disgrace, Grandmother scraped together the necessary money and sent him abroad to study.

Father went reluctantly. He would have preferred to remain at home with the family, but elders had to be obeyed. He went on to study law at Oxford, and later left for the United States for another degree from Columbia University. When he returned to China ten years later, at the age of twenty-three, he was a severe young man, old for his age, bookish, withdrawn, and melancholy.

One of Grandfather Chan's closest friends had been Liao, a brilliant and wealthy young man from a family of prominent scholars and politicians. As activists in the early days of the Sun Yat-sen revolution,* the two had engaged in such radical acts as cutting off their pigtails, or queues, in defiance of the degrading Manchu ordinance that required all Chinese to wear pigtails as a symbol of their submission to the foreign Manchu rule. (Chan did not live to see the culmination of the movement that finally overthrew the Manchus. But Liao was able to join the revolution in later years, becoming friends with many of its principal leaders. He became a cabinet member of the first

---

* Sun's revolution, launched at the turn of the century and climaxing in the fall of the Ch'ing Dynasty in 1911, was both Nationalistic and Republican, aiming to expel Manchus and foreigners alike, and seeking to bring an end to thousands of years of imperial rule.

Republic of China in Peking, and served as foreign minister while his brother, Liao Chung-kai, was prime minister.)

To seal their friendship, Chan and Liao made a pact, long before either was married, to link their families by wedding a future son to a future daughter. Chan went on to have five children, while Liao fathered a family of ten, including two girls who grew up to be celebrated beauties and fashion setters in turn-of-the-century Peking. They were raised in the hothouse glamour of mansions carpeted with thick *Tientsin* rugs, draped with crystal chandeliers, and adorned with priceless knick-knacks of porcelain, jade, and ivory.

The daughters went to school in England, France, and Italy and spent summer and winter vacations traveling. They soaked up the arts, took music and languages—French, German, Spanish, Portuguese, Japanese—and glowed with the refinements of privilege.

It was to the older of these two enchanting girls, Isabelle, that Chan's son was betrothed.

My maternal Grandfather Liao was liberal, worldly, enlightened; but in matters close to his heart—a daughter's marriage, for instance—he was stubbornly conservative.

He was serving a term as Chinese ambassador to Cuba at the time and wanted the prearranged wedding to take place in Havana. He sent for Isabelle, by then a student in London. But she meanwhile had fallen in love with an Englishman and had no desire to marry a stranger. In the end, Liao had to send one of his brothers to bring her back, willful but heartbroken.

Father and Mother were married in Havana in December 1918.

They went to Washington, D.C., where they had Cynthia, their first child, and returned to Peking three years later. Father taught law at Peking University (where Mao Tse-tung had been a librarian) and also worked as a chief editor for the English *New China Morning Post.*

Four years later, Mother was again with child.

I was born in 1925—the year of Sun Yat-sen's death and Chiang Kai-shek's rise to power. It was the Year of the Ox, which, in the book of Chinese astrology, portends a life of hard effort.

I was not my parents' last disappointment. After me, there would be four more girls, the six of us constituting misfortune bordering on tragedy. We were named in the Chinese tradition, after flowers—Chrysanthemum, Plum Blossom, Water Lily, Orchid, Bamboo, Peach Blossom—each symbolizing a special set of qualities: strength and stability, purity and integrity, romance and gentleness, charm and daintiness, humility and wisdom, energy and hope.

They named me Sheng Mai (Plum Blossom): a winter flower that braves snow and storm and is a metaphor for purity, integrity, and beauty. With all the hard work ahead of me, imposed by the sign of the Ox, I needed a name to look up to.

We grew up in Peking, first in the vast home of my grandparents, later in a large house of our own. But it is the first home, where I lived from the first few years of my childhood, that I loved the best. Relatives, servants (maids, cooks, gardeners, seamstresses, carriers, messengers, ricksha men), visitors, and old friends came and went in a ceaseless stream. There was no end to the holidays and festivities: birthdays, New Year, the Moon Festival, Ancestor Worship Day, the beginning of spring, the Seventh Day of the Seventh Moon, the Eighth Day of the Eighth Moon, and so on.

This immense household was orchestrated by Grandfather Liao, a man of stature in every sense: tall, erect, and imperial even in his baggy pyjamas. His features, his temper, and his expression were as open and generous as his nature. He radiated intelligence and humanity—the stuff of grand portraits and marble busts.

Grandfather was a scholar and diplomat, one of the few ranking government officials of his time who had been educated in the West. He had studied in England and France during the early days of the Sun Yat-sen revolution though later, in a period of truce, had accompanied General Lee Hung Chang, last Army Chief of the Manchu regime, to Europe and the United States.

While in America, he had fallen in love with and married a Chinese girl raised in Washington, D.C., whose forebears had set out for California in the late eighteenth century, as merchants plying a trade between the West Coast and southern China.

Like his family, they too were originally from Fukien, a coastal province in South China with a high yield of renowned poets, authors, artists, and politicians through the ages, among them Lin Yu-tang, perhaps the best known popularizer of Chinese culture. (Legend attributes this native Fukienese creativity to a benign chemistry contained in the water and soil of the province.)

Grandfather's family was Hakka, descended from the "guest settlers" of the southern coast. Seafarers and adventurers by tradition, their early origins are vague, but they are believed to stem from the north, from as far up-country as Shantung (the birthplace of Confucius), Anwhei, and Honan.

Gradually driven out by persecution during the third millennium of the Ch'ing Dynasty, the Hakka pushed farther and farther south, settling eventually in Kiangsi and Kwantung provinces. (This theory is often put forth to explain why the Hakka dialect is closer to Mandarin than to Cantonese.)

Liao brought his new wife back to Peking, where they settled in an exclusive residential district. Number sixteen Tung Chun Pau Hu Tung was an imposing gray-stone mansion. It was there, amid the bustle and glitter of my grandparents' social life, that I spent the early years of my childhood.

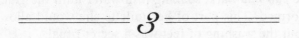

I can still see the house very clearly: green tile roofs and curved lintels, japanned doors and polished floors, red and gold pilasters and halls leading to courtyards within courtyards. A child could hide or get lost in so vast a maze, but we children were safe, so long as we followed our noses. The sweet scent of incense could be traced to the prayer rooms within, the fragrance of jasmine and gardenia to the gardens outside, the aroma of rich broth to the cauldrons bubbling in the kitchen.

The kitchen was a kind of central depot where important things happened. Here, servants ate and argued, great meals were planned and prepared, and the huge coal stoves were the first to be lit at the crack of dawn.

The room was hot and greasy, but large enough for our dozen or so servants to sit down to communal meals. From the ceiling hung sides of beef, cured hams, dried spices, and strings of onions and garlic, but the "icebox" was out in the yard, a deep hole in the ground where cabbages and turnips, bought by the truckload, were stored through the winter months.

I remember sitting in the pantry that was next door, a room filled with the aged, piercing odor of dry goods: fruits, mushrooms, truffles, shrimp, scallops, walnuts, peanuts, sugar crystals, and, in a special ceramic jar, such delicacies as sesame candy, peanut brittle, and walnut cookies. The cook would reach into this ceramic jar up to his elbow and either reward or bribe us with its contents.

On days when guests came to dinner—every other day, so it seemed—Cynthia and I would be fed in the pantry, watched over impatiently by our *amahs*. We each had an *amah*—a wet nurse in baby Connie's case—who fed and clothed us, and put us to bed. Mine, Li Ma, was a young woman in her twenties, supple and small-boned, with a pleasant, dimpled, guileless face and a topknot of lacquered hair. She extracted the lacquer from the *pao-hua* bark, soaking it in water until the gluey substance formed. This part of her toilette she would allow us to watch, but the washing of feet was a secret ritual.

Li Ma's feet were not "golden lilies" or "fragrant lilies," which is to say they were not bound, as were her mother's and grandmother's and all their maternal forebears' since the tenth century. Her generation had discarded at last that grotesque symbol of both sex and suppression, the broken, bandaged foot. Li Ma's feet were normal: small, but not much different from a man's. She needn't have been ashamed of washing them in public. There was no bandage to unwrap, no festering smell of unwholesome flesh, no deformed and withered stub of a foot to excite the lurid imagination.

But the humiliation of centuries dies hard, and Li Ma's feet may as well have been bound for the shame instilled in her. Sometimes, we would see her fill an enamel basin with water and carry it into her room. Following quietly, Cynthia and I would peep through a crack in her door. The room was a mere cubicle, most of it filled with the *k'ang,* a sleeping platform built over a coal stove. In one corner was a porcelain image of a household god; in another, a wobbly stool.

But the room was impeccably clean, like Li Ma herself. Her light blue jacket with the mandarin collar was always starched, her black pyjamas crisp and clean. Even her cloth shoes, which she sewed and embroidered by hand, and her white cotton socks were seldom soiled.

As we watched, she would set the basin of water beside her and begin to take off her shoes. Cynthia and I would titter and pinch each other with excitement, though neither of us knew what the secrecy meant. Once, I asked Grandfather Liao what it was all about, why Li Ma wanted to hide her feet.

"Perhaps they are dirty," was Grandfather's vague reply.

And so for years we engaged in this harmless but titillating spying.

Li Ma's nature was placid and agreeable for the most part

but her temper could snap at a moment's notice—when she caught us spying, for example, or when we lingered over our food at the pantry table.

"Eat, eat," she would say, eager to move on to more important pursuits: trading gossip, eavesdropping, and gawking at the guests who would soon arrive.

The edge in her voice always brought out the defiance in me. I would start to play with my food, picking up noodles by the strand with my chopsticks.

"Eat!" she would threaten. "Eat or I'll tell your mother."

"Go ahead, tell," I would challenge her. "I don't care. She's busy, anyway. I dare you."

Cynthia would intervene then, urging me to hurry. "Come," she would whisper, "let's go to bed." Unlike me, she could scarcely wait for the ghost stories.

In the kitchen next door, the habitual quarrel between the cook, Lao Wong, and his assistant, Huang Ma, would be underway. Wong was a bachelor, Huang Ma the head butler's wife. Yet the two could have been husband and wife, or brother and sister, so familiar and protracted were their arguments. The mutual scolding went on all day, an endless exchange of charges and complaints, sniffs and snorts and meaningful sighs. Nothing ever came of this gentle faultfinding; it was only a way of communicating.

The two were alike even in shape and size: round and soft and doughy to the touch, like dumplings that had risen, sweating, in the hot pressure of the kitchen. Their overheated bodies seemed to emit steam at all times; a sudden splash of water on such piping hot flesh might have sizzled.

Their conversations would go something like this:

HUANG MA: (muttering) Messy, messy . . . and I'm always stuck with the cleaning. . . .

LAO WONG: My job is to cook, fat one, not to clean. Cleaning is your job. If you could cook like me you wouldn't be cleaning.

HUANG MA: If you're such a good cook, what are you doing

here? Why aren't you cooking at the Peking Hotel or the fancy Tien Hua-lo Restaurant? Tell me that.

LAO WONG: (as if the choice were his entirely) I prefer to cook for the honorable Mr. and Mrs. Liao.

HUANG MA: Then you'd better start cleaning up.

LAO WONG: (at a loss) All right, old woman Huang; enough out of you. Go fix the noodles and rice and leave me alone.

Upstairs in our room, Cynthia and I would sit on the bed with anticipation, while Li Ma would fold clothes.

"Tell us ghost stories, Li Ma," Cynthia would start.

"No, don't. I don't want to hear," I would say, but really wanting to hear.

Then Cynthia, pleading: "Tell us about the corpse."

"What corpse?" Li Ma would ask.

"The corpse that woke up."

"What corpse that woke up?"

"The woman corpse that woke up and chased the man."

"What woman corpse that woke up and chased what man?"

"Li Ma! Stop pretending!"

Li Ma would give in at last. "All right; I'll tell about the painted skin.

"Long, long ago a man was walking down a road when he met a beautiful young woman. She told him this tale of woe: 'My parents,' she said, 'are so money-hungry that they sold me as a concubine to a rich man. Now my new master is a kind man, but his wife is terrible, a terrible jealous woman who never misses a day of scolding or beating me. I can bear her cruelty no longer, and so I have run away.'

"When he heard this story, the man took pity on the young concubine and led her back to his house, where he hid her in his library. He said nothing about this to his wife.

"But one day he returned home and found the library door locked. This made him uneasy, so he went outside and climbed the high wall to his library window. He peered through the window ... it was a foggy night and he could barely see. He breathed on the windowpane and rubbed it softly with his finger . . . and what do you think he saw?

"Bending over the bed in the library was a horrible green-faced demon with long pointed teeth just like the edge of a saw.

"The demon had a piece of skin spread out on the bed and was painting it with a thick brush. When the job was done, the demon shook out the skin, which had been painted to look like a human skin, with eyes, nose, hands, feet, and so on. She threw it over herself like a cloak—and turned into the concubine.

"Shaking with fright, the man ran to a shaman for help. He was crying like a baby. 'What shall I do? What shall I do?' The shaman told him to go home and hang a fly-brush over his bedroom door to keep out the demon. The man did as he was told, but when the demon saw the fly-brush, she snarled and gnashed her teeth and burst through the door in a rage, charging at the petrified man . . . and tearing out his heart before his wife's horrified eyes.

"The wife fainted. But when she recovered, she went back to the shaman to tell him what had happened. The shaman investigated and learned that the demon was posing as a chambermaid in a nearby house.

"Grabbing his wooden sword, he went straight to the house, and struck down the demon. As the ghastly creature fell to the floor, her human skin came loose. Suddenly, she was grunting and groaning and writhing—until she vanished in a spiral of smoke.

"Now the wife pleaded with the shaman to bring her husband back to life.

" 'Go to the edge of town,' the shaman told her, 'and you will see a raving lunatic who grovels on the ground like an animal. He has the magic power to raise the dead.'

"The woman followed the shaman's directions and found the lunatic. When she begged him to help her bring her husband back to life, the lunatic only mocked her and laughed and beat her with a cane in front of everyone in the street.

"But in the end he gave her a huge pill and told her to

swallow it. The woman was not sure that she could get it down her throat, it was so big. But she was willing to do anything. She coughed and coughed, almost choking, but at last managed to swallow it. 'Now go home,' ordered the lunatic. The poor woman went away with a heavy heart, thinking she had been tricked.

"Later that day, she began preparing the corpse for burial. When she saw the gaping wound in her husband's chest, where his heart had been plucked out, she began to cry. Suddenly, she felt a lump rising in her throat. It grew larger and larger until it pushed its way into her mouth and fell out into the dead man's wound. It was a human heart, and as it lay in the wound, it began to throb.

"Trembling, the woman quickly closed the wound and squeezed it together. Then she bound a piece of silk around her husband's chest and rubbed his body to bring back the circulation.

"When she removed the silk bandage during the night, she saw that her husband was breathing. By the next morning he was awake and alert. Where the demon had torn out his heart, only a thick scar the size of a large coin remained."

The story over, I would turn to Cynthia. "Can I sleep with you tonight?"

"No! Now tell about the corpse, Li Ma."

"You and your corpse!"

"Please, Li Ma. I'll tell the beginning, then. 'Once upon a time, four travelers went to an inn where the innkeeper's daughter-in-law had just died.' Now you tell . . ."

"All right, but this is the last story: The four travelers got to the inn. But the inn was full and the only room left was in the women's quarters where the corpse was laid out while the coffin was being made. The travelers had come a long way and were too tired to go on, so they told the innkeeper that they wouldn't mind sharing a room with the dead body. The innkeeper showed them into the quarters where the corpse lay, dressed in paper robes. The travelers were so exhausted that as soon as they lay down, they fell fast asleep.

"But one of them was a light sleeper, and in the middle of the night he was awakened by the sound of rustling paper and a creaking bed. He opened his eyes and saw the dead woman getting up from her bed and crawling toward his companions. She wore a scarf around her head and her skin had a greenish-yellow tint.

"When she reached the sleeping bodies, she blew on them one by one, then crawled toward the terrified man. He quickly pretended to be asleep, shutting his eyes. The corpse got closer and closer to him, and when she was by his side, she blew on him, too. . . . At last he heard her shuffle across the floor. He listened, motionless, to the rustle of her paper robes and the creaking of the bedsprings as she settled back into bed.

"The traveler waited until he thought she was asleep, then very quietly but very quickly began putting on his clothes. But the minute he started out the door, the corpse leaped out of her bed and began following him."

By now, Cynthia and I would be huddled together.

"The man began running toward the highway," Li Ma would continue. "He was too afraid to stop and call for help, because the corpse might catch up with him. At last he came to a monastery. He banged frantically on the door, shouting for help. But the priest was alarmed at the sudden noise and refused to open the door.

"Now the corpse had almost caught up with the half-crazed man. He knew he couldn't stand at the gate any longer. When the corpse was only a few feet away, the man dodged behind a poplar tree. The corpse pounced this way and that, round and round the tree. At last she grew impatient and lunged at the tree trunk as though to embrace it, hoping to catch the man.

"But the man escaped by falling backward onto the ground, while the corpse smashed into the tree and knocked herself unconscious.

"The next morning, the priest opened the gate and found the traveler lying on the ground, speechless with shock. The corpse was still hugging the tree. She had used such force that her fingers had sunk into the bark like arrows."

And so each night we were put to bed with the stuff of nightmares. These tales of the dead and the damned were the sedative fed to every child by the *amah*. They were our opiate as well.

When Li Ma had gone, Cynthia and I would steal out of the room, Cynthia leading me by the hand, and I dragging along my red woolen blanket with the other.

We would tiptoe out to the head of the marble staircase and kneel behind the banister for a view of the main hallway, where the parties would begin. At the main gate outside, guarded by twin stone lions, the guard and three ricksha and sedan-chair men would be waiting for the guests to arrive in their horse carriages, automobiles, rickshas, or sedan chairs. The red lanterns would be winking in the trees in the courtyards. And in the guardhouse, the guard and the errand boys would be hunched over a gambling table, smoking water pipes and cheap cigarettes and clicking dominoes, until the guard's parrot would squawk from its cage, "The guests are coming, guests are coming!"

Then the guests would trickle in: the men in dark European suits or formal mandarin gowns, the women in silk and brocade *cheongsam*, with painted bow-lips and eyebrows like new moons. Grandfather and Grandmother were dazzling, he in his Parisian suit, tall and handsome, and she in a sequined *cheongsam* that seemed painted onto her youthful body.

The band would be playing, the chandeliers sparkling, the floors turning into a thousand mirrors. But our spying never lasted very long. The marble underneath us would turn to ice, and Cynthia would begin to pull on my blanket.

"Give me some!"

"No!"

"Give me!" She would tug until I began to cry.

One of the *amahs* would appear at that point, scolding and herding us back to bed.

Later, I would creep into Cynthia's room and shake her.

"Wake up!"

"I'm awake. What's wrong?"

"I'm scared."

"So?"

"Let me sleep in your bed," I would beg.

"No, you take up too much space. You kick in the night."

"Let me. Please. I won't tell Mama about the cod-liver oil if you let me." (Cynthia used to feed her daily dose of cod-liver oil to me, threatening all kinds of punishment if I dared to squeal. I was a rotund child, and for years I blamed Cynthia and her cod-liver oil for this.)

At last she would draw a line down the middle of the bed with a red pencil. "All right. That's your side. If you cross the line, out you go."

Later, she would shake me awake, saying, "You crossed the line, you crossed the line!"

But I always pretended to be asleep, and after a while she would give up and fall asleep herself.

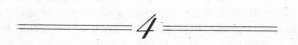

Early on Sunday mornings, Grandmother Liao could be seen sitting on a bench in her courtyard, brushing the hair of her two Pekinese nestled obediently in her lap. She would be wearing a bright pink or blue dress, looking far younger than her years. On the bench beside her would be a jewelry box of lacquer and inlaid mother-of-pearl, holding an assortment of multicolored ribbons for the Pekinese: a different color for each day of the week. They were a nervous, overactive pair, with the unendearing habit of wetting the laps of people to whom they did not take a fancy. But Grandmother was blind to their faults as only a mistress can be who orders for her pets custom-made miniature sofas with carved legs and brocade upholstery.

I remember trying to sit on one of those dwarf sofas, and Grandmother exclaiming, "No, no, you'll break it!" and the dogs yapping and scratching at my leg until I burst out, "Stop that! Son of a turtle!" It was one of those swear words we learned from the cook, without understanding its meaning, or effect, but which we knew was worse than calling someone a son of a bitch.

Grandmother recoiled with shock. "Don't ever say that! Who taught you such a bad word?"

At that moment, Grandfather Liao, his thick silver hair uncombed, strolled into the courtyard in his rumpled plum-colored pyjamas. Grandmother reported the bad news: I was picking up foul language from the servants. But Grandfather only smiled, reassuring me that I could do no wrong in his eyes.

Grandmother's four-and-a-half-acre garden was typical of the formal Chinese garden of those times, built on the classical model described by Shen Fu, an eighteenth-century aesthete. It was cunningly landscaped, following Shen Fu's model.

A wild landscape, perhaps better arranged and more artistically planned than nature, but still a bit of nature itself, with trees, mounds, creeks, bridges ... a patch of vegetable fields, fruit trees, and some flowers. Dotted in this natural landscape are the human structures, the bridges, pavilions, long-winding corridors, irregular rockeries, and sweeping roofs, so perfectly belonging to the scenery as to become a whole with it. There are no even-cut hedges, no perfectly conical or circular trees, no symmetric rows lining avenues as if in battle formation, and no straight pavements—none of all those elements that contribute to make Versailles so ugly in Chinese eyes. Everywhere we see curves, irregularity, concealment and suggestion. . . .

In the summer, the tall drooping willows would sway to the

music of the birds by day, of the cicadas by night. We used to play among the fruit trees, singing nursery rhymes and dancing sometimes in Mother's old dresses, so long that they trailed in the dust.

Once, we had made ourselves up heavily with rouge and lipstick and had draped ourselves with jewelry when Mother and Father came into the garden.

Mother burst out laughing, but Father stiffened with disapproval. "Disgusting," he said. "Go and wash your faces at once."

I started to run out of the garden, but Mother stopped me. "Wait, where is the other earring? You have only one on."

I touched my ear, frightened. "I don't know."

"It must have dropped off somewhere," Mother said.

"How many times must I tell you not to play this foolish game!" Father shouted angrily. "Now you've lost your mother's earring. It is gold. Gold is worth money. Money is not a fruit growing on trees. Now go and wash your face."

I ran from the garden, crying, into Grandfather's study. At once he comforted me, "Don't cry, my little Boo-Boo."

I can remember sitting on his lap while he told me stories, the caress of his huge hands on my head, like the blessing of a benevolent giant. He was the largest and greatest person I knew, and at our Sunday afternoon meals, he towered above us all at the head of the table, directing our lives the way a king guides his beloved subjects. He would examine each member of the family by turn, asking questions, scolding and praising, and all the time savoring, appraising, and commenting on the food.

Those Sunday lunches were elaborate multi-course affairs lasting several hours, a typical menu featuring "Lion's Head" (a chopped pork and cabbage dish, and one of Wong's specialties), roast duck and pancakes, beef steamed in its natural juices and spiked with *ginseng* (for adults only), meat dumplings, white rice, wheat noodles, pickled cabbage, pickled turnip, steamed vegetables, and a special bean curd with hot pepper.

The bean curd always brought on one of Grandfather's favorite stories.

"There was once a scholar who went bankrupt," he would begin, scooping the bean curd onto his dish. "It happens a lot to scholars. This man wanted to invite his friend, another scholar, to dinner. But the friend was wealthy and he, having no money, couldn't afford any meat. And what was a special meal without meat?

"Then he had an idea: He would serve rice and bean curd, which he could afford, and pretend that he was serving such simple fare on purpose, because of its nutritional values.

"So when his friend came to dinner and they sat down to eat, the poor scholar picked up the dish of bean curd and exclaimed, 'Ah, bean curd . . . the elixir of life!'

"The rich scholar said nothing, but ate heartily, thanked his friend for his hospitality, and took his leave.

"Several weeks later the poor scholar received an invitation to dinner at his friend's house. Knowing that his friend was both wealthy and generous, he anticipated the most sumptuous of meals. When the day came, he was not disappointed. His friend had set a lavish table, piled high with marvelous meat and vegetable dishes—and also a dish of bean curd.

"As soon as they sat down to dinner, the poor scholar reached out for a meat dish. 'Ah, meat!' he said longingly.

"With a little smile, his host said, 'But, my friend, I thought you said that bean curd was the elixir of life.'

" 'It is, it is,' said the other impatiently. Then, overcome with sudden appetite, and taking a huge mouthful of meat, he said, 'But who cares about life when you can have meat?' "

Grandfather would begin his exhaustive critique of the food which was passed on to the cook by Lao Huang, the head butler, who stood behind him and craned his neck to catch every word.

"This isn't quite salty enough," Grandfather would say, tasting the duck.

"Yes sir, yes sir," Lao Huang would reply, bowing.

"The pork should fall apart at the touch of a chopstick. See how it's not tender enough?"

"Yessir, yessir."

"The vegetables should be crisper."

"Yessir, yessir!" (more bowing and grinning).

After lunch, Cynthia and I would run around the room, mocking Lao Huang, bowing to one another and singing, "Yessir, yessir!" Lao Huang would chase us outside into the servants' yard with a feather duster. There, the exhausted Wong would be lounging flat on his back while an errand boy fanned him with a straw fan, counting the strokes: "Ninety-six, ninety-seven, ninety-eight, ninety-nine, one hundred . . . there. Finished!"

"More, more. Fan me a little more," Wong would beg.

"Then give me some more cash."

"All right . . . ten more cash [a form of Chinese penny] for another hundred strokes. Robber! Bandit!" And Wong would sink back to enjoy the expensive breeze.

Sundays were also the days when Grandfather would prowl the antique stores, usually returning home with a couple of porcelain flower pots to add to his already mountainous collection. His library was filled with these and other finds: carved figurines, delicate silk scrolls, ancient faded paintings.

I loved the smell of polished wood that permeated the room, the book-lined walls, the thick spongy carpets, and, most of all, the sight of Grandfather reading in his armchair.

To this day, one of my most comforting memories is of squeezing into the armchair when I went to bid him goodnight, and feeling the drowsiness wash over me as we sang together: "Shallow flow the streams, high fly the dreams, follow the wind, follow the sky. . . ."

Before we could finish, I would fall asleep and never know when Li Ma came to carry me to bed.

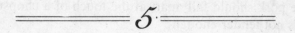

Graham Greene once said that there is always a moment in childhood when a door opens and lets the future in. Literature was that doorway for me. And it was Li Chieh, my elementary school teacher with the ink brush eyebrows, who pointed me in that direction.

A graduate student from Peking University, Li Chieh was in his mid-twenties when he came to teach us at the Kung Te School. He was an energetic, overworked man, of medium height and build, sober-looking in the blue cotton mandarin gown that was the uniform of university students in the thirties, but with a shock of insubordinate black hair on which he took out much of his exasperation.

My first week in Li Chieh's composition class ended with a miserable grade—the equivalent of a D—and a written summons from him: "See me after class tomorrow."

Mother, with her knack for rooting out trouble, got wind of this and gave me a long lecture.

At school the next day, torn between dread and impatience, I fretted through the day's classes.

The bell rang at last. I ran to the teachers' conference room where Li was waiting.

"Sit down," he said, "and let me hear you read your paper."

I obeyed, squeaking like a mouse. When I had finished, he said, "What do you think of the writing?"

I found it a strange question, since I had never stopped to think of my own writing.

"Well then," said Li, "let me tell you what *I* think. But first you should know that more than three-quarters of the class were given Ds and Fs on this assignment. So you are not alone.

"But that's not why I've brought you here. You are here because I think you could become a good writer—that is, if you follow my advice and work hard. By the way, your handwriting is just awful. You must work on your calligraphy. Now, this piece of work is messy, but it does show you can write with imagination and feeling. You're very observant for a child your age, but you didn't bother to organize your thoughts. You were just trying to finish the assignment in a hurry.

"I want you to spend more time reading. And I want you to get into the habit of keeping a diary. The entries can be long or short, but they will improve your script and writing."

Then he handed me two books to read and said, "Next week, when we have time, we will talk about Chinese literature."

From then on, every Wednesday afternoon after class, Teacher Li would select a few students and call them to his room to discuss reading and writing.

One day Li said, "If you don't mind, I'd like to read your diary." I didn't mind at all. Maybe I had already begun to write self-consciously, knowing that others would read what I wrote. I had followed Li's suggestions and recorded my thoughts on books I read, and on authors I especially liked.

On fine weekends, Teacher Li would take us on picnics, to the famous West Mountain or somewhere else out of the city.

Peking was a city of clear-cut seasons: hot humid summers, long frigid winters, short melancholy autumns, and fragrant, even shorter springs.

In November, winter blew in with sudden freezing blasts from Mongolia in the Northwest, a cold, dry season of clear blue skies.

When spring came—usually in early April—the tall poplars would break out in furry growths that soon littered the ground. The air held the sweet scent of young blossoms, until storms and high winds swept in yellow sands from the Gobi Desert that powdered the surface of the city and settled in everyone's nose and hair.

Summer was a month of indecision for the family. Where would we go for the season? To Kuling, for the crisp mountain air? To Mo Kin Shan, near Nanking? Or to Bai Hai, where we could swim? Perhaps we should simply make a short retreat in Central Park, once part of the Forbidden City.

The shadows of the leaves danced with indecision and sparrows paced hesitantly on the flowering boughs.

It was in the summer of my tenth year that I memorized the famous Three Hundred Poems, and it was the following autumn when I wrote the poem that would result in my first publication.

The red maple leaves carpeted the hills and cushioned the mountain paths we followed, led by Teacher Li. Along the banks of leaf-strewn streams we would stop to write short verses. Ankle-deep in the rust-colored sheddings of ash, willow, and poplar, I wrote that first poem, "Autumn."

The next year we were introduced to Western literature in translation: the novels of Louisa May Alcott, Charles Dickens, Somerset Maugham, and others. We saw a distant world, full of bracing curiosities: a family of four girls that bore hardship with touching grace, a great revolution in France and the heartbreaking sacrifice of Sydney Carton, and the disappointed and lonely Europeans in Asian lands far away from home.

It was also the year I discovered movies—great romantic spectacles filled with magic, swashbuckling wanderings, and chivalrous love.

Whenever I talked about becoming an actress, I saw frowns of disapproval. But aspiring to be a writer seemed to invite no opposition. It was my nature to be defiant. But this was one case where I actually enjoyed doing the acceptable thing.

I decided to be a writer.

But that, and a lot of other ambitions, had to be shelved in the years of war that followed.

The Book of Rites

6

The war, in fact, had been going on for years. It was a strange sort of war, undeclared and without a battlefront. It began in 1931, when the expansionist Japanese military had engineered the Mukden Incident "in self-defense" to justify their annexation of Manchuria. In order to take control of the provincial capital of Mukden, Japanese troops had set off an explosion along the railway they controlled and used the alarm as a pretext to take over the capital. Since then, they had found one excuse after another to invade China's major cities—Peking, Tientsin, Shanghai, Nanking, and Hankow—taking care to label each thrust "self-determination" or "self-defense" by the people of Manchuria.

For the next six years, they continued to penetrate Inner Mongolia and North China both politically—through arrangements with puppet governments—and economically—by trafficking in both opium and Japanese goods.

The Nationalists kept on retreating from Nanking to the triple city of Hankow-Hanyang-Wuchang (Wuhan), farther and farther back, using China's vast expanse as their principal defense against the enemy.

We, too, moved from city to city after the Japanese troops reached the outskirts of Peking. Then, in 1937, just before the

Marco Polo Bridge incident,* Father decided to move us all—Mother and the six of us—to Hong Kong, while he went abroad on an assignment.

He had been dividing his time between teaching and journalism. At Peking University he had taught law and English, and had gone on to become dean. He also started an English-language newspaper, one of only three in Peking. Now he was joining the foreign service as consul general in Mexicali, Mexico.

His separation from us was explained in terms of economic practicality. A civil servant's salary was small, and we would be more comfortable in China, with the built-in benefits of servants and relatives. (It was clear that Grandfather Liao would have been more than happy to lend financial assistance, but Father was not about to accept such favors.) Also, we would be getting a Chinese education, which Father considered of over-riding importance.

The truth was that my parents had reached the point of diminishing contact and conversation. There was no explosive friction—only a correct civility in their day-to-day dealings. There are opposites that attract, but the opposites of my parents' personalities—austere scholar and fun-loving socialite—were the kinds that did not.

As for the distance between Father and the rest of us, I suppose it was no different from the formality in most Chinese families, where intimacy with one's father is limited to a polite question-and-answer exchange at the dinner table. Still, we left for Hong Kong with the vague expectation that we would join Father overseas before too long.

As it turned out, I didn't see him again for twelve years. By then Mother had died, he had remarried in San Francisco, and

* A small Japanese garrison at the town of Wan P'ing on the outskirts of Peking staged an incident near the Marco Polo Bridge to provoke the Chinese guards into an exchange of gunfire, and used this as an excuse subsequently to launch a large-scale attack on the city of Peking itself.

I was planning my own marriage in Shanghai. The year was 1948.

It was in Hong Kong that I got my first taste of Communism, in the person of Madame Liao Ho Hsing-ying. Madame Liao was our grand-aunt, the widow of Grandfather Liao's brother, Liao Chung-kai, who had served as the first prime minister of the Republic under Sun Yat-sen.

Like Grandfather Liao, who was two years older, Liao Chung-kai was a scholar, an activist, and an astute politician. The two brothers came from a large family; exactly how large was undetermined, since the full number of children had never been tallied up. With so many wives and concubines involved, it was hard enough to keep track of the male offspring. The females were of so little consequence that they did not even figure in a head-count.

Grandfather Liao and his brother pursued parallel careers, but in personality and style they were as different as water and fire. Grandfather Liao was modern but moderate, westernized in outlook but Confucian in approach. Though fervently patriotic, he was not an extremist. To him, reform was an evolutionary process rather than a sudden upheaval. His brother, on the other hand, was a radical in the romantic mold: reckless, impatient, and full of defiance.

On the eve of a huge political rally he was to address, his advisors brought him the rumor: There was to be an attempt on his life. But Liao Chung-kai is said to have brushed off the warning with this reasoning: "If I'm going to be the leader of a country, how can I cancel speeches on the strength of a rumor? Anything can happen to a leader, he has to take chances."

Liao Chung-kai took his chances and went to address the assembly. He talked simply and emphatically, without any of the pedantry that could easily have accompanied his cultured background and learning. He spoke of the warlords who divided China at the time; of the need for change, of the crumbling remains of the old order which he, as a young revolutionary, had fought so hard to dismantle.

At the end of his speech, he walked out of the assembly hall. Out of the mammoth crowd that had listened spellbound, a gun was fired.

Liao fell to the ground and died within minutes. He was forty years old.

The police arrested several suspects, including one prominent journalist who had been openly critical of Liao Chung-kai's radical leanings. But in the confusion of that behemoth crowd, it was impossible to determine where the shots had come from, how they had been fired, or who had fired them.

Liao Chung-kai's widow demanded an investigation. She was a woman accustomed to making demands—a tireless crusader, a rigid intellectual, and an uncompromising adversary. It was said that she could wear down or shout down anybody, including her husband, who had not been able to stand up to her.

The Nationalist government did carry out an investigation. Witnesses were questioned and confessions made. But the inquiry, as far as Madame Liao was concerned, was half-hearted and inconclusive, suggesting, to her, the government's indifference.

She complained, lodged protests, made more demands. Then she began nominating her son, Liao Chung-chih, for various positions in the government. Insult followed injury when none of her efforts bore fruit. It was a slow process of disenchantment with the Nationalists, and in the end it was complete.

Prime Minister Liao Chung-kai was assassinated in 1928. By the time we reached Hong Kong in 1938, Madame Liao, her son, and her daughter were active Communists, though we did not fully realize it at the time. The daughter, Liao Moon-sheng, married a member of the Chinese Communist Party who later became a party executive, a regional committee member. The son, Liao Chung-chih, went on to become Mao Tse-tung's special assistant, was China's chief negotiator with the Eastern European bloc, and was also responsible for conducting the first trade talks with Japan after the Revolution.

While we were in Hong Kong, they were odd, mysterious figures who alighted in our midst and took off again like will-o'-the-wisps, elusive and flickering in their movements (and wisely so, considering the Hong Kong government's watchfulness at that time).

The son, for whom we had no other name than "Uncle," was a handsome, aloof young man whose air of reticence suggested secrets too involved for casual revelation. He used to appear suddenly at a family dinner, polite but uncommunicative, and just as suddenly disappear.

At the time, I was twelve years old and baffled by their comings and goings. It was only years later, when I went to Shanghai toward the end of the war to live with Grandfather and Grandmother Liao, that some of the mysteries of the Liao family were unraveled.

It seems that throughout the war, the Liaos made repeated trips to Chungking, the wartime capital of the Nationalist government, where the son, in fact, was arrested more than once for his underground activities. But in deference to his father, the late prime minister, the authorities had released him each time. Then he disappeared and nothing was heard of him for years, until it was revealed that he and his brother-in-law had made the Long March to Yenan with Mao Tse-tung.

At war's end, when the Communist position was weakening, party leaders began initiating talks with the Nationalists. One of Mao's representatives sent to Chungking for negotiations with Chiang Kai-shek's men was a Mr. Lee, Madame Liao's son-in-law. On his way from Yenan to Chungking during one such mission, he was blown to pieces by a Japanese bomb.

For Madame Liao, this misfortune destroyed the last shred of whatever goodwill she may have had toward the Nationalists. First, her husband had been assassinated and they had not fully avenged his death. Then, they had slighted her son. And now, even though it was not directly their doing, her son-in-law had been killed on his way to negotiate with them. From then on it was all-out war.

Eventually, Comrade Liao became one of the principal women leaders in the Chinese Communist Party, the head of the women's political committee, a member of the Central Committee, and the chief commissioner for the Overseas Chinese Committee, a powerful body that protects the social and cultural well-being of expatriate Chinese.

But in those early Hong Kong days, Grandaunt Liao was just an eccentric old woman who lacked humanity while preaching it. We were going to St. Paul's Convent then, and I remember how we were obliged, every couple of weeks or so, to go and kowtow to her. Inevitably, she would begin to denounce first our school, and then all religion.

"There is no God," she would tell us with chilling conviction. "Only stupid people believe in God. God is for those too weak to face the reality of life."

Then she would lecture us on any visible signs of vanity or frivolity. Mother, who was still in her thirties and an attractive, even glamorous woman, was singled out for using cosmetics, which were somehow decadent and corrupting.

To prove a point which none of us could understand, Madame Liao did her best to look homely and frumpish. Her hair was cropped short, the bluntness of the cut bringing out the hardness of a face that registered both a moral and physical objection to smiling. Her sober suits were almost always gray, ill-fitting, and drab. She had what the Chinese call a face of ice and iron, with matching hair, eyes, clothes, and posture. Everything that detracted from the cold, harsh purpose of Communism as she saw it was a felony.

Yet Madame Liao, for all her dedication to equality and her opposition to social injustice, was not above arranging her own son's marriage, handpicking the woman she thought he should marry, and then mistreating her daughter-in-law to such a degree that the girl kept trying to run away from home.

At New Year's Eve, when the rest of our relatives were giving us red envelopes containing lucky money, Madame Liao denounced the custom as yet another useless form of capitalism. We never could figure out what capitalism was, only that it provided an excuse for Grandaunt Liao to withhold the presents to which we felt entitled.

Two years ago, when I learned of Grandaunt Liao's death in Peking, I sat down to write an article for a Taiwanese newspaper recounting my brief acquaintance with her in Hong Kong, and I remembered a jingle that was circulating at the time.

She had taken to giving public speeches in Hong Kong—a bizarre forum for a woman in those days. Sprinkled throughout her speeches were dire predictions, many of which turned out, surprisingly, to be true. She predicted, for instance, that the war would last longer than most of us expected. Certainly, few expected it to last another eight years. She anticipated the advent of communes in Hong Kong, a prediction inaccurate only as to locale. (And, though she herself was unprepared for the personal tragedy that the Japanese invasion would bring, she had all of us in the family prepare for the impending food shortage by making endless rice cakes.)

But no one seemed to take her speeches seriously, and whenever she went before a crowd, a titter would break out, somehow reducing her tragedy to a cruel joke.

The jingle that was often heard went something like this:

Madame Liao, whenever there is a meeting, always attends;
Whenever she attends, she always gives a speech;
Whenever she gives a speech, she always talks about her
     dead husband;

Whenever she talks about her dead husband, she always cries;
Whenever she cries, she needs a cool drink;
Only after the cool drink does widow Liao, the public speaker,
     stop crying.

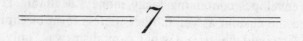

Early one morning, before leaving for school, I went as usual into mother's room to kiss her good-bye. Ordinarily, she would still be in bed, but this time she was up and dressed, folding clothes and stacking them in a suitcase.

"Where are you going?" I asked, then remembered her doctor's appointment. "But I thought you were only going in for a checkup."

She had her back to me. "Oh, it might take a few days," she said, and turned suddenly to hug me. "If I have to stay in the hospital, you'll take care of the house and your sisters?"

I nodded, still confused. At the door I said, "Maybe I should stay home today?" The idea didn't seem curious to her. "No, you go on now," she replied quietly, "but come see me at the hospital after school." A sudden sadness came over us both. I said nothing, but something unpleasant stirred between my chest and stomach. Suddenly, school seemed an impossible burden.

I went through the day in a state of impatience that could barely be contained. Lunch went uneaten. I couldn't apply myself to anything.

The bell rang at four o'clock, releasing the tight coil in me, and I sprang up from my seat to rush for the door, startling the teacher, Miss Yang Shu-ying.

"Here, Sheng Mai. Where do you think you're going?" she said sharply. "Come back and explain your bad manners. Who told you to leave before I dismissed the class?"

I stood at the door, my back to the class, afraid to turn around and reveal my trembling mouth. Then I lost control. "My mother is sick, my mother is sick!" I shouted, and ran out.

On the bus, I found I had only a ten-cent coin in my pocket. If I used it then, I would have to walk home from the hospital. I got off the bus to walk. It was a shorter distance from school to the hospital than from the hospital to our house. The November wind was a stinging slap across my face as I raced down the street.

At the hospital, a nurse showed me to Mother's room, where she lay in bed half-asleep. I went to stand beside her.

"Mother, are you all right?"

She opened her eyes. "Oh yes, I'm all right; the doctor just wants to take more tests. A few more days and I'll be coming home."

Seeing my alarm, she took my hand. "Don't you worry, everything will be all right." But there was no assurance in her voice.

I stayed until the nurse came and asked me to leave. "It's getting late. You should go home and get some rest."

"Little girl!" she added, with sudden pity.

I looked at Mother. "Can you help her?" I said to the nurse.

"Of course. You needn't worry." She thought I meant immediate help, but my question really was, "How sick is my mother?"

Mother smiled at me. "You're no more a little girl—you've grown up. I'm depending on you."

For the next six months, I went to visit her every afternoon, staying with her till dusk. Often my limbs would turn leaden with fatigue, but I could never fall asleep in her presence, for fear I would wake up and find her gone.

In my prayers I called to Grandfather Liao. If only he were there, he would know what to do. But my grandparents were still trapped in occupied China. They claimed to be too old and enervated to escape. Anyway, what would they live on in Hong Kong? Their property, investments, and ties were all on the mainland.

I prayed too for Father's return. Why was he off in some remote country instead of at Mother's bedside? How could he leave her in the care of six young daughters? When Loretta, the youngest, was born—the sixth disappointment in a row—he didn't even come to visit his wife at the hospital. At thirteen, I just didn't understand Father's seeming lack of concern for Mother. And no one was around to offer any sort of explanation. Cynthia was a boarder at Queen Mary's Hospital Nursing School, and I knew the rest were too young to grasp the seriousness of Mother's illness.

The disease took root, keeping her in a state of terrible equilibrium. When weeks passed without improvement, I asked to see the physician in charge, a man who happened to be one of Mother's distant cousins.

He was visibly uncomfortable at having to discuss a patient with a thirteen-year-old relative.

"Where is your father?" was his first question.

"In Mexico," I replied. "He is consul general there and can't get home on leave. Wartime regulations," I added automatically, but without conviction.

"I can't tell *you* much about your mother's sickness," he said. "It may be ulcers, it may be some other internal problem. We may have to operate, but right now she is too weak."

Winter melted into spring, but the very renewal of life, the blossoms and the birdsong, seemed lifeless that year. She never got stronger. First she stopped eating. Then she stopped sleeping. Finally, when disease and pain had ground her down into skin and bone, the diagnosis was made: terminal cancer. It was a new word to me, but it branded me for life.

The last month was a continuing nightmare of pain, and, toward the end, even when the needle probed her wasted arms, there was no relief. As the needle emerged, she would cry out for another, driving me out of the room, hands pressed to ears, with the force of her agony.

One rainy afternoon I took her a bouquet of carnations—her favorite flower—and set them quietly on her bedside table because she was asleep. When evening came she awoke and turned to me as if she knew I had been sitting beside her all along. "Boo-Boo, let me hold your hand."

I reached out for her hand—it was so shrunken—and she held

it with surprising strength, as if to deter me from some hasty act. Her voice sank into a whisper.

"Mother," I pleaded, "please rest, don't try to talk."

She held my hand tighter. "Let me talk. I might not be able to after tonight."

She began to breathe unevenly. "Boo-Boo, you'll be fourteen soon; you're no more a child. I expect you to take my place."

"Oh, no! Mother, you mustn't leave us! Please!"

"Boo-Boo, be brave." The words were a stern order, as sobering as if she had seized me by the shoulders and shaken me.

"You will take care of the family."

After a while, she said, "I am only sorry I won't be able to see you all grow up. And I so miss your grandpa and grandma in Peking. When you see them again, tell them I love them."

That evening she sank into a final coma.

She died on a Sunday morning, as if she had chosen a day when both Cynthia and I could be by her side. She said a few words neither of us could understand. A nurse came in to take her pulse and looked at us. It was over.

Cynthia and I knelt beside her bed, trembling. Neither of us could cry.

Mother's death left me head of the household with a monthly budget of three hundred dollars. For a family of five—Cynthia had returned to nursing school—this meant cutting corners and learning to do without. I had always wanted to take piano lessons. But the budget could bear the cost of only one student, and so my sister Theresa, being as keen to study as I, was the one to enroll. (The sacrifice I made was not wasted for, to this day, Theresa, who lives in Houston, Texas, and is a computer programming genius, plays the piano consistently and well.)

By the following year, the strain had caught up. There was simply no way I could go to school and simultaneously manage a household on so little money. I was beginning to feel my sisters' resentment keenly. I had become the disciplinarian and taskmaster—unbearable in a sibling.

With Father's written permission, I got us all into boarding school at St. Paul's, a French convent. The fee was fifty dollars per boarder. After room and board, each of us was left with an allowance of ten dollars, out of which came monthly expenses—clothing, books, and other incidentals.

At some point in those years when budgets and bank accounts were a daily headache, I made a vow: If ever I had enough money to live comfortably, I would never budget again.

Luck has been with me. I never have.

Boarding school meant limited freedom: We were allowed out only twice a month. In the long intervals between holiday weekends, we had to find other ways to amuse ourselves. Fantasy was often the best entertainment, and, since it was a time when we were absorbing classical and romantic literature, we poured much of the resultant sentimentality into weekly letters to boyfriends in neighboring schools.

As editor of the school paper with a facility for speedy composition, I was also resident scribe, charged with conducting most romantic correspondence. Each Saturday afternoon, after my own letter writing was done, I would sit down to compose love letters for four or five of my girl friends. This required reading their mail—a privilege that gave me a certain amount of power. Intimate knowledge of their secrets meant that they were willing to do just about anything for me: iron my uniform, make my bed, and run other menial errands.

These long-distance courtships were by and large fleeting, but there was one with a happy ending. In my class was a painfully shy girl, a brilliant student in science and mathematics but unimaginative in the realm of romance. It so happened that the young man courting her was a college student with a remarkable literary flair, plainly visible from his letters.

Every Saturday for two semesters, I gave him my best effort under my friend's name. It was only after they were wed that the truth emerged: Not only was the bride unable to recite the famous Chinese poems, she had never even written her own love letters.

Ten years ago, I met this couple, still happily married, in Taiwan. He was a distinguished writer and publisher, and she was dean of a girls' school

How we laughed over those early letters!

"You really had me fooled for a whole year," he said. "I didn't know I was courting you instead of my wife."

"Nonsense," I said, "you *were* courting her. J iust translated her profound feelings for you." And everyone was satisfied.

Not all my efforts as a literary mercenary were so successful. One of my clients was found out, sending her boyfriend into a fit of rage, with accusations of gross dishonesty. He demanded an apology from me, which I gave. Still dissatisfied, the young man insisted we meet. I declined. But at the end of the last year of high school, it happened that I won a writing contest—and taking second place among the ninety-nine other contestants was my old pen pal.

When we went to receive our awards, we studied each other with curiosity, for we were intimate strangers.

He was tall, handsome, and self-assured and I was young and smitten. But he was suffering the humiliation of defeat at the hands of a girl.

"From now on you'd better be a little careful," he said, half joking, half warning. "You're showing too much of your brain." He made me feel indecent, as though I had shown too much of my underwear.

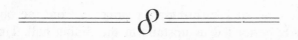

8

The fateful explosion of Pearl Harbor struck us in Hong Kong a day later: December 8, 1941.

At eight o'clock in the morning, I was brushing my hair in front of the mirror in my room when the first violent concussions shook the dormitory. The image of my own panic, caught

in that mirror—mouth agape, eyes wide, hairbrush suspended—
is burned into my memory.

The building trembled with each profound blast, followed by
the shrill chatter of antiaircraft and machine guns.

In the corridor outside, voices were echoing the same question: "What is it, what is it? What's going on?"

I turned on the radio beside my desk and again stood trans-
fixed. A calm British voice was speaking in the deliberate tones
of an announcement. "War . . . Japanese planes . . . Kaitak Airfield . . . ships in the harbor . . . ground fire . . . attacking
places . . ."

Mother Superior had started directing traffic. "Everybody
down to the shelter. Please hurry, hurry now."

I turned off the radio, took a warm coat from the closet, and
went out into the hall to look for my sisters. We gathered together and started down to the basement shelter. Through the
window of the stairway landing, I could see across Hong Kong
Bay toward Kaitak Airfield in Kowloon. A giant mushroom of
smoke had sprouted out from the bombed airport.

The basement shelter was cold and choked with damp mist.
We sat on wooden benches shivering, listening to the muted
sounds of war: the stutter of machine guns and the thunder of
detonating bombs. After each earthshaking explosion, a thin
shower of dust fell from the ceiling beams and hung in the light
of the shaded ceiling bulbs. A few small children began to cry.

We prayed and said countless rosaries. Hours passed, the
wooden benches grew harder, the children could not be consoled.

Night came at last, bringing a surcease from the bombing.
Mother Superior led us upstairs to the dining hall. Tired and
stiff from the long hours on the hard benches, we wolfed down
a supper of dry bread and milk.

It was the first of many unnerving days.

In the beginning, Mother Superior kept predicting an early
Japanese defeat. But, by the fourth day, rumors were circulating that the Japanese had not only captured Kaitak Airport,

they had also landed on Kowloon. The peninsula was now occupied by the Royal Army of Japan.

Mother Superior crossed herself. "Keep praying, and leave
everything in God's hands."

Each morning before dawn we rose, washed, pulled on warm
clothes, and went down to the shelter to shiver until nightfall,
returning to our dormitories only to sleep.

But sleep was difficult on an empty stomach. With all the
food shops shut down, we were running out of supplies. One
morning, Mother Superior announced an austerity drive: All of
us, about fifty nuns and boarders, would have to get by on one
slice of bread for breakfast, and half a bowl of rice for supper.

In later years, I met a woman who had spent four years in a
concentration camp. The prolonged hunger, she told me, had
left her with an obsessive appetite.

It is only an accident of metabolism that has spared me a
similar scar.

The war grew in intensity as Christmas approached, making
a mockery of Mother Superior's hopeful prediction. The bomb-
ings continued through the night, keeping us prisoners in the
basement, where we slept on mattresses and shared blankets on
the stone floor.

Three days before Christmas, a bomb struck one of the
school buildings, almost directly above our shelter. Now all
water and electricity were cut off. News of the outside world
came from the servants who bravely ventured forth during lulls
in the bombardment. The stories they brought back were heart-
stopping. The Japanese definitely had taken Kowloon and part
of Hong Kong, looting, raping, and killing wherever they went.

Christmas Eve came and went with an uneasy calm. The
bombing had stopped; an ominous silence followed. There
were rumors that the British had surrendered.

At midnight Mother Superior shepherded us to the chapel to
pray and sing Christmas carols by candlelight. The sky was
clear and cold, studded with stars that seemed chipped from
ice.

Between prayers, I asked a silent question: "O God, do our prayers mean anything?"

Once I turned to a nun kneeling beside me in the chapel. "Suppose we are doing the wrong thing by praying?" I said. "Suppose God and the Blessed Virgin are sick of hearing us beg?"

The answer came back, firm but uninspiring. "Nonsense, child. Just have faith and pray."

On Christmas Day we heard the announcement: The war in Hong Kong was over, the British had indeed surrendered, the Japanese were in control. We knew it was only a matter of time before they would come to the convent. Two weeks later, they were there.

"They're coming up the stairs," someone cried.

The hammer of heavy boots began pounding the wooden stairs. We had seen them coming from our dormitory window above the courtyard, and imagined the worst. The two servants in the school had carried bloodcurdling reports about robbery and rape by the Japanese victors. Young girls were gang-raped and disembowelled, they said, while their parents or husbands looked on, held helpless at gunpoint.

In the dormitory we stood huddled in small groups, mesmerized by the terrible rhythm of stomping boots moving closer and closer toward us.

Across the hall a key grated against a lock. We could hear the timbre of Mother Superior's voice—and the unevenness of our own breathing. Then the key turned in the lock of our door and it swung open.

Behind Mother Superior were ten or more Japanese soldiers in filthy uniforms, reeking of alcohol and onion. I couldn't take my eyes off their boots; they were thick with mud.

Mother Superior's round, usually placid face wore an expression of arrested fright. "Girls," she said, in a quavering voice, "give me your watches and fountain pens."

We hurried to obey, rummaging for the articles and handing them to her as she stood stiffly in the doorway. With stern formality she distributed the pens and watches among the soldiers. They shook the watches, holding them to their ears, then unscrewed and examined all the fountain pens. The Chinese interpreter spoke up: They wanted more.

Mother Superior shook her head and spread her arms. "There is no more." Huge sweat stains had spread on her white sleeves under her arms.

The soldiers lingered, arguing among themselves in guttural outbursts. Then, grumbling, they tramped away.

At the bottom of the stairs, the interpreter turned to say, "We will return tomorrow and search the whole place."

I threw myself on the bed and lay staring at the wall, dry-eyed, though tears would have been a relief. The danger was over for the time being, but I was still shaking.

We sat out those six months in the convent compound behind locked doors, cold, hungry, but unmolested. We had almost nothing to eat but beans: dried beans, red beans, black beans, green beans, but always beans and more beans, only occasionally replaced by cabbage leaves. The leaves were the part of the cabbage which once had been too coarse even for pigs.

At the time of the bombing, I had been accepted to True Light High School, an elite and academically respected day school. Though the change was inconvenient—I was still boarding at St. Paul's with my younger sisters—I was grateful to be among the hundred and fifty chosen out of three thousand applicants.

I kept busy during those difficult months, in stiff competition at True Light, commuting to St. Paul's, and, in addition, teaching the first through the fifth grades. I was ready for college, but the nearest one—Lingnan University—had moved to the interior of China near Kweilin, and I could not have moved away from the convent without protection, even if I could have left my four younger sisters.

Not that I wanted to leave at that point, because, by then, Bill Wong had arrived.

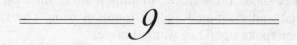

He was a young architect visiting his parents from Chungking and, though he was ten years older, I fell in love with him instantly, without premeditation, just like a fifteen-year-old.

He was to have returned to his job after the new year, but, like countless others, was trapped in Hong Kong when the Japanese attacked. For the three weeks of battle that followed, we saw and heard nothing of each other. Mail had ceased, news was sketchy, and the only steady source of information was gossip and rumors. Time was a dead weight threatening to sink us into despair, but I fought it with a daily exercise: writing to Bill. I took great care with those letters, even though they would not reach him for some time, if ever.

Now, for the first time, I was writing love letters of my own, not the formula worked out for my classmates. The technique acquired as class correspondent was not serving me very well. I tore up more sheets of paper than I saved. It wasn't so easy to speak from the heart.

But the letters eased the strain of the three weeks until the surrender of Hong Kong, when Bill could come and visit once more at the convent. He had no missives to offer, but there was more than relief in the way he said my name again and again, so that the nuns watching us were embarrassed and looked down at the floor.

He had brought small packages of food for me and my sisters—a merciful change from the dried beans that sustained us during those months.

The curfew was from six in the evening to six the next morning, so his visits were always during the day. Our hideaway was a tiny courtyard behind the school. In winter months the stone steps facing the lily pond were too cold for comfort, but it was our sanctuary, a place to clasp hands, read to each other, and exchange vows of lasting devotion.

We read all the modern Chinese classics there: *All Men Are Brothers, The Golden Lotus, Strange Stories from a Chinese Studio, Romance of the Three Kingdoms, Adventures of the Monkey.* We would interrupt each other to read out a phrase or passage that struck us. Once, I put down my novel, *Dream of the Red Chamber*—which I had read at least three times—and stared at the dragonflies catching the sun's glint on the lily pads.

"What are you thinking?" he asked.

"About marriage. I'll never get married in China."

"Why not?"

"Look at all these women," I said, shaking the book, "they have no life of their own." I read him several pages. He thought for a while and said, "It is not true, China has changed a great deal and will continue to change."

"But look," I said. "The men are never true to their women. They're all unfaithful."

"But in the old days," said Bill, "the wife expected her husband to stray; she even found excuses for him. That was the custom, the mark of respect for a husband."

Then he looked very serious, an expression he put on whenever he was teasing. "Men are naturally polygamous and sensible women have always made allowances for their occasional lapses," he said. "That's why modern women are so unhappy. They may win equality and independence, but they are fools to give up their glamorous position as lovers and concubines."

"Are you serious?" I asked, bristling.

"Of course not," he said, mocking my indignation, and went back to reading, smiling at the page to let me know the teasing was over.

For those six months, from December 1941 to May 1942, my sisters and I remained holed up in the convent, waiting for official permission from the Japanese to leave Hong Kong. With schools, shops, and most offices closed, there was little to distract us from the long uncertain wait for that crucial piece of paper.

We didn't know at the time that the Japanese would have little reason to detain a group of useless children amounting to nothing more than a drain on food supplies. Feeding a population of half a million, on an island that depended on the mainland for all its staples, was becoming a serious problem.

In May, the papers came through at last. Bill had planned on leaving with us, but he had delayed his own application for a permit so long that it was doubtful whether he would get one in time. He could have left three months earlier, but he had risked waiting for us, determined to escort us and his sister, Arlene, through the war zone to the interior.

On the eve of our departure, he came to the convent again to make sure we were ready. "Let me see your luggage," he said, when everything else seemed in order.

With Cynthia, who had joined us from nursing school as we prepared to leave, I led him to the hall and showed him the twenty-four pieces of luggage we had packed the night before. We had left out a lot and were proud of it. But he clapped his hands over his head. "Where do you think you are going—on a pleasure cruise?"

"Start repacking right away," he ordered. "My God, don't you know the time may come when we have to carry our own bags without any help?"

"Sorry, Bill," I said.

"Sorry, Bill," Cynthia said.

We started throwing things out: clothes, books, mementos of Peking.

Early the next morning we arrived at the Star Ferry for the first leg of our trip, in plenty of time to make the six-thirty crossing to Macao. But Bill wasn't there to see us off. He was usually punctual; something terrible must have happened.

Then we saw Arlene running toward us. I had an impulse to race forward and wrest the news—good or bad—from her. But I kept sitting on my bag as though bound to it, until Arlene stood before us, catching her breath and wiping her brow, and handed me a note.

I remember how the piece of paper shook as I read it out loud: Bill had left Hong Kong the night before and would meet us in Macao. I offered a silent prayer of thanks before reading on. He had heard a rumor that the Japanese had stopped issuing exit permits to able-bodied young men seeking to leave Hong Kong. Afraid to take a chance, he had left hurriedly just before the curfew. The note ended with a simple line: "Be brave—for your sake and mine."

I folded the note and stuffed it into a pocket on the inside of my quilted jacket, vowing silently to preserve it through the war. And I did.

Now, with Arlene, we were seven frightened young girls. We moved on to customs inspection, terrified that the Japanese inspectors might spot-check and find Mother's jewelry sewn into our coat seams. Without that secret fund, neither the trip nor mere survival would be possible.

The last to pass through inspection, I was about to move on when one of the customs officials laid a hand on my shoulder. I can still see his face now, flushed, red-eyed, and alcoholic. The grip tightened on my shoulder as if he needed support. He swayed slightly as his face broke into a foolish, lecherous grin. Then he released me with a gentle pat, satisfied, I suppose, by his brief moment of sadistic fun.

The boat ride from Kowloon to Macao gave us a preview of the delays, setbacks, and chance perversities that would mark the rest of our journey into the interior. We boarded, expecting to reach Macao in two to three hours, the normal length of time. Instead, the journey stretched out to three days.

It was the end of May, the southwest monsoon was in full ferment, the heat and humidity of the oppressive rainy season had set in. On the lower deck, buffeted by wind and waves, we managed to shoehorn ourselves into a few empty seats before the desperate crush began. For the next three days we remained glued to our seats, sleeping in shifts and going to the bathroom by turns, lest our places be seized by others.

Packed to the gunwales with refugees, the boat was dangerously overloaded, held up by frequent Japanese inspections from other boats, and festering with refuse. By the time we reached Macao, at least one passenger had died, several were sick and had to be carried ashore, and the rest were almost delirious with hunger.

So great was the relief of seeing Macao at last that I have preserved the memory of crossing the Pearl River to approach it. The picture in my mind is of small granite hills and houses washed in pastel pinks, yellows, and greens. Best of all, I remember two young men on the jetty, waving and jumping more vigorously, it seemed to me, than others in the waiting crowd.

One of them was Bill.

Father had sent word from San Francisco that he would have money delivered to a Catholic church in Macao. But when we got to the mission, the priest knew nothing about us or the message or the money.

We spent about a week in Macao while Bill and his friend Bob Yüeh, another young architect, made inquiries about guides and routes to our next destination, Kwang-chouwan in the Bay of Canton. We needed to find a reliable escort, one with experience in transporting refugees inland. This meant a black market transaction involving astonishing sums of money.

There was no alternative but to part with a piece of jewelry—the first of many appalling losses we would have to take along the way. This one was Mother's seven-carat diamond ring. It fetched a pitiful seven hundred dollars, but the cash bought us the promise of passage to free China. By then we were a party of nineteen: Bill and his sister Arlene, Bob Yüeh, the six Chan girls, and ten other refugees who felt it would be safer to be part of a larger group, and an armed escort.

It would be a roundabout route, through areas too impover-
ished for hospitals or doctors—a detour necessary to avoid the
Japanese and the Communists. The journey, we were told,
would take a couple of weeks.

As it turned out, we were on the road for a total of two
months.

The Book of Liberation

10

"How long will it take us?" I asked Bill.

"Twenty-seven to thirty days at our present rate. If no flood or other catastrophe stops us, and if we're not rained off the road for a few days."

The refugee trails crisscrossed wartime China like a crawling centipede: a slow-moving stream of footsore families, overloaded wheelbarrows, and sickly pack animals, all fleeing from occupied areas.

The people limped on diseased, blistered, often shoeless feet; the animals buckled under the strain; the carts sagged and dragged under piles of shabby belongings surmounted by the very old, the very young, or the very sick.

We stumbled along roads pitted with ditches and potholes the size of craters. The hot earth seared our feet. The winds showered us with powdered grit that clogged the throat and stung the eyes and rubbed sores along the sweat creases of the skin. Yet when the rain came down, filling the potholes with slush, the road was a minefield of muddy traps.

Scraps of furniture and discarded baggage littered the roadsides, picked clean by beggars and scavengers. Other tokens of disaster marked the trails: graveyards and isolated graves every mile or so, an overturned truck here, a broken-down ox cart there, and fallen wheelbarrows everywhere.

After a while people seemed to stop talking, plodding along

with eyes fixed ahead on the ground, or squatting against their packs by the roadside with open mouth and heaving chest.

How long would it take? The question made the rounds every few miles. It wasn't so much curiosity as a ritual of complaint.

Twenty-seven days! "I'll have muscles like a peasant," I complained.

"And a good deal more understanding of what China's peasants have gone through for centuries," Bob added gratuitously.

Bill's friend had a way of turning chitchat into heavy polemic. He was beginning to get on my nerves.

"Bob, are you a Communist?" I asked him. He didn't like being confronted squarely.

"Some of the reforms the Communists promise are not altogether bad." He said this with a certain smugness, as if he alone were privy to those reforms.

"Look at them!" he said, pointing to a peasant family plodding through the dust. "After a lifetime of donkey work, they don't even own enough to pack a cart."

I felt somehow responsible—for their hardship and ours.

"Are you sorry you offered to escort us?" I asked.

"Sorry? No. Why should I be sorry? My feet are blistered, my throat is burning, my back is breaking, but it's been a holiday."

Bill gave me a look that said, "Ignore him."

I turned to Bill, changing the subject. "I wonder how our poet Li Po traveled when he was banished to Yunan?"

I was thinking of the cold afternoons in the convent courtyard. No matter what we read, we kept coming back to the T'ang poets.

"Not like this," Bill said. "Not in such style. I mean, he didn't have you."

The compliment confused me. I never knew when to take him seriously.

Still, it was as though I had taken a sip of hot, sweet wine.

We came to a bridge where two men with rifles slung across

their backs were cursing at an old man. They had drawn him off to the side of the road. Five women, obviously related to the old man, stood at a respectful distance, wringing their hands.

Seeing us, the bandits fell silent. The old man eyed us with a combination of misery and hope. The bandits studied us with predatory curiosity. They probably would not search the women, for that would bring nine years of bad luck, but they could torture the men until the women broke down and paid a ransom for them.

Maybe they felt there were too many of us. Maybe they saw we were only minimally armed, which suggested we were of modest means. Maybe their rifles were empty. In any case, they waved us through.

"But how can we leave the old man in their hands?" Cynthia asked, as soon as we were out of earshot.

"How can we *not* leave him?" Bob replied. "It's every man for himself and his own."

Seeing us agog, he said, "The old fellow will bargain his way out for a few coins or a sack of rice."

We moved on toward the next village. There, two Japanese soldiers stood guard at the gate, ostensibly on the lookout for Communists or illegal travelers—though everyone knew that these itinerants were gold mines of extortion and squeeze. We had to split up to find shelter. Four of us, Bill, Connie, Sylvia, and I, went to a small inn choked with the stinking black smoke of a *tung* oil lap. On the dirt floor of the outer room, bodies lay like fish in a hold, limb over limb, three deep in places.

The innkeeper stepped over them with careless ease. He sized us up with peasant cunning. We were dirty, exhausted, beggarly in appearance and spirit, but he read us for better quality. He led us to an inner room and pointed to a wooden platform, about six feet long by four feet wide, covered with a filthy quilt, and quoted a shocking price.

Too weary to bargain, we started to walk out. The innkeeper jumped to grab Bill's arm, planting one foot squarely on the face of a sleeping client. What would the honorable gentleman consider fair? Bill offered a figure as outlandishly low as his was high. The man accepted with a bland smile.

Everywhere around us were prostrate bodies, most of them old, giving off the unwholesome odors of medicine and mold and unwashed flesh.

"Well, what else can we do?" Bill said in apology. "I can't have you lie on the ground outside. It will be cold by morning, and this country is full of leeches."

"Let's make the best of it," said Connie, bravely trying to set an example. "But how?"

"Here, you lie this way, and you lie that way," Bill directed. Then he went to find floor space for himself amidst the tangled bodies.

Further along the way, in Kwangei province, at another inn, we found a dead rat in our bed. When we screamed, the innkeeper charged in, alarmed. "What is it, what is it?"

Cowering in a corner, we pointed to the rat.

The innkeeper shook his head and clucked with annoyance. "Women! Why all the fuss about a dead rat?"

He picked it up by the tail, swung it playfully once or twice in front of our faces, and tossed it out the door.

Across the occupied areas, the procession grew longer by the day, joined by thousands who had hung onto home and property until the last minute. They carried in their packs everything they owned: frayed quilts, straw slippers, cheap images of household gods, pots and pans not worth small change, and a few precious packs of seed to plant at journey's end (though most would be devoured at some desperate point along the way).

Traders and hawkers were living off rumors of gross inflation within the cities and offered to divest the wayfarers of their remaining possessions for paltry sums of money. Barter of all sorts went on. Everything had its value: not just gold, silver, jade, pearls, amber, and perfume, but a handful of cured seed, mismatched sneakers, torn mosquito nets, and clay cooking pots, cracked and glued together again. Thieves and beggars flourished, despite brutal whippings and canings.

No stray dogs ran through the encampments, because hungry people would eat any animal available.

Once, outside a teahouse, we saw a sedan chair, covered with yellow dust and guarded by a haggard servant. The owner was sitting inside the teahouse, sucking up a large dish of noodles and snails with loud snorts, like a pig snuffling for truffles. He wore fine silk brocade, but loose flesh hung from his face in quivering folds, like a turkey's wattles.

"Would you believe it?" he said to us, through a full mouth, "nineteen days on the road with almost nothing to eat except the sweetmeats I brought with me! While peasants like you were shovelling in real food because you had your own cooking pots."

"We were counting weevils and worms in our food and jealous of the one who had the most," Bill said in his haughtiest Mandarin.

The rich man looked startled. "So you travel poor, my friend? Is it worthwhile?" He answered himself. "Perhaps so, perhaps so. Five times I was squeezed for taxes. Three times more my guard had to fight off bandits." He was inhaling his noodles by now, scarcely using his chopsticks.

When his plate was empty, he poked around for hidden scraps, then ordered another. "I will probably be poor myself by the time I reach Chungking," he said. "But I hear these are the last noodles on the way. At least I will enjoy what I can. This ugly city is bursting at the seams. It has never known such prosperity." And he addressed himself to the precious second helping as though he, too, had never known such prosperity.

Food was becoming prohibitive. The harvests had been commandeered by the Japanese; the penalty for black-marketing was death. But farmers were still hoarding scant rations. Food was distributed by the occupying forces for sale in towns along the trail, but what they supplied was so spoiled or weevil-ridden that their own soldiers spat it out.

"You see who suffers in every way?" Bob was working up to one of his harangues. "The peasant. It's always the peasant. The backbone of China, but nobody gives a damn about him, not even his own people."

"Isn't that what the Nationalists are fighting for, too?" Bill asked.

"That," Bob said obtusely, "is a coin with two sides."

Staples and vegetables grew scarcer and less appetizing. But eggs were always available, mostly boiled in tea. If only we had made more of those rice cakes recommended by Greataunt Liao! She was right about some things, after all. Now and then we would find game—rabbit or pheasant or wild duck—but always at impossible prices. We ate pickled locusts and dried grasshoppers, mountain berries, sunflower seeds, and lotus seeds (the best and most expensive of all). But fresh fruit was strictly overpriced.

"If we allow ourselves one section of a pear a day," Sylvia calculated, "they will stretch as far as Liuchow. But who wants to eat rotten pears?" She looked defeated at the prospect.

Bill laughed at the earnest calculation. "We are not that hard up—yet. Let's feast lavishly on a pear a day. At least it gives a little moisture and strength. The only strength we get from the rotten vegetables is in the weevils."

Sylvia made a face. "They're hard to eat, even with your eyes shut."

"Nonsense," said Bill. "Weevils and worms are meat. Didn't you know? That's what the Japanese tell us."

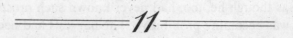

We had been on the road for two weeks and were to spend the night in Kwangchouwan, then move on to Liuchou in Kwangsi province. There were two reasons for avoiding delay: The Japanese were said to be getting closer, and Kwangchouwan was spilling over with refugees. The inns and rest houses were packed, private houses were filled to capacity, and the overflow were bivouacked out in the streets.

But I had come down with fever and chills, and my strength was ebbing by the hour. The group held a conference to decide whether to stay in Kwangchouwan, or to forge ahead as planned. Staying entailed the hopeless task of finding shelter, but moving on would mean an almost murderous scramble for a sedan chair to carry me along.

There was a heated argument between Bill and Bob, ending in an icy standoff. Bill wanted to stay, at least for a day or two. Bob was self-appointed spokesman for those in favor of moving on. He was sick of the whole trip by now and never let us forget it. He gave in finally to Bill's overruling—we would stay and Bill would find accommodations—but with thunder on his face and a hiss in his voice: "Women, stupid women!" It was all a woman's fault—it usually was—but he couldn't forgive a man who let his judgment be impaired by a woman's illness.

Bill had a contact in Kwangchouwan, a manufacturer of firecrackers. He apologized for not being able to put us up; his house was packed tight, like a can of sardines, but we were welcome to his factory warehouse.

It was a windowless box of a building, covered with a rusty corrugated roof. By day it trapped the intense June heat like an airless furnace; by night it was an icebox. When it rained, the dirt floor dissolved into a series of cesspools. We longed to throw open the double doors to the factory to let in some fresh air, but dreaded the armies of mosquitos that even the burning incense could not repel.

The worst of the illness was not the fever that left me so parched as to bring on nightmares about being eaten up by flames. Nor was it the demonic chills that made the bed itself shake, so that my younger sisters recoiled in fear. It wasn't even the hallucinations and cravings for certain foods—a taste of meat, a dream of walnut candy—that was the hardest to bear. It was the lack of a toilet in the warehouse.

The nearest available spot was out in the fields behind the

warehouse, and when the dysentery was at its meanest, I had to drag myself outside, an effort so painful that it brought on vomiting and shivers along the way.

For almost a week, fever and delirium took their hold, despite the Ten Thousand Miracle Oil, guaranteed to cure everything from ringworm to gout; despite quinine, fast dwindling in supply; despite a quack's evil elixir of leaves and herbs, boiled over charcoal through the night and gagged down before dawn; despite the thrust of an acupuncturist's needles into my stomach.

The acupuncturist chanted like a witch to my cries of pain.

"Cover her with a mosquito net and burn mosquito-chaser joss sticks," she whispered. "For three days, don't call her by her real name or say anything about her getting well. Otherwise, the evil spirits may hear and send the illness back upon her."

I heard Bill and Cynthia holding a whispered conference. When I turned my head, I saw their faces in the candlelight, owlish with fatigue.

"Leave me here," I said. I felt indifferent, drained of feeling. "You all go on. I'm not going to make it." I sank into a deep sleep.

When I woke up, almost a day later—and you may call this a miracle—both fever and dysentery had abated.

Bill hired a sedan chair left vacant by an old man who had died of a heart attack in it, clawing for air as he went under. The carriers simply laid him in the gutter and looked around for a new passenger. It cost us more sea salt and some precious jasmine tea, but gave me time to recover on the way to our next stop.

The carriers made good time, spurred on by their terror of ghosts. These spirits wandered along the highways at night, weeping, abandoned in a strange place without directions to heaven. Lurking in the darker stretches of the highway at sundown, they called out the names of passersby. And woe to him who was stupid enough to answer; they would then claim his body.

Before we reached Liuchou we stopped at a village near Yülin where an innkeeper said, "I can give you robes while you leave your clothing in the bathhouse. When you awake, they will be as sweet as spring air. There is oil for afterwards to ease the sores of travel."

Two steaming tubs filled with clean water! And privacy in the form of a low partition for separation! The Japanese laughed about this ridiculous Chinese modesty. They themselves made a casual social occasion out of a communal bath, inviting friends in and serving tea and wine while scrubbing themselves.

But there was the problem of the jewelry, sewn into the folds of our clothes. Soap and water wouldnt't hurt, but a hot iron might.

"I'll speak to the innkeeper," Bill said. "They cannot soak quilting in any case. It would take days to dry, and might wad up. They must have some method."

When the innkeeper stuck his head in the door to ask if we wanted salt to scrub with, the matter of the hidden treasure was explained.

"Never fear," he said. "We have learned to outwit the louse and bedbug. We turn the clothing inside out and dampen only along the seams and stitches. Then we run the tip of a hot iron over that part. That is where the bugs hide, and it forms a narrow line of steam which detonates them. After that, we scrub the surface with an almost dry lather. This picks up the soil and sterilizes the clothing. When it has fully dried, we brush it off. Nothing in the wadding is affected."

We took our leave of the innkeeper who had deloused us. It was an odd little farewell ceremony, an exchange of gifts that would be meaningless now: a jar of Pond's cold cream for us, a package of salt cake for him.

"It is sea salt, not mountain salt," Bill told him. "It contains iodine. It will be useful for trading in countries where many wear their heads on one shoulder because of goiter."

The steam iron protected the jewelry, but we lost most of it anyway. With luck and ingenuity a person could dodge disease, starvation, even death. But there was no escaping the swindle and fraud of a wartime economy. Once, a respectable looking man offered us safe passage in return for the fee in advance. We ripped open a quilted robe and handed him a diamond brooch. We never saw him again.

I told Bill about the time I had overheard Mother's transaction.

One afternoon in Hong Kong, about a year before Mother died, I came home from school more impatient than usual. I couldn't wait to tell her about the green jacket my best friend had worn to school.

I was going through that phase of girlhood when the ideal is a mirror image of one's best friend, and I wanted a jacket just like hers.

We were living in an apartment, sixteen Golden Dragon Terrace on Causeway Bay. I went racing through the rooms, shouting for Mother.

Ah Su, the old amah, came shuffling out of the kitchen, a finger on her lips. Be quiet! She motioned to me, pushing me away from the door to Mother's room.

But I could already hear the voice inside. It was a woman's voice I hadn't heard before, saying, "Mrs. Chan, these are elegant. Exquisite. Without question you would do better if we were not at war. But you must know these are hard times. The future is uncertain. No one really wants to waste money on jewelry. I'm afraid I can't offer you more than what I offered yesterday."

I had to strain to hear Mother's reply. "But these are bracelets my mother gave me on my eighteenth birthday. . . . "

There was a long silence.

Then Mother's stricken voice. "Surely they're worth more? My husband works for the government. But what he makes just isn't enough to see six children through school. . . ."

I turned away from the door, ears burning with shame. Mother was selling off her jewelry, reduced to haggling like a fishwife, and I had overheard the degrading transaction.

All of a sudden, I saw what it meant: her mysterious telephone conversations, the figures quoted, the way she kept going to her safe-deposit box to get jewelry we never saw her wear.

In my room, I burrowed into bed and sobbed. In Peking we had been reared like silkworms, in cocoons spun of infinite wealth. Now the cushioning was falling apart and the threat of poverty was terrifying.

The lesson was clear: From now on, I would have to do well at school. I would have to provide for Mother and free her from the soul-destroying fear of poverty. There was no choice.

"How I cried," I told Bill.

"You'd be crying much more without your diamonds," he said in his matter-of-fact way, "in a concentration camp."

One day, he brought out a ring of his own to use as barter.

"But it's an ancestor ring," I protested.

"So? Maybe it will save my worthless body to join my worthy ancestors someday."

12

We marched on toward Kweilin. Along the way, we had met an old man riding atop an overloaded ox cart, clutching a broken umbrella against the sun and crying out, "Water, water!"

Bill had been saving four pears, protected in a square of matting and nursed in his pack. In return for two of these pears, the owner of the ox cart had let us load our packs onto his cart, around the old man.

Late that afternoon, the sun a halo behind his head, the old man sat sucking on his last pear with the concentrated selfishness of the senile.

"Ai ya, ai ya! The drink of heaven!" he called down, greedily licking his fingers. "I thank you humbly, and bless your ancestors."

He smiled and bowed to Bill with foolish servility, letting out a long sigh of contentment that rattled a little at the end. Then he fell back on the load with eyes wide open and lay still as though to contemplate the vastness of the sky.

To prepare for the old man's funeral, the women in the family were dispatched to find a water teacher, a fortune-teller, and a spirit vendor, while the old man's son, the farmer, went off to negotiate for a graveyard with the owner of the land. His small son was left to guard the cart, though the corpse was already protected by a host of jealous demons.

Bill wandered off to barter for a square of honey as offering for the dead. He found not only the offering, but firecrackers to frighten away the evil spirits until the grave was filled.

The firecrackers were sold by a vendor, one of dozens who had joined the ragtag funeral procession. There were even orchestras and opera troupes, jugglers and singsong girls, fortune-tellers and shamans. It was a traveling sideshow, reassuring in its vulgarity.

By dark, the procession had dwindled down to the stragglers, the old, and the invalid. Bandits exacted their toll from them, restrained from outright plunder only by superstition. For to strip a person of all possessions and cause death by starvation would leave the victim empty-handed at the entrance to the spirit world, thus inviting the vengeance of his ghost, and avalanches and flash floods upon the oppressor. The funeral procession would pass unharmed.

The farmer signaled for the women to begin their dirge. It was more a singsong chant with the deceased than a lament, the women reassuring him that he would be missed, reminding him not to change his winter underclothes too soon, and cautioning him to keep away from too much hot sauce in heaven, as that could aggravate his ulcer.

The water teacher and fortune-tellers had chosen the grave site, on a peaceful slope beneath a red-gold maple tree. Stout local peasant boys had been hired to dig the grave, while the farmer built the sacrificial altar. Then, with his son's help, he rolled the corpse in matting.

The funeral party wound its way toward the hill in the dark, guided by the dim glow of a candle lantern and the occasional flares of firecrackers. When the body was lowered into the ground, the spirit would see the gaudy altar, festooned with colored strips of paper and fabric, and holding the slender offerings of the survivors: a square of honey, a couple of bruised, discolored pears, a bowl of rice, a handful of nuts, a turnip, an ear of corn.

Moaning and jabbering last-minute instructions, the women sent the corpse on its way. The last firecrackers exploded in the grave, paving the way for the body, hastily lowered and buried before the demons got wind of its whereabouts.

We repaired to the farmer's hut, where the women had prepared a feast. The grain was the farmer's own, and the vegetables—cabbage, corn, sweet potatoes—were not rotten. There were walnuts, hazelnuts, chestnuts . . . and pork.

The women sang sad songs. ("Dear Master, you were always generous on Earth. Now that you've gone to the other world, walk slowly and take care of yourself, walk slowly and take care of yourself.") They sang to the accompaniment of a crude, wavering lute, wavering a little themselves after the homemade wine.

Through the curtain of dust, the sun looked like a dirty coin. We munched on handfuls of parched wheat.

Bill spotted a respectable looking family and addressed the head of the household, the former mayor of a village. The family was pushing an overburdened wheelbarrow with anxious haste, intent on reaching the next town before dark.

The mayor was reluctant to do business. "We have a little food, but we are many mouths and we have many *li* to go."

"We have sweet potatoes," Bill offered, "but no fuel."

"Sweet potatoes!" The mayor's eyes lit up. "We've been living on turnips and corn gruel. And we have fuel."

"Then we can cook and cut the potatoes into shares," Bill suggested.

The mayor smiled broadly. "We cannot cut the gruel, but we can divide a little into each cup."

We all stopped beside the road to make a fire in an open

brazier. The travelers thinned out to a trickle. We had half a cup each of tea, only slightly stronger and darker than hot water, but refreshing.

"I'm hungry," little Loretta said—for the fourth time that day. She was always hungry and cried for food others were eating, but was bearing up as bravely as the rest.

A water carrier came singing, "Sunrise to work, yao ho-ho; sunset to stop, yao ho-ho."

Bill stepped out to the road to hail the bent wire of a man springing up and down under the weight of two large jars hanging from each end of a bamboo pole across his shoulders. The haggling went on for half an hour, Bill shouting, "Thief! Robber! Murderer!" and the water carrier screaming, "Landlord! Warlord! Slave owner who would steal a poor peasant's last meal!" From the vehemence of the transaction, it was difficult to believe it was only tea and not blood that was at stake. In the end, they settled the price with their fists, hitting them together to bind the bargain. Pleased with the exercise, they both grinned from ear to ear.

13

Toward Kweilin, the land changed abruptly from stunted foothills to gaunt peaks that pierced foggy skies. The mornings were uncomfortably damp and chilly, warming up only around eleven o'clock. Then the sun beat down on the rock faces, making us sweat, until a cloud blotted it out and left us cold and damp. By late in the afternoon, the sun had vanished; for the rest of the day, we moved in chilly valleys of dreamlike gloom.

Kweilin rose out of the dawn mists of its myriad of canals. Ripe pomegranates flashed through the green fretwork of trees. A spicy incense threaded the air, issuing from tender leaves and weathered barks. Kweilin was quiet but open-faced and unconspiring—not a city that crouched behind innumerable high walls like Peking.

We knew we would be here about a month, waiting for money from Father. Soon the group would be splitting up. We decided to spend a week on the Liu River.

Because passage was cheap, we took a boat, rowed by the boatman's wife and daughter. The boatman himself sat smoking his waterpipe, paying stern attention to the business of filling and refilling it with tobacco. Occasionally, he would deign to point out some landmark of note. The banks were dotted with terraces, temples, and teahouses. When we passed the Wooden Dragon Cave, the river turned and broadened, opening up onto gaudy mat-and-bamboo sails of pleasure boats flitting over the sparkling water.

It was hard to imagine such a thing as war.

The river cut through a mysterious grotto, a chain of high caves scooped out of the surrounding hills. Light shot through the water and clarified it. Down below, great schools of gold-and-silver fish were darting past like showers of miniature arrows.

Loretta leaned over the boat to scoop up a drink. Then, face dripping, she hollered into the caves and smiled at the thousand answers that echoed back.

The hills had locked us into a fortress of bare, rugged rock, softened only by bursts of red dodder that foamed in places. In the backwaters of the river, snow-white duckweed swayed to gentle currents. Up ahead, the river wound in a strip of porcelain blue through bare dun hills. Finally, on the crest of the hills, it rushed out of the sky in a cascade of golden mist.

We stopped at the foot of the Huanshan Hill, then climbed through an endless series of rocks and miniature shrines to the Lover's Tomb. Legend told the story of a Ming minister whose politics had cost him the life of his beloved. He brought her remains here, the most exquisite view he could find on the river, and built a magnificent tomb where he spent the rest of his life writing poetry with the eloquence and dedication of the brokenhearted.

  : We started back as sunset cast gaudy banners across the sky. The hills were shadowy and forbidding, but the water stayed crimson with the boat's reflection as we approached the arched silhouette of the Bridge of Ten Thousand Years. The evening star hung high and bright above. Below, the fishing boats sent out flickers of light, like fireflies drifting lazily on the darkening river.

The boatman's daughter, no longer needed at the oars, beat time with bamboo chopsticks on a little porcelain plate and sang despairing love songs. As if her sweet voice had moved the moon, it spread its golden light behind the black profiles of the hills.

The boatman's wife lighted incense on a tiny altar decorated with white duckweed, while holding a cup of clear water drawn from the cave.

"If you make a wish now, the water god is bound to grant it," she said, "for you have caught the moonrise."

I looked at Bill, whose face was in the shadow, and felt his hand touching mine.

Now every minute was precious. Cynthia would be leaving for Kunming, to join the Fourteenth Air Force as a nurse. Connie, Sylvia, and Theresa would leave with a group of students for their school near Kweilin, and I, keeping little Loretta with me, would be going to college at Lingnan University, about five hundred miles away. The others in our group were heading in different directions. Though we didn't know it then, Bob would end up with the Communists, never to be heard from again. And I would be parted from Bill. We had not allowed ourselves to dwell on this moment, pretending instead that the separation was only temporary. Bill had a job to do in Chungking, I had college to finish and younger sisters to take care of, we were both young, we would keep in touch, there was time.

But when the time came to go our separate ways, I panicked. Suppose I never saw him again. Suppose he forgot me. How would I manage without him? Whom would I turn to? I had seldom felt so abandoned and bleak. Then I saw with surprise the look on his face: He was fighting to control himself.

"I promised your teacher, Miss Chan," he said in an odd voice, "that I would take care of you as long as you let me. Now I am breaking that promise."

"But you aren't breaking a promise. You've taken care of me. You've saved me; you've saved all of us." I was crying by now, the tears falling unchecked, my fingers threaded through his in a tight knot of solace.

I felt older than he suddenly; he needed consoling.

"I said I'd look after you as long as you let me. Does this mean you've ceased to let me?" In his misery, he was torturing us both with impossible questions.

"Don't forget me," I pleaded.

"Don't you forget me. And write."

We wrote and sent messages until the flimsy thread that binds wartime romances was cut and lost in the chaos of the following years. When I saw him again it was long after the war, and we were both married to different people.

My husband General Chennault had bought me a house in Shanghai which needed remodelling. An architectural firm was recommended to me and I arranged to have the firm's president meet me at the house.

The servant showed him in. For minutes we just stood in the living room, looking at each other speechlessly. He was the first to speak. "How strange it is. I always wanted to go back to Kweilin to find you. At last, when I could get back, you were gone. Now here we are, together again, just when we stopped searching. I am so sorry."

I reached out for his hand. "I am sorry, too, Bill."

"That's war," he said simply.

"Yes, that's war," I agreed. And we were strangers no more.

At Lingnan University, we learned to live with constant disruption. In keeping with their policy of raining bombs on institutions of learning—first in Korea, then, since 1937, in China—the Japanese were bound to attack us, too. It was their way of striking at the core of national consciousness: the radical student body.

Fearing that Lingnan University would be a target, we kept shifting the campus from village to village. We started out in the north of Canton, in a small village that had never seen electricity or running water.

The school cottages were perched halfway up a hill in rolling, watercolor country. They were rude buildings: four brick pillars with wooden joints to support a tiled roof, matted bamboo walls, and a mud-and-mortar finish over the entire structure to give it a sturdy look.

The classrooms and dormitories were spread out in the scattered cottages, a precaution against concentrated bombing. Sometimes the Japanese pilots flew so low that we could make out their moustaches.

Steps had been cut into the hillside between the rows of cottages, above the clean geometric curves of terraced paddy fields. On a clear day, they stretched out and beyond, green steps climbing to bright blue heavens. In the fields behind were golden cornfields, thick bamboo groves, and fishponds filled with carp.

I finished college in only three years. They were taxing, makeshift years spent running to bomb shelters, scurrying like rats from village to village, bathing in cold water drawn from a well, and studying by candlelight. But they were oddly satisfying times, filled with purpose and optimism.

We read about the war in Spain, the Italians bombing Ethiopia, the Germans invading Austria and Czechoslovakia. There was a sense of common struggle against the enemy which, while it wore different masks in different places, always had the same hideous features of fascism underneath. Each day our cities were bombed, our people killed by the thousands, yet there was a feeling that final victory would be ours. The enemy was making a mistake, we said: the same mistake Napoleon had made in his advance on Moscow.

We had a small theater where we put on plays and poetry readings, music groups, bridge, and Ping-Pong competitions.

Literature sustained me: the *Shih Ching* with its plain tales of the human condition; the songs of the T'ang poets Li Po, Tu Fu, and Su Tung Pao; the picaresque novels of the Ming period, with their rich modern characters and funny sexuality.

My model and mentor was Professor Wu, a stocky, fortyish scholar who always came to class with an air of having forgotten something. He reminded us of a cartoon, with his wire-rimmed glasses and his clownish hair parted in the middle and bristling like the quills of a porcupine. But behind his glasses his eyes swam about like some shifty crustacean's, taking in everything.

He wore shirts that looked as though someone, mistaking them for rags, had rolled them up to wipe the blackboard. They were always wrinkled and, like his eyebrows and hair, were always snowy with chalk. But on his feet, absurdly at odds with his scruffy European shirt and trousers, were a pair of immaculate Chinese cloth shoes.

Sometimes, in the middle of a classroom assignment, I would look up to find Professor Wu sitting sideways at his desk and proudly holding up a foot for a private inspection. If he caught me watching him I would drop my eyes, flushing. When I dared look up again, he would still be watching me.

They used to tease me about being his favorite. I of course had to deny this, but it pleased me secretly to think this might be true, that this scholarly man who could recite the classics backwards and forwards, who lashed out at some poor student's inability with a tongue as stinging as a whip, who gave us backbreaking assignments and had such power over us, that this awesome man might secretly be in love with me, a girl in her teens.

To please him, I worked hard. I wrote and published my first short story, searched for books he mentioned in passing, and, with his help, had two job offers lined up even before I was graduated.

It was only an adolescent infatuation, but I can still see the candlelight flickering under his breath as he read to us in his loud voice. The war was going on outside, but we listened, hypnotized, to Professor Wu, nursing cups of strong Fukienese tea so bitter that it had to be sipped slowly, the way those T'ang poets used to sip wine.

It was six months since we had left Kweilin; we were just settling into school when we had to move again, this time to Kueiyang. Having gathered my sisters together, I had arranged to join a group of students in yet another trek, worse in many ways than the earlier stretches made with Bill.

We were fleeing westward through harsh, rugged terrain now, on foot, by train, by truck. Connie, Sylvia, Theresa, and Loretta all took turns getting sick along the way while I, miraculously, was spared. Now I was alone in charge of them, for Cynthia was working in Kunming. I didn't know what we would do for money in the long run, and I was worn out by months of crushing responsibility.

It was the spring of 1943, and the Japanese had begun the drive that would lead to their capture of the important southern cities: Ch'angsha, Hengyang, Kweilin, Liuchou.

The truck driver was directing the disposal of bundles on the roof of the truck, while engineering ways to crowd in two people where there was barely room for one. One of the passengers, a grotesquely fat man, was threatened with ejection but in the end was allowed to remain. He was a Chungking official, too impatient to await his turn on one of the unpredictable, overcrowded government planes.

The truck waited, chugging, spitting smoke and steam. It was an antediluvian machine, the remnants of an American truck on its last legs, held together with twine.

The truck driver gave the signal to board, standing to one side like a feudal lord surveying his indentured servants and puffing on an expensive imported cigar. He was one of the Yellow Ox agents trafficking in refugees. These agents' fees were astronomical, but at least they were fixed prices and you didn't have to worry about your seat being given to a higher bidder.

I saw a man slip the truck driver a small package, obsequiously addressing him as "Esquire." The bribe, a supply of quinine, was for two end seats where there would be a little more air to breathe.

The driver got in when the last of the herd had been penned, fastened the doors (pausing to tickle his two concubines), and started up the engine. The truck began to shudder with groans and barks.

"Is it going to explode?" Loretta asked.

"We won't know until it does," Connie said comfortingly.

We began crawling forward in the foggy dawn, guided by the tung oil lantern that served as headlights. The dim beam exposed layers of mists that rose from the rivers and canals.

Soon we were careering down the road, the truck driver laughing and talking while one of the concubines cleared the road ahead of stray pedestrians with unexpected blasts from a shrill mouth horn. The pedestrians would spring into ditches as the truck tore by, shaking their fists at us and shouting curses.

As day broke we saw the streams of refugees, many of them young men fleeing conscription to Japanese labor battalions. Their footwear alone told stories of endurance and ingenuity; some were made out of closely sewn layers of cloth, some out of truck-tire scraps, some from blocks of wood.

Ricksha boys were pulling along towering loads of bric-abrac—on which their clients took turns riding—straining uphill like animals in harness, the knotted muscles in their shoulders and calves as tense as strung-out rope.

We coasted in neutral on long downhill stretches, the musical concubines leaning out periodically to toot their horns. Once, an old peasant, too deaf or too infirm to make way, was side-swiped by the truck on a turn that overhung a gorge. His pack shot out in the air, leaving his body as it disappeared over the edge.

Even as we wound up the hillside, the scavengers were pouring down the sides of the gorge, hurrying to save not the old man but his pack.

However, there were generosity and compassion, too. Children, lost or abandoned, were soon adopted, often by families already in danger of starving. A jar of tea was shared here, a rice cake there. There was always someone to revive an old man or woman whose strength, or will, had given out.

Robbery and theft occurred, but not as often as might be imagined. Even the mountain brigands had their own rough code. They would not lay hands on women and children, even though most carried whatever valuables they had hidden in their clothing. They usually left the elderly alone. And when they came upon a small party or a lone traveler—usually after dark, when the road was almost deserted—they might exact a toll, but not an unreasonable one.

One band of robbers was said to have escorted a group of women to the next town without molestation, charging only the usual porterage.

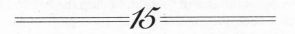

At a town called Chin Chung Chang (nicknamed the Gate of Death) in the province of Kweichow, I remember a slimy gruel of rotten vegetables and moldy rice, peppered with worms and weevils. With desperate humor, we made a game of it, pushing the bugs to the edge of our tin plates and counting them to see who had the biggest "meat treat."

The town, once called Chin Chung Chiang (The Golden River City) and only recently renamed Gate of Death, was on the rail route from Kweilin. It was a town of such meanness and squalor that it was known for its "deficient threes": no three hours of steady sunlight, no three *li* without hill or gorge, no citizen with more than three dollars to his name.

There were other deficiencies: no water safe enough to drink without boiling, yet no fuel to boil it with; no salt to provide iodine, and no cures for the resultant goiter.

Against this backdrop of desolation and filth, the invalid and the war-crippled dragged past. There was little solace from the townspeople, themselves caught in an eternal cycle of poverty, plagues, epidemics, famines, and other disasters.

They moved with an odd stiff-necked gait, heads twisted to one side by the huge goiters that symbolized their hideous fate. They lived in earthwall huts too poor for a table or a wooden stool, one suit of clothing to a family.

Now their luck was turning. They could get a new suit of clothing or a box of cooking utensils from some defeated refugee, simply for carrying his load to the next town. The very louse-ridden floorspace in their earth-wall huts was worth money. Even their foul water had a price. Now at last the accumulated misery and anger could be unleashed; they could swindle and curse and bully the strangers at whim. And they could sink with a vengeance into opium.

These were sterile hills where nothing would grow—except opium poppies the size of lotus and hemp the height of a man. Drugs had been the answer to starvation and brutish poverty since the British spread the habit. Later, the British had fought a war to keep the emperor from forbidding their manufacture. But by then it was the women in regions like this who promoted the habit by feeding drugs to their sons who otherwise would have fled their insufferable homes.

The trains were already crammed, the open windows framing crowds of panting, sweating, grinning, and grimacing faces. Cotton and mat-covered bundles clogged the corridors, along with broken furniture, crates jammed with screaming livestock, and baskets of squawking infants.

We had found room as second-class passengers on the roof of a box car. Families were pressed together like fish in a net. Three men—grandfather, father, and son—managed somehow to occupy a space large enough only for one on the sloped side of the roof, their only protection a raised footrail that ran along the edge.

It was an hour past sunrise, but each inquiry about the train's departure brought the same irritable warning from the conductor. "Right away. Don't leave the train!" Those wanting to stretch cramped legs, or to relieve themselves, did not dare go back into the station rooms and risk being left behind. They chose instead the nearest track to squat in plain view of the leering audience aboard the train who applauded their efforts with cheers and catcalls.

By mid-morning, the crowded human bodies gave off heat and steam that trapped the stale air beneath the roof like an old unused furnace. The young whined and fretted. The old kept up a steady litany of gloom and doom.

Now and then the car would jolt and trundle a few hundred yards down the track, then double back for no apparent reason. The more experienced travelers—those who had been back and forth to collect refugee families, or merchants with business in the interior—said the train could sit there for five days. On the other hand, it could take off in five minutes. Who could tell?

The platform was a chaotic bazaar, with throngs of hawkers selling everything from hard-boiled eggs pickled in tea, to rice cakes and lucky papers. Fortune-tellers shouted out omens and predictions. Fruit-and-nut vendors kept up a hoarse auction. One businessman was busy selling old American fruit jars with screw tops, demonstrating the miracle of airtight design.

Others carried lighted charcoal braziers on one end of a bamboo pole, weighted on the other end by earthen jars. They would stop and squat to cook noodles, vegetables, fish, or soup on order, shouting all the while dire prophesies of starvation ahead: "Your last chance, your last chance for a solid meal! Why hoard coins you will never live to spend? And even if you live, there is nothing to buy. The Japanese will tell you, they have already bombed the land bare."

The Japanese guards seemed to enjoy the humor.

On the train, a young man expressed disgust. "Everything to build morale. We frighten and rob our own worse than the Japanese do." He looked like a student, but was traveling alone, rare for students.

"But not so effectively," a merchant next to him said. "The difference is that the Japanese don't bother robbing the poor."

The student appraised the merchant's overdressed concubine. "Wouldn't you be wiser to travel as a poor man?"

The merchant drummed on his ample stomach. "What can I do to hide this? In any case, there is no more danger. They have got everything I owned." He turned to give his concubine a squeeze. "Except this one remaining flower in my lonely desert."

But the student was more interested in his financial affairs. "I thought they were pursuing a policy of coexistence and leaving the merchants alone to develop trade?"

The merchant laughed at the sober catch phrase. "In a way, yes. If the merchant doesn't have ready money, he is quite safe. But if he does, he is lost."

"They confiscated all your property?"

"Not exactly. Because business in my city was going heavily

Japanese, they assigned me a Japanese partner. In a matter of months, he found that I owed my own business sixty thousand pieces of silver."

"A debt to yourself?"

"Ah, that was the point. As he was now a full partner, I owed thirty thousand of that to him. He took me to court. The court found me guilty of misappropriation, and attached my home and art works to pay off the debt.

"Then my partner decided that since I had fallen so low in arrears with my own business, I was not a very good business-man. So he sued again for dissolution of the partnership. This time the court awarded him the business upon payment to me of a fair quitclaim for my equity. But, alas, as he had been operating the business, my equity had shrunk."

"What did he pay you?"

"Ten thousand silver."

"Of your own money?" The student couldn't contain a grin.

"So it goes."

"Maybe we needed the war to wake us up," said the student. "Maybe this is the only thing that could knock some sense into us; another Asian nation that has been smart enough to adopt Western culture."

An old peasant looked insulted. "The Japanese have become westernized, yes, and they've invaded us. But I don't think that makes them smarter."

"What?" said the student, mocking. "You have a worthy thought?"

"Take me," said the peasant. "I was the best farmer in my village. I had a fine house, almost a palace, three rooms, all solid against the blasts of winter. I had a fine courtyard with a pond, ducks, geese, a real pigsty, and a stable for my buffalo. The Japanese came and ate my animals. They made a motor park out of my fine land—five *mou* ruined by grease and fuel and rotten rubber. They chopped my orchard down for fire-wood. Now they occupy the land, but what good is it doing them? The land will not grow anything for ten years. And they have lost the man who farmed it."

He shook his head. "Five mou! Imagine. An estate it had taken ten lifetimes to accumulate. And they use it for a motor park."

He fell silent, staring into space, shocked afresh by such a picture of waste.

"How much land is five mou?" I asked.

"About two acres."

When the sun was high above the corrugated iron roof of the depot, there was the deafening shriek of a whistle. Railway workers shouted orders and counter-orders. Japanese guards bellowed out commands while paddling the backsides of women with their rifle butts, to hurry them up the ladders. The train began to jerk into movement. On the platform, those left behind pressed in against the barriers, their faces and flailing arms registering all stages of despair.

Suddenly, a concerted cry broke out, mixed in at first with the din of skidding wheels and banging cars, but rising to drown out every other sound. It lasted for several minutes until it was shouted down by the train's whistle.

The crowd broke loose. The barriers were thrown down as if by stampeding elephants. Whistles blew again and again, senselessly. A column of Japanese guards beat an opening through the human wall, knocking down bodies and stepping over them. Then the hordes surged forward, clutching at ladders and doorways, snatching at windowsills, waving arms, and overhanging feet. They fell off, screaming as they landed under the wheels or between the bucking cars.

All through the suburbs they ran alongside, making sudden lunges but managing only to slam against the train and bounce off, badly hurt.

A middle-aged man succeeded with his eight-year-old son in one arm.

"Did others come with you?" someone asked.

"Eleven," the father said. "But it does not matter. This is my eldest son. Today our family has been blessed."

"The son, the son! Or, the father, the father!" I, like many around me, was crying hysterically by now. "Never a thought of the mother or wife or daughter if a man is in danger. What are women, still animals?"

"Don't cry," Sylvia said, crying. Seeing us in tears, Loretta started to bawl. "I'm hungry!"

The next accident happened on the high trestle bridge that curved over the deep gorge of a river. We could see one end of the train as it leaned on the curve to double back on itself, catapulting a man out into space. He had fallen asleep on one of the front cars, and his feet had slipped off the footrail that was his only protection. His cry fell clear to the river.

The train rushed on, stopping for no one. Not for the pregnant woman who, compelled by modesty, was trying to relieve herself from a ladder between two cars and fell under the wheels. Not for the child who had been snatched by an erratic wind off the car top, leaving a screaming mother: "Stop, stop! My daughter! My daughter has fallen off."

"Don't cry," her husband consoled her, "If she's alive, someone will find her and take her for a slave girl. At least it was not one of our sons. Don't cry, woman," he said with quiet resignation, "the train won't stop."

When, at midnight, the train suddenly ground to a halt, Japanese guards streamed alongside, barking through megaphones. No one was to venture more than ten yards from the tracks under pain of being shot. No fires were to be built, no songs sung.

The passengers kept up a chorus of soot coughs, exchanging gossip of calamities along the way.

The train stood still until dawn. When the first stains of daylight began to seep through the sky, the engines gave notice with three shrill blasts and, without further warning, started to buck into movement.

Suddenly there followed the same desperate farce of people rushing to get on, running fruitlessly alongside, banging on the sides of the train with feeble fists. Three women on bound feet shuffled along at the pace of frantic snails, their fate as painfully clear as that of the woman who stood rooted to the ground in the gray mist of dawn, paralyzed by the panic.

In a fit of diabolical mockery, the train trundled back in the direction from which it had come, retracing its murderous tracks across a bridge and coming slowly, spitefully, to a halt near a water tower.

Japanese megaphones broadcast warnings of water pollution, but the crowds were uncontrollable, falling upon the reservoir like desert animals at a salt lick. For those who could still afford tea, tea eggs, and rice cakes, vendors rose out of the morning mists like genii.

Sunrise brought a squadron of Japanese bombers gliding overhead in unhurried sequence, tagged by fighter planes that snarled back and forth across the rail tracks like angry hornets.

In the distance, a whistle shrilled, a cue for the refugees to stand flat against the train while an armored troop and supply train came by.

It stayed on the siding until afternoon. Meanwhile, local peasants were rooted out and put to work in a human production line. They chopped the coal out of a nearby hill and packed it across the ditched fields in baskets slung over the shoulder.

A hot-towel vendor came by our car, straining under a bamboo pole loaded with a stove at one end, a cauldron of filthy water at the other. He fished out grimy rags from the cloudy water with a stick, wringing them out with hands as red and swollen as brine-cured hams.

Filthy or not, the towels were in great demand. Grit and grease was smeared all over the flesh as thick as lard. Scraped away, it stung the skin and opened up patches of raw sores.

"Pee in your hand a little and wipe it over the sores," an old peasant woman told us, meaning well.

We passed through all kinds of bad weather, in which the elements bore down with mercurial spite. First the cold shrieked down from the mountains. Then the rains spat ice in the sudden gales. Sometimes the train stopped, and we clung to the slippery roof, shivering, greedy for each other's warmth. There were times when the west winds were let loose from the high snow peaks, and old women whimpered because it was too much to bear, and old men gave up and let go their hold on life.

Yet life went on, mischievously. Babies were born and survived. The strong sheltered the weak against winds and showers. And after soaking rains, the train top looked like a flying laundry, the cat's cradle of lines strung out to hold flapping, brightly quilted clothes.

Still, the sores festered, the eyes itched, the skin burned and broke out in rashes, the throat was raw and tight from coughing.

Once, at midnight, three piercing whistles brought me sitting bolt upright.

"Lie flat, lie flat!" a voice shouted. We fell onto the boards.

The sound of the engine changed suddenly into a dangerous underwater roar. There was a deafening confusion of echoes, then the thick fumes of coal gas.

I remember the spreading itch of gooseflesh along my arms as a man's voice began to howl like some pain-crazed animal. We were spared the sight by the sudden crowd of gawkers, but details of the accident followed us throughout the rest of the trip, and for a long time I had nightmares about the merchant, his concubine, and the low tunnel that knocked off her head.

In the dream I saw shadows twisting in the moonlight while the train rushed on heedlessly. The merchant would be holding another shadow to his heaving chest, a shadow whose shape was somehow wrong. And I would hear a sickening, bubbly sound coming from where there should have been a head.

Toward the end of our journey, we managed to find space in a car. But near Kueiyang, the train stopped suddenly. Japanese troops were taking over. In the wild stampede of outgoing refugees, I was carried forward by an inexorable wave, the hysterical cries of my sisters ringing in my ears. While I was buffeted forward, they were helplessly beaten back by the surging, panic-stricken crowds.

The wave propelled me forward, to throw me out of the door, onto the heap of bodies washed up on the platform, all crying from the relief of surviving such a catastrophe.

The train began to lurch forward. Now I was one of the desperate masses running alongside the moving train, yelling and banging uselessly on its sides and falling back at last to wail and curse as it sped away—carrying my sisters with it.

I must have stood crying on the platform for a long time. When the crowd thinned out, a few people began to ask me what was the matter.

I kept repeating the same lament over and over again: "My sisters are gone! What shall I do? I have all the cash with me."

"There's nothing you can do about the train now," someone said. "Best search in nearby villages. They may have the sense to get off at the next stop, who knows?"

It seemed vastly improbable that I would find them wandering around in an adjacent village, but I had to try. Strangers offered to join the search. For the rest of the day we walked from village to village, shouting my sisters' names.

By the time the sun went down I was stumbling from fatigue and defeat. About the rest of the day I remember only that we took shelter in a farmhouse, which we left at the crack of dawn. Another day of fruitless wandering followed, ending in another desolate, dog-tired night. Then still another day, another night; and several more without success.

My original companions had dropped out of the search, leaving me in the care of others who, incredibly, in the midst of their own troubles and hardships, took time to plod along with me mile after mile, through paddy fields and over stony paths.

This went on for a week, until one afternoon a convoy of American soldiers in a truck stopped to ask if I needed help. When I told them that Cynthia worked for General Chennault in the Fourteenth Air Force, they said, "So do we!" and offered to drive me to Kweiyang. They would also send a message to Cynthia in Kunming.

I wasn't in Kweiyang for long when everything began to happen. Cynthia sent word that she had sent the news of our lost sisters to Father. He in turn had sent a special request to General Chennault, whom he had met in San Francisco just before the general was sent to China, in 1937, to authorize a search for his daughters. The General was doing everything he could, and I was to remain in Kweiyang until I received further instructions.

One morning, the good news reached me. The General's men had found Sylvia, Connie, Theresa, and Loretta in a box car somewhere along the railway route from Kweiyang to Kunming!

The soldiers had searched train after train along that route, comparing hundreds of almost identical little girls with photographs supplied by Cynthia. Later they laughed about the way they finally found them. One of the men pointed to four sad, frightened young girls sitting between a middle-aged man and woman. "Look, look," said the American soldier, who knew Cynthia. "Doesn't that one look like Cynthia?"

And he was right.

They were hungry and tired, but otherwise safe, protected by the kindly couple who had taken them under their wing.

We had our reunion in Kunming, where I arrived in a Fourteenth Air Force truck. But we were not together for long.

Father had sent instructions for us to leave China and join him in the United States. Shaken by his daughters' escapades, he had decided the time had come to remove us from the dangers of war to the safety of the United States, where he was established with his new wife, Bessie.

It was all arranged. We would be flown over the Hump, landing in Calcutta, to embark on a boat trip to San Francisco.

But I was not about to leave China. I still remembered Father abandoning us during the war and leaving Mother to die alone. And I did not like the threat that had accompanied the message. If I didn't leave for the United States, he would stop sending me money and I would have to fend for myself.

It was the kind of challenge I felt compelled to take on. I had been through devastating times and was proud of having survived. I felt confident that I could make it on my own. I was a good student, I could work hard, perhaps teach on the side, and I would be free to do as I wished, released at last from the burden—I was still only sixteen—of looking after my sisters.

The prospect of independence exhilarated me, and, though I felt bereft when they left, I was also freed. When Cynthia asked me to hand over the jewelry I had been guarding throughout the war, I did so willingly, keeping only the tear-shaped diamond ring that had been Mother's favorite.

It was not the most valuable or the most striking piece, but I'm glad I kept it. To this day it reminds me of Mother—both because of the diamond and because of the tear.

Anna with General Chennault, 1957.

Anna with the late President Kennedy, 1963.

Anna and friends with General Westmoreland in Saigon, and Anna with General Nguyen Cao Ky, former Vice-President of South Vietnam.

Anna with the late FBI Director, J. Edgar Hoover, and former CIA chief, Vice-Admiral William F. Raborn.

Anna with President Nixon at the White House.

Anna at the White House with President Ford and friends, 1976.

Photo taken at Mrs. Ford's residence (left to right) Mrs. John L. McLucas, Mrs. Ford, Mrs. George S. Brown, and Anna.

*Anna with President Chiang Ching-kuo, Taipei, Taiwan,
Republic of China.*

Anna with General John Alison, a member of the 14th Air Force. Picture taken in 1976 at the National Air and Space Museum in Washington, D.C. in front of a P40.

The Spring Annals

17

While still in college, I had two job offers, from a local magazine and from an evening daily. But my sights were set on larger publications. So when Kao Chih Shih, an official at the government information office and an old family friend, mentioned the opening at Central News Agency, I jumped. CNA was the government news bureau and wire service headquartered in Chungking, and the bureau chief was Chen Shu-tung, a close friend of Kao Chih Shih. If I liked, he could introduce me.

"When do you want to start working?" Kao asked, as if the choice were already mine. I wasn't so confident. But my friend was stubbornly optimistic. "They're looking for a young reporter they can train, and I've seen your writing." It wasn't until just before my interview that he brought up what might, he thought, be a slight drawback. The agency's policy was to hire only men as correspondents.

I said, "If that's the case, they'll never hire me. I'll never . . ."

"Never is a strong word. Let's say they haven't hired women until now."

Kao drove me to Chen's residence for the interview, at the end of which the bureau chief told me what I'd expected to hear. My qualifications were good, but company policy was against me.

I had prepared my argument. "Try me out," I said, "before

letting headquarters know. If you're satisfied with my work, you can recommend me to them. If not, it will have been a short trial and headquarters need never know."

Chen considered this. "How would you like to start next Monday?" he said.

On the way home, Kao was exuberant. "You see how easy it is?" He sighed. "Ah, to be young and beautiful and talented!"

I started out as junior assistant editor, under a Mr. Shaw, the editor-in-chief. I read all incoming news releases, edited copy, and wrote heads and subheads.

Those were the days when telegraphic news in Chinese was still decoded manually. The vocabulary of journalism used some nine thousand characters, each with its corresponding numerical code, from 0001 to 11,000, and higher for the more complicated characters. By the third week, I had memorized the keys to about three thousand numbers and was decoding wire service news—a laborious process involving minute checking of facts and spellings—and editing. It was required journalistic training, a test more of patience than mettle, and it served me well—especially in 1962 when I compiled two telegraphic code Chinese-English dictionaries while working for Georgetown University.

At CNA I worked the night shift from five o'clock to midnight for the first six months, until my first "real assignment": cultural and educational news. After two months on the beat, I was asked to cover the United States Forces stationed in Kunming. It wasn't an earthshaking development—except for me. At age nineteen, I was the first woman war correspondent for CNA.

The pay was low, but so were my expenses. Room and board were provided by a rich businessman and his concubine, in return for my tutoring his two young sons. They had an establishment on the Sei Bank or West Bank of Kunming, and put me in the guest house across a wide courtyard. The family treated me with touching formality and respect, as if I were a renowned scholar. The job was not unpleasant. I was expected simply to help the boys with their homework every afternoon and to improve their reading and writing. As a calligrapher my qualifications weren't entirely impeccable—Teacher Li would have had much to find fault with. But they were apparently good enough for my employers. I saw only smiles of satisfaction at the boys' progress.

A year later, when I was earning enough from CNA and other free-lance publications to afford an apartment of my own, I found a small room on Hundred Flowers Street, across the avenue from Morning Glory Avenue. It was a lovely address, but still inferior to Grandfather Liao's Shanghai street: Bubbling Well Road.

The war ended less than a month after I turned twenty. I remember when the news first reached our office on the evening of July 14, V. J. Day. A cheer went up in the newsroom as we rushed from desk to desk congratulating each other.

Out in the street, people were hugging, laughing, crying, singing with euphoria. Eight years of war had done too much injury to be remedied overnight, but to the people in the street it was a day for unrepressed rejoicing.

The government was preparing to shift its headquarters from Chungking back to Nanking, with many of its agencies returning to Shanghai, Peking, Canton, and other points of origin. It was the era of rehabilitation and reconstruction, and CNA was reassigning correspondents from Chungking to cover the administration's transitions to the major cities, and from Kunming to cover war-crime trials in Shanghai. The assignments were given mostly to senior correspondents. I took a chance and asked to be transferred to Shanghai. I had heard that my grandparents were living in Shanghai and was eager to track them down after the eight-year-long separation.

"If you can find a way to get there," said the editor, "the job is yours." I could tell he thought I would never get airplane space on such short notice. What he didn't know was that General Chennault had written to a friend, an officer, with a request to provide transportation for me. The General had left China by then and was in fact on his way home to the United States. But his instructions were honored by the efficient officer, who promised me a seat on a U.S. air transport plane departing for Shanghai within a week.

At Wu Char Ba Airport, in Kunming, I almost forgot my luggage in the excitement. It would not have been too devastating a loss, for I was looking forward to buying a new wardrobe upon reaching Shanghai. I felt the need to make up for the years of sobriety and deprivation that marked the war. Never would I be poor again, I vowed. I would just have to avoid poverty at all cost. But in return for the effort, I promised myself soft comfortable beds with fresh linen, the luxury of being driven from place to place instead of having to walk. I had done enough walking for a lifetime: a thousand miles from Hong Kong to the interior alone, to say nothing of daily treks back and forth to school, home, and office in abominable weather. No, when I wanted exercise I'd get it on the dance floor. The lean years were over.

Shanghai was one big, bubbling well of returning expatriates from Kweilin, Chang-tu, and more remote cities, most of them with wads of money to spend. They had a lot to compensate for. The reunited husbands and wives, parents and children, friends and relatives often did not even recognize one another. Nightclubs and restaurants came to life, the loud saxophones and trumpets replacing the air raids and bomb explosions, the frenzied dancing replacing the running and hiding.

It was to be only a short interlude. Before long, another war would begin, tragic and brutal as only civil wars can be, and splitting families apart in more lasting ways—with the kind of spite only family feuds can generate.

My early days at CNA could have been bewildering to the point of defeat, for I was young and inexperienced. But I was fortunate to have the guidance and help of generous colleagues, many of them not much older than I, who were themselves struggling with the difficulties of reporting on a war in a government controlled press. Among these hardworking and thoughtful associates was a woman, Fong Tan, whose help to me was invaluable.

Fong Tan was about seven years older than I, but she gave the impression of having been a reporter all her life. Her dedication was impressive, but her reputation mixed. She was thought to be a brilliant woman, but difficult, intimidating, and eccentric.

Fong Tan and I were friends at first sight. We met at a news conference we were covering together, and almost instantly found ourselves talking like old school friends and confiding to each other our most intimate ambitions and fears.

She was the only daughter of ultra-conservative parents, wealthy landowners in a backward province of southern China. Raised in an atmosphere of overprotective provincialism, by a family whose creed was that a woman should never venture into a world of career and ideas, Fong Tan's childhood was difficult, her coming of age unbearable.

A voracious reader and an independent thinker, Fong Tan was obsessed at an early age by all the possibilities that lay outside her immediate reach: education, experience, challenge. By early adolescence, she was determined to test the limits of her ability. This meant breaking away from her family and rejecting their support. Her parents and brothers had wanted her to marry the man of their choice, a wealthy landowner, and her refusal to do so resulted in their disowning her. When her parents died, her brothers inherited the family estate, while she was left destitute.

She moved to Shanghai and began writing, a hazardous way of life, especially for a writer ahead of her time. She wrote articles and columns on women's issues and rights at a prodigious rate, translated literature and poetry, and generally lived like a pauper until, by a stroke of luck, she was hired for a desk job by CNA.

It was Fong Tan who showed me, by the example of her struggle, that the impossible is there to be challenged. At the core of her determination was a fierce integrity, an intellectual purity that came through in 'her personality and habits. She argued and fought passionately about everything that to her was worth believing in and defending: individual freedom, the ethic of hard work, friendship, loyalty, honesty.

Her tragedy was that her crusade for equality and fairness was doomed, for she was pitting herself against men in a man's world. She was more capable, hardworking, and dedicated than most of her male colleagues, but promotions would never come her way. Still, while most men resented her for the threat she posed, she made and kept several close male friends who treated her as an equal.

I admired her great courage, and the strong sense of direction that had led her into the difficult field of journalism. But sometimes her fierceness and dogmatism were too much even for me, and we would end up arguing for hours. They were stimulating, provocative arguments, however, usually taking place on weekends, when we would drive out to the countryside to read and write and discuss our favorite writers. She had translated some Shakespeare and Byron, and I remember how taken I was with one particular translation of Byron's "When We Two Parted," which appeared in one of the evening papers—an extraordinarily sensitive and haunting rendition.

When Shanghai fell to the Communists, Fong Tan went south to Hong Kong, where she eventually established a reputation as a columnist, following her vocation as a suffragette. It was an inhospitable climate in which to air such views, for Hong Kong in the late fifties was a desolate place both in literary and in cultural terms. Writers could seldom practice their craft and make ends meet, and even well-known columnists could rarely hope to make more than ten dollars an article. To supplement the subsistence-level fees earned as a writer, Fong Tan took on translation assignments and wrote under a variety of pseudonyms.

We kept up our correspondence all through those years, until General Chennault started Civil Air Transport (CAT) and

Fong Tan joined us to help out in the public relations. Eventually, she returned to Hong Kong, a lonely voice in a world where the only thing that mattered seemed to be business, tourism, gambling, and the price of gold. I imagined her among her precious books, steeped in literature and ideas, while around her spun a great shopping center of neon.

She died ten years ago of cancer, leaving a void in my life that no other woman friend has quite been able to fill.

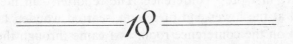

In 1923, a large crowd gathered near El Paso, Texas, to watch the Fort Bliss Air Force maneuvers. As the pilots arrived on the field, an old woman in a long dress boldly tottered up to one of them. The crowd saw them talk for a while, then the pilot shook his head.

Her jaunty red bandana fluttering in the breeze, the old woman went from pilot to pilot, all of whom shook their heads.

Suddenly, the announcement came over the loudspeaker, introducing Grandma Morris, age eighty, who had arrived in Texas in a covered wagon half a century ago. Grandma, it seemed, was eager for a ride in one of the planes, and as a special, unscheduled favor, she was getting it.

The crowd clapped and cheered as the old woman was hoisted into the cockpit of a two-seater. The pilot buckled her up, hit the propeller, and the engine roared. The old woman waved to the crowd.

Just as the pilot was about to climb in, the plane jerked forward without warning, throwing him onto the ground.

"Jump, jump!" cried the horrified crowd.

But the plane was already taxiing down the airstrip, gathering momentum, tilting suddenly up into the air, and brushing past rooftops and treetops. Higher and higher it climbed, wheeling and banking wildly, until at last it plummeted toward earth. The crowd began running in all directions.

But, miraculously, the plane pulled out of its fall, barely missing the field, then rising to loop and roll in the air like a giddy bird. Again it did a tailspin earthward, again it pulled out and skimmed the ground, this time for a perfect landing.

Out of the cockpit leaped Grandma Morris, peeling off bandana, wig, eyeglasses, and dress to reveal a laughing, uniformed pilot, Captain Claire Lee Chennault.

It was my first press conference. The reporters—all men—had gathered at the lower end of a long, scarred wooden table, A hush fell on the conference room as I came through the door. Someone whistled, a silly indignity men got away with in those days.

"Come in, Anna," said Bob Fong, a young reporter and a colleague at CNA. He left his chair and ushered me in.

"Gentlemen, Miss Anna Chan, our new lady reporter. As you can see, I wasn't lying." Whatever it was he might or might not have been lying about, they studied the evidence closely.

A heat wave passed over my face.

I had hardly sat down when a door at the far end of the room swung open.

"The Old Man," Bob said.

I half expected Grandma Morris to come cackling into the room, but instead a lean, dark-haired American officer strode in, full of brisk purpose. His face was dark, grooved, and weathered, like the bark of a tree; he had an air of just having climbed out of a cockpit. On the shoulders of his leather flight jacket were twin silver stars. Behind him followed a Chinese colonel and two other Americans, a colonel and a lieutenant-colonel.

The General's gaze scanned the room. "Good afternoon, gentlemen. And lady," he added, with a smile that explained his nickname, Old Leatherface.

Afterwards, I went to see his press officer, Lieutenant Colonel Hutton, about some background questions.

"He's part Chinese, you know," said Hutton. "You can tell by the eyes. Don't you think?"

"Are you joking?" I said.

"Yes, I'm joking. Now what do you want to know?"

He was a fifty-year-old American from the southern United States, thirty-one years older than I, married, the father of eight, a major-general in the U.S. Air Force, and a great liberator. He was so different, he could have come from the moon.

But there are chapters in one's life when the future, not the past, is prologue, and so it happened that when I met the man I was to marry, our future together had begun to take shape long before.

In 1925, the year I was born, he was sent to Ford Island, in the middle of Pearl Harbor, in Hawaii.

There, as commander of the Nineteenth Fighter Squadron at Luke Field, he acquired a taste for the interests that would mark his military successes in the China-Burma-India theater of World War II. He developed, for example, the nucleus of his stunningly efficient air-raid warning system used in both the Sino-Japanese War and the Second World War—a system that began with nothing more complicated than two spotters using powerful binoculars on top of a field tower equipped with a loudspeaker.

He also introduced into the curriculum at Luke Field a radical element: the tactics of acrobatic aerial combat. It was a radical concept demonstrating that firepower could be concentrated in a way impossible in traditional dogfights.

After Hawaii, he went on to teach flying at Brooks Field in Texas, where, in addition to the loops and rolls of aerial acrobatics, he began experimenting with flamboyant paratrooper techniques until he was ordered to "stop that paratrooper nonsense before someone gets hurt."

But by then the paratrooping maneuvers had caught the attention of Russian militarists who came to make him an offer, armed with vodka, chocolate, caviar, and talk of $1,000 a month in salary. (As a major in the United States Air Force he had been making $360.)

He turned them down. The paratrooping, he said, was just a sideshow. He was a fighter pilot, and, though he had studied under Clayton Bissel,* a World War I ace committed to 1918 dogfighter tactics, he had his own ideas about how fighter planes should be flown.

As a student at the Air Corps tactical school at Langely Field, Virginia, and later as senior instructor in fighter tactics at Maxwell Field, Alabama, he was in the forefront of a dispute that would preoccupy the Air Corps for years to come: the fighter versus bomber controversy.

It was the age of Giulio Douhet, the Italian general whose theory was the bible for air strategists in favor of bombers. Their showpiece was a heavily armed Martin B-10, the 235-mph forerunner of the modern bomber. In addition, the 1930s were the Depression years and Air Corps funds could barely cover gas for the four hours a month in the air required to collect flying pay.

But Chennault felt that the fighter plane's shortcomings, the result of outdated tactics, could be remedied. There was too much of "an air of medieval jousting in the dogfights," too much dispersion of firepower. He lectured that planes, like infantrymen, should fight in teams, augmenting their power.

The concept was hardly original. Oswald von Boelcke, an early German ace, had advanced the idea that two planes fighting as a team could inflict double firepower on the enemy. The theory was refined by another German, Baron Manfred von Richthofen, and dramatically staged by his Flying Circus of

---

* It was Bissel who suggested that the only way a fighter could knock down a modern bomber would be to drop a ball and chain into its propeller.

World War I. (The Circus remained invincible until Richthofen was shot down and Hermann Goering took over, leading the Circus back into individual dogfights—and its eventual downfall.)

Officially, the U.S. Air Corps was still a proponent of dogfights when Chennault, with the blessing of the tactical school commandant, organized the "Three Men on a Flying Trapeze," an Air Corps acrobatic team.

For the next three years, the team performed all over the country as awestruck audiences craned their necks and held their breath to see the barrel-snaps; slow- and double-rolls; loops, spins, and wingovers; chandelles and Immelmanns; squirrel cages and triple turns in close formation.

But despite these daredevil stunts, Chennault had to admit that the Air Corps by and large remained unimpressed and "considered fighters in the same dodo category as sausage balloons."

By 1936, the year the Flying Trapeze gave its farewell performance, the tactical school had stopped teaching fighter tactics altogether.

The following year Capt. Chennault, age forty-two, lay recuperating from an attack of chronic bronchitis in Louisiana, half-deaf and thoroughly depressed by the boredom of an early retirement.

He had a fear, as he once wrote, of getting "caught in the drudgery of trying to eke a living from cotton farming in a losing battle against palmetto root, bad weather, fluctuating prices, and the passing years," and wanted at all cost to avoid what he called "flying a desk."

So, when an offer to study the Chinese Air Force came from Madame Chiang Kai-shek through friends in China, he accepted without equivocation.

It was 1937, the Japanese had been gnawing away at the north for four years, and our family had left Peking to resettle in Hong Kong.

It was all I could do, during that first press conference, to follow the briefing. I was mesmerized by his delivery: well-paced and unfaltering. But it was the person, not the statement, that arrested me.

Afterwards, Bob Fong glanced down at my notebook and smiled slyly.

"You're impressed, aren't you?"

"What do you mean?"

"You didn't take any notes."

As we stood up to leave, I saw the General walking toward me.

"Miss Chan?"

"Yes."

"Your father wrote me recently asking how Cynthia was getting along and he mentioned that I might be seeing another of his daughters soon."

"I am so glad to meet you, General."

He inclined his head politely. In my nervousness I was almost whispering.

"If you don't have to rush back, won't you have a cup of tea with a few of us?"

"I do have time. I'd love some tea."

He let me walk ahead of him through the door into a smaller room where several American and Chinese officers were sitting.

They rose as we entered and General Chennault introduced them, adding, somewhat paternally, "Miss Chan's father, a friend of mine in San Francisco, asked me to keep an eye on her."

Over tea and cakes the nervousness left me. I was enjoying myself, heady over the privilege of bantering with the General and his senior officers.

But I still couldn't take my eyes off him. And I hoped he did not think of me only as Chan's daughter.

The more I learned about him, the more I wanted to find out. Research led me beyond the press releases and newspaper clippings, though many of the complexities and connections came to light only years later.

His forebears had come to the States in 1778 from Alsace-Lorraine as volunteers in Lafayette's Independence Army. After the Revolutionary War, one branch of the family went from tobacco farming in Virginia, south to the frontier region of Tennessee, and still farther south into the Carolinas.

The Chennaults continued the search for wilderness until they reached the delta country of Louisiana, where Steven Chennault, the son of John Nelson Chennault and Hannah Houston (first cousin of Sam Houston of Texas), married Frances Thompson, who bore him a son, John Stonewall Jackson Chennault. The boy was as much a hunter, fisherman, and pioneer as his forebears, and possibly more of a marksman, going down in local history as a gunslinger who ran crooked horse traders out of town by grazing their hat brims with well-placed bullets. John Stonewall Jackson Chennault later married Jessie Lee, whose father, Dr. William Wallace Lee, was a cousin of Robert E. Lee.

Claire Lee Chennault was the son of Jessie and John, born in Commerce, Texas, where his parents had traveled, but raised in the Tensas River region in Louisiana.

Another hunter and fisherman, Claire prowled the woods as a boy, vanishing from home for days at a time. Once, he set out in a small boat down the Tensas River, Mississippi-bound. His head filled with the adventures of Ivanhoe, Treasure Island, Ben Hur, and Tom Sawyer, he floated downstream until he spied in the distance the glow of lanterns at his destination. The fantasy was almost complete.

But the light turned out to be an old paddleboat, churning the river and upsetting the small craft in its wake. The boy stayed afloat by clinging to his rifle, and reached shore frightened and bedraggled. In the shelter of a farmhouse, it took him a week to muster enough courage to write to his father.

Unlike his antecedents, he went on to college. After Louisiana State University, he taught school in Athens, Louisiana, where he organized a baseball team of note and cracked the whip on unruly high school students by inviting them to step outside.

When World War I erupted, he enlisted, served throughout most of the war as a first lieutenant in the Aviation Section of the Signal Reserve Corps, and, later, as a commissioned officer in the Air Service of the Army.

Eight-and-a-half years passed before "radical Chennault" was made captain.

By then his byline was showing up frequently in the service magazines, over articles advancing his theories on military aviation.

When Chennault first arrived in China at Madame Chiang Kai-shek's invitation, the Chinese Air Force was controlled and run by the Italians under General Scaroni—a low-cost proposition for the Italians, who paid their expenses out of Italy's share of the Boxer indemnity.

At the Italian school at Loyang, a prestigious institution for the sons of elitist Chinese families, the prevailing tradition—allowing every cadet to graduate—summed up the caliber of the program. The Air Force itself, while officially made up of five hundred planes, had only ninety-one in fighting condition, most of them acquired through an odd method of fund raising, by which subscriptions were sold to planes named after different cities. Rallies would be held in each city, at the end of which a new plane was flown in and the name of the subscribing city painted on the fuselage. The same plane was then flown to the next city, where the new name would be painted over the previous one, and so on.

The Sino-Japanese war began within weeks of Chennault's arrival. Suddenly he had the task not only of overseeing an Air

Force of Chinese pilots and international mercenaries, but also of training pilots who, despite a record of destroying almost half the planes in take-off and landing accidents, considered it an admission of weakness to practice.

He devised new night-fighting tactics, set up a vast radio and telephone network to signal the approach of Japanese bombers, and in frustration periodically offered his resignation to Madame Chiang Kai-shek, who duly refused to accept.

By the summer of 1940, more than a hundred Japanese planes were bombing the city of Chungking daily, but the Chinese Air Force was unequal to either the number or the agility of the Japanese Zeroes or Kate fighters which could "turn on a dime" and shoot almost straight up. (The workhorse for Chennault's Air Force was the P-40 Tomahawk, a durable plane, but slow, and burdened by a liquid-cooled engine.)

By mid-October Generalissimo Chiang Kai-shek had decided to send Chennault to the United States to ask for more planes and pilots. It was a ticklish mission, for the United States was not yet an official participant in the war, and was reluctant to risk anything more than the obsolescent fighters already committed to China. The enormity of the task confronting Chennault was brought home by a visit to his old Air Corps acquaintances. Not only were most of them staff officers "flying swivel chairs," but it took headquarters, interested mainly in the European War, an hour to find a map of China on a scale worthy of military inquiry—and then most areas of current strategic interest had to be penciled in.

Such was the effectiveness, however, of a small but powerful circle of friends in the White House and cabinet—T.V. Soong; Dr. Lauchlin Currie, President Franklin D. Roosevelt's special advisor on China; New Dealer Thomas G. Corcoran, the President's right-hand man; and Soong's two close friends, Frank Knox, Secretary of the Navy, and Henry Morganthau, Secretary of the Treasury—that, on April 15, 1941, an executive order was issued under FDR's signature. The unpublicized order authorized reserve officers and enlisted men to resign from the

Army, Navy, and Marines in order to join the American Volunteer Group in China.

The AVG was a crack force of one hundred twelve pilots, drawing a salary of $250 to $750 a month and a bonus of $500 for every Japanese plane shot down. The first contingent of the still secret AVG met unobtrusively at the Mark Hopkins Hotel in San Francisco on July 7, the fourth anniversary of the night the Sino-Japanese War began.

Before leaving San Francisco, Chennault stopped by at the Chinese Consulate to pay a courtesy call, where he met the consul general, my father.

Based in Toungoo, Burma, the AVG training school took on a personality of its own, typified by its frightful planes, painted raffishly at the snout to look like grinning sharks—a trademark borrowed from a British squadron in Africa. The mascot, created by a Walt Disney artist and painted on the side of the plane, was a Bengal tiger with wings.

Under Chennault, the Flying Tigers learned tactics geared to the P-40's strengths, concentrating on accurate gunnery, fighting in pairs, and generally staying out of the range of the enemy's defensive power to avoid a mistake which Chennault used to call "non-habit forming."

The Flying Tigers were ready for combat about the time of Pearl Harbor, when radio reports from Kunming announced the Japanese bombing of the city on December 8. The AVG forces, split between Burma and China, went into daily combat without replacements or spare parts, keeping their aircraft afloat with the proverbial chewing gum and wire and armed with homemade bombs and whiskey-bottle incendiaries.

So eclectic were the improvisations that one of the pilots speculated that it would take only the addition of a periscope to turn the P-40 into a submarine.

By 1942, the AVG was on the offensive, dive-bombing Indo-China—though it was really the earlier air battles over Rangoon, Burma, that had brought it fame.

In seven months of combat in the China-Burma-India Theater, the AVG had destroyed around two hundred twenty-nine planes, possibly one hundred fifty-three more, while its own casualty rate for Tigers killed in aerial combat was four.

By war's end, the Tigers had destroyed over one thousand two hundred Japanese planes, with about seven hundred more probables. Their own losses came to five hundred seventy-three planes.

After the fall of Rangoon on March 7, 1942, Chennault withdrew his last few planes from Burma to China. From headquarters in Kunming, they defended the shattered cities of western China and continued their protection of convoys on the Burma Road which by this time was transporting about twenty thousand tons of materiel a month into China. The United States by now had entered the war, and there was no longer any need for a private air force. The AVG was consequently disbanded on July 4, 1942, and was incorporated into a regular Army Air Force unit, under the command of Chennault, by now a Brigadier-General.

The China Air Task Force, as the new unit was called, was forced to subsist on the local economy, cut off as it was from the rest of the world. The idea of an aerial supply line was as yet too dangerous to be practical, and only an occasional army plane came over the treacherous spur of the Himalayas known as the Hump from India. Living off the land, the CATF grew rice and bean sprouts, raised chickens and pigs, and used bamboo and straw to build dummy P-40s for the airfields. They capitalized on interior lines of communication, a local warning net, seasonal weather, and the strengths of their planes to seize the initiative. With sudden thrusts at sporadic targets, they threw the enemy off balance and kept the larger forces on the defensive.

In nine months the CATF demolished one hundred forty-nine enemy planes in the air, possibly eighty-five more, and lost only sixteen P-40s. It was the smallest American air force ever to be commanded by a general.

A year later, in March, the combined chiefs dissolved the old CATF, promoted Chennault to Major-General, and placed him in charge of the Fourteenth Air Force in China.

20

The Fourteenth was doomed to an uneven career, born at the lowest point—between the spring of 1942 and the autumn of the following year—in the Allied marriage of the China-Burma-India Theater. In Burma, General Joseph ("Vinegar Joe") Stilwell had taken a "hell of a beating," the Battle of Rangoon had dealt the Allied defense of Asia a hefty blow, and opinion was split on the question of how to regain the initiative.

In Washington, the policy of the Roosevelt administration was to keep China in the war, armed and equipped, to fight Japan. Strategically, this called for a supply line through which large amounts of war materiel could be delivered to China. Then, in tandem with an upgraded Chinese army, the ultimate offensive could be launched: strike at Japan from the air and, from the sea, at her islands in the Pacific.

The British, on the other hand, preferred to supply China with only enough materiel to keep her *in* the war—not victorious and strong after it. Britain's concern was summed up by Anthony Eden when he expressed to Roosevelt, prior to the Trident Conference, concern over the danger of "Chinese running up and down the Pacific." Far better to concentrate on India as the bedrock of the colonies.

Stilwell's prescription was to retake Burma, but the British had no appetite for yet another campaign in the hellish Burmese jungle. Churchill wanted instead to direct the main drive in Asia toward the archipelago—first Sumatra, then Singapore—

likening the recapture of Burma to "munching a porcupine, quill by quill."

Stilwell's rationale for his obsession with Burma—that strategically it would open the door to China—was meaningless to Chiang Kai-shek. Why should he assign his troops to another abortive Burma campaign when his Fifth Army had already been wiped out by Stilwell's bullish tactics?

The animosity between the two had simmered almost to boiling point, with Stilwell hard put to conceal his contempt for the "Peanut," as he nicknamed the Generalissimo—"a stubborn, ignorant, prejudiced, conceited despot who never hears the truth except from me and finds it hard to believe"—and Chiang Kai-shek in turn seething over Stilwell's lordly interpretation of Lend-Lease. It was clear everywhere, except in Washington, D.C., that "Vinegar Joe" was the wrong man for the job.

Lend-Lease was the pivot on which the American war machinery in China was mounted, and Stilwell was determined to control it absolutely. He felt that Lend-Lease should be subject to quid-pro-quo: U.S. support in return for Chinese action.

Regrettably, his temperament was unsuited to the job. Tactless, obsessive, and full of righteous anger, his approach was so impolitic that Roosevelt felt it necessary at one point to recommend better manners toward Chiang Kai-shek, Supreme Commander and Chief of State. "One cannot speak sternly to a man like that," he said in a matter-of-fact memo, "or exact commitments from him the way we might do from the Sultan of Morocco."

Several months later when a policy shift led FDR to take a harsher tone vis-à-vis Chiang Kai-shek, the result was less than satisfactory. While providing Stilwell with malicious but momentary amusement, the tough note only ended in an awkward retraction. Stilwell had to be recalled and a replacement found, proving that FDR's original caveat was a wise one after all.

But at this stage Stilwell's carrot-and-stick administration of Lend-Lease was just beginning to get on the Generalissimo's nerves. He saw it as policy discriminatory to China. Otherwise, why were the British allowed control of their own quota of Lend-Lease while the Chinese were required to go on bended knee?

So long as Stilwell was in charge, he would keep flogging the idea of ground campaigns, waged by an infantry much in need of reform, and supplied by a costly and hazardous route over the Hump, the fifteen-thousand-foot Santsung Range in the Himalayas.

After the Japanese conquest of Burma in 1942, the Hump was the only supply route from the United States to China. From bases in Assam, war materiel had to cross the five hundred miles to Kunming over this air route of terrifying winds and blinding monsoon rains, above peaks "aluminum-plated" with the wreckage of planes.

It was the longest and costliest of supply lines, beginning with the twelve-thousand-mile sea journey from the United States to Karachi or Bombay, across India by rail for the next one thousand five hundred miles, then via the "Toonerville Trolley," a decrepit railway between Bengal and Assam, and ending in the final murderous flight across the Hump to Kunming.

When forward air bases began operating out of East China after 1942, the supplies continued on an even longer trip—for another four hundred to seven hundred miles from Kunming by cart and truck, and, in the case of gasoline, in drums rolled for a hundred miles at a time.

For these reasons alone the idea of an air campaign supported by ground action, as laid out by Chennault, had far more appeal for Chiang Kai-shek. The combination would conserve valuable ground troops while taking on the enemy in the kind of warfare so robustly demonstrated by the Flying Tigers.

Confident that his Air Force, given the proper support and authority, could flatten the enemy, Chennault proposed to defend the Hump route, cut off Japanese sea lanes, and undermine the enemy's air power over Burma and Indochina.

The idea appealed to Chiang Kai-shek for the many difficulties it would obviate. If American air power could win the war, there would not be any need for the Burma campaign; reorganization of the Chinese Army—a job he felt he could ill afford to take on at that point—would not be necessary; and, finally, he would not need to expend the soldiers and materiel that could be put to future use in the brewing civil war bound to follow in the wake of World War II.

The original Roosevelt-Churchill decision of December 1941 to favor the European War meant that in Europe both air and ground campaigns on a massive scale were affordable, while in China-Burma-India only one or the other was possible.

It was inevitable, therefore, that the leading advocates of the conflicting schools of thought should clash.

By now, Chennault's reputation was legendary. His stuntmen pilots had taken on superior Japanese forces and trounced them time and again. They had prevented the enemy from terrorizing the skies over East China, and had saved Chungking from a fourth season of raids. In their remarkably brief career, they had made history.

With Wendell Willkie's visit to China in October 1942, Chennault had won a valuable ally. The plan was to defeat Japan with a mere one hundred five modern fighters, thirty medium bombers, twelve heavy bombers, and the necessary replacements.

The cause was taken up in the United States, reaching the height of its appeal with Madame Chiang Kai-shek's visit to the U.S. in November 1942. In Washington, she made it clear, in public appearances, and in her address to a joint session of Congress, that air war was the answer.

By the fall of 1942, enthusiasm for a ground offensive in Burma was waning on all sides. The debate was continued at the Trident Conference in 1943, ending in a compromise favorable to Chennault's plan. He was to launch his air offensive, and to this end was to receive a priority on supplies over the Hump until the end of October.

Now it was the spring of 1944 and supplies continued to be scarce. But the Fourteenth, operating out of East China air bases, had been hitting hard at Japanese rail lines and offshore shipping. In retaliation, the enemy were sweeping south through Hankow, trying to take the main north-south rail line and the East China urban bases. To keep them from falling into Japanese hands, the Fourteenth was exploding airfields and ammunition dumps. The panic had set off the frantic exodus westward. It was a season of despair and suicides. By late summer, China was falling apart from inflation, hoarding, droughts, floods, and famines.

The country was near breaking point on other fronts as well. Stilwell resented Chennault's continued reassurances to the Generalissimo that air power, requiring more supplies, was the answer. Chennault blamed Stilwell for holding up those supplies.

As early as February, Chennault had warned Stilwell, the theater commander, of a mammoth Japanese offensive, but the warning fell on deaf ears. Stilwell, champing at the bit to retake Burma, had, since November 1943, plunged once more into the jungle, from which—with the exception of several brief, unproductive meetings with Chiang Kai-shek—he would not emerge until the summer of 1944.

By the time he resurfaced, the Japanese offensives were well underway. The giant pincer was closing around the East China airfields and the north-south corridor was being laid.

The Japanese had encountered their first resistance in May 1944, in the city of Changsha. Defending it was General Hsueh Yüeh, who successfully fought off three attacks and earned for himself the sobriquet, Tiger of Changsha. When Changsha finally succumbed to the protracted siege, the Japanese moved on to Hengyang, where the Tiger once again fought tooth and claw.

Hsueh was commander of the Tenth War Zone in the province of Honan, at a time when people were reduced to eating tree bark and peanut husks, handfuls of dirt, and, in the end, the dead. His troops were made up of half-starved and shoeless farm boys, dying off day by day from disease and malnutrition.

They fought on with only decrepit rifles and the residue of captured Japanese equipment, a pathetic refutation of the argument that the Chinese were incapable of putting up a fight except under U.S. command.

The Tiger of Changsha, a brilliant tactician with the manners of a scholar and the presence of a field commander, effected a close collaboration with "Big Tiger" Chennault, the commander of the Fourteenth Air Force. The coordination was evidence of the accuracy of Chennault's conviction, that air power backed up by ground forces was the winning formula.

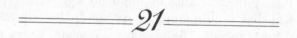

To keep up the Fourteenth's frantic attacks on Japanese supply convoys, Chennault had not only spent the allotted gasoline, but had dipped into reserve stockpiles for additional loans. The attacks were containing the enemy offensive, but, without adequate supplies for either air or ground forces, resistance was crippled.

Chennault had persisted in his pleas for more supplies and had even proposed, as a desperate measure, to divert about a thousand tons of his allotment to Hsueh Yüeh for the defense of Hengyang. But Stilwell by now had decided that Chennault was undeserving, that Hsueh Yüeh had lost Changsha and would therefore lose Hengyang as well, and that Chiang Kai-shek was unreliable. In this spirit of mistrust, he not only refused to send them the crucial supplies, but demanded, at a critical juncture in October 1944 (with the fate of Kweilin and Liuchow still hanging), that Chennault repay the stockpile loans. Stilwell was determined, in his own phrase, to "let them stew."

When Kweilin and Liuchow collapsed and Kweichow lay next in line for Japanese attack, an alarmed Chiang Kai-shek issued the Allies an ultimatum: Take the pressure off the Chinese at Lungling by directing the Burma divisions toward Bhamo, or face the withdrawal of his Y-force back across the Salween River to protect Kunming.

The message was wired by a furious Stilwell to General George Marshall in the midst of the second Quebec Conference, where Roosevelt and Churchill were at loggerheads over Germany, and the joint chiefs over planning and logistics, but where no one knew what to do about China.

Discouraged by the progressive collapse of East China, and worn out from three consecutive terms in office, Roosevelt could muster no interest in China beyond keeping her in the war. In this spiritless frame of mind he signed the reply to Chiang Kai-shek's ultimatum, a six-hundred-word telegram composed by Marshall. The message was plain. Break off the action on the Salween, and Chiang Kai-shek would have to "accept the consequences and assume the personal responsibility." Place General Stilwell in command of all Chinese forces, or risk the cutoff of American support.

Stilwell carried the "hot firecracker" to Chiang Kai-shek himself, taking ghoulish delight in the task, and reporting the scene in his journal after he "handed the bundle of paprika to the Peanut and then sank back with a sigh. The harpoon hit the little bugger right in the solar plexus and went through him."

But the hot firecracker backfired. It was too crude an affront, both to the dignity of China and to the integrity of her Chief of State. Not only did the Generalissimo refuse Stilwell the command post, he demanded his recall.

Forced to back down from the ultimatum, the War Department ordered Stilwell out of China on October 19, 1944, sending in his place Lieutenant General Albert C. Wedemeyer.

When the message from my father arrived asking my sisters and me to leave for the United States, the General called me to his office to relay the command. Afterwards, we fell silent, lost in our own thoughts. Finally, he said, getting up from his chair, "You're not a child; you don't have to go if you don't want to."

He stood facing the window while I stared at his back.

I took the cue without hesitation. "General," I said, "I don't want to leave. I'm going to stay on."

He turned slowly from the window, his silhouette solid against the backlighting of the sun. The force of his answer was undeniable. "All right. That settles it."

Why was I so elated? He had said nothing, except to suggest that I needn't leave if I didn't want to. But I was absurdly happy, and in my happiness could think of nothing else to say. It was raining hard outside. The tea on the table between us sat cold and untouched. I got up to go.

At the door, he said quietly, "I'm glad, Anna." That was all. But that was enough.

With Wedemeyer as theater commander, and the supply flow much improved, the Fourteenth was putting on an impressive show, challenging the enemy in the skies, keeping the north-south corridor out of commission, and destroying their ground troops, supplies, railroads, and shipping.

By June, the Japanese had loosened their hold on the captured portions of East China, burning and demolishing in their wake. With the enemy in retreat in Asia, with the May 8 victory in Europe, and with the Allied capture of Okinawa, there was no longer any need to protect the China coast.

It was the beginning of the end of a chapter, not only of the war, but for Chennault himself. In the inevitable reorganization, the Fourteenth was to be cut to the size of an air wing, with Chennault as wing commander, and George E. Stratemeyer as air chief in China.

The well had been poisoned ever since Stilwell's return to the United States. Chennault resigned on July 8, 1945, eight years to the day after his first arrival in China.

The round of farewell parties for him in Kunming was unending. I was invited to some of them. Then came the last, given by the officers and staff of the Fourteenth Air Force. One by one all evening they sought brief moments with the General to say good-bye, a ceremony that took forever. It wasn't the small air force of two hundred men and a few dented planes he had started out with. It had grown to thirty thousand men and a thousand planes.

Hours later, the crowd thinned out but the remainder looked implacable, the kind that would never leave.

I was standing alone with him for a change. "It's late," I said finally. "I'd better go."

He seemed a little unsettled, as if trying to decide whether to press me to stay or to show me to the door. "I'll have Wang drive you home," he said, and walked me to the side door closest to the parking lot where Wang kept vigil in the old Buick sedan.

We stopped at the door and lingered awkwardly.

"So. Good-bye?" he said.

I was afraid to look up. "I'll be at the airport to see you off."

He touched me on the shoulder. "But that may not be the best place to say good-bye."

I looked up at last; he was holding out both arms.

He kissed me. Again I was afraid to look. I heard him say, "I'll be back."

A voice from behind started to tease. "General, you are blocking traffic!" It was one of his "boys," grinning indulgently.

The General was overcome with confusion, reduced to an errant teenager.

But when the intruder had gone, he kissed me again.

On his last day, the crowds—hundreds, thousands, a million, perhaps two million—clogged the streets, windows, and balconies of Chungking, waving and cheering. The General's car could barely inch along, touched and patted forward by hundreds of reverent hands until the chauffeur simply cut the engine and let the car be borne along by the surge of goodwill.

The drab buildings of the wartime capital were hung with multicolored flags, banners, bunting, and cloth Flying Tigers leaping in the breeze. The ideograms on billboards and banners shouted out farewell messages. "Chen-o-de Chang Chun, we'll never forget you in a thousand years."

Nor will I, I thought. Nor will I.

The crowd pushed the automobile into an open square. In the middle, a raised platform was decorated with more flags and Flying Tiger emblems. The General squeezed through an archway of pine branches and flowers to stand for the rest of the day on the platform, while the procession of thousands of well-wishers filed past with Chinese scrolls, embroidered silk, assorted gifts, or hearty handshakes—a barbaric custom, but the exception was gladly made.

The evening before, he had been decorated by the Generalissimo with the Order of the White Sun and Blue Sky, the first ever for a foreigner. General Wedemeyer had pinned a second Oak Leaf Cluster to Chennault's Distinguished Service Medal. And, on his farewell tour of China the week before, he had presented Hsueh Yüeh with the old Sam Browne belt from his prewar uniform. The Big Tiger had embraced the Little Tiger, who wept openly.

Late that afternoon, the crowds lined the runways for the takeoff. Firecrackers snapped and crackled as the C-47 rolled down the runway, clearing the devils from Chen-o-de Chan Chun's path.

My throat was suddenly tight and dry, as though I had been shouting along with the crowds. Actually, I watched mutely as the plane disappeared in the direction of the Hump.

So this was what it meant to be alone.

22

He was still in the skies, flying over Egypt on his way to Athens, when news of the Japanese surrender crackled over the radios.

I went off to Shanghai, where CNA was opening a bureau.

"It won't be a temporary assignment," they told me. "It's a permanent transfer—and a promotion."

It was a coveted beat. I had requested it, but I couldn't believe, or accept without questioning, my good fortune. "Why me?"

"Several reasons. You've been covering foreign news, and Shanghai is like a foreign city. Your work is good, your English is good. And one more reason."

"What?"

"They want someone there quickly. You're the only one with access to a U.S. military plane."

I took an agency letter verifying my war correspondent status and went to the commanding officer in charge of transportation.

The officer glanced at the letter and smiled. "Congratulations, Anna! When would you like to leave?"

"You mean you'll have a seat for me?" I wasn't expecting immediate success.

"I think I can manage it, since you don't take up that much space. You can leave Friday. Or you can wait till next week."

It was still only Tuesday. I'd have time to pack and say my good-byes. "Friday, then." I held out my hand. "Thank you, General!"

"Glad to do it for you." He paused. "And for the Old Man, too! Before he left he asked me to help whenever I could."

The thought warmed me. Amid the preparation and rush before leaving, my General had thought to plan ahead for me.

The Kunming office gave me a farewell dinner where *shaosh-ing* (yellow wine) flowed and *gan-bey* (bottoms up) and *shwey-byan* (as you please) flew back and forth.

It was good clean fun until the fruit arrived for dessert and one of the reporters turned to me, a few sheets to the wind. "I understand General Chennault kissed you at his farewell party." Fortified by the wine, I decided to be direct.

"Yes. He kissed me good-bye."

He studied my body, taking liberties which, in sobriety, he would never have allowed himself. "Lovely face and figure, good mind, good education—all for a foreigner. What a waste!"

I felt flushed—not solely from the wine—and turned my back on him. But I was shaken. *Foreigner.* What a word. Yet there it was, casting an ominous shadow.

Darkness fell as my plane circled Shanghai for the landing at Kiangwan Airport. Down below, the huge city was an illuminated checkerboard. I had never been to Shanghai before, but there was an air of familiarity about the tall buildings, bright street lights, trolley cars, and gaudy shop windows of the sprawling city, even though I missed the ancient cobbles of Kunming.

War had left few external scars. The Sun Company department store, the Pacific and Park hotels, the race course, and the Majestic Ballroom ... all the famous landmarks were there, unscathed.

Grandfather Liao was in his study when the servant let me in. This was not a mansion like the great house in Peking, but it was sunny and spacious, with the unmistakable touch much in evidence: books, scrolls, and beloved antiques.

Although he had aged, his voice and eyes were as youthful as I remembered them.

"Boo-Boo!" he said, over and over, "little Boo-Boo. We've been expecting you, for I knew we would see each other again."

He called to Grandmother, who rushed to me with laughter

and tears pouring out simultaneously. Only then did I realize how much I had missed them.

The day after Christmas, 1945, I was glancing through U.S. wire service reports, when a brief Associated Press item caught my eye. The words "Major General Claire Lee Chennault" jumped out at me. " . . . boarded a plane in San Francisco bound for Shanghai, China . . . refused to discuss his mission with reporters."

He was coming back!

Three days later I was at Kiangwan Airport. He stepped off the plane looking younger and more relaxed than I remembered him. "Anna!" he exclaimed, through the cluster of reporters. He reached out to seize my hand, ignoring the first few questions. I stepped back and asked a few of my own. His answers were uncharacteristically vague. He wanted to help China recover from the war, and was looking into ways of so doing.

Before he left the airport in a private car provided by friends, he whispered in my ear, "Let's have dinner tonight. I'll call you."

I nodded, my heartbeat racing like a trip-hammer.

Five o'clock came and he hadn't called. Did he know where to find me? If I left the office, would he know to call Grandfather Liao's house? Should I call him? But where?

The telephone rang at five-fifteen, as raucous as a fire alarm. "I'll pick you up outside in five minutes."

"But I'm not dressed for dinner, I'll have to go home and change . . ." I had of course been dressed and ready for hours.

His answer was perfect. "You look lovely."

"Five minutes," he said and hung up.

When I got into the car, he told the driver, "Park Hotel."

We leaned back against the cushions, spent with expectation. He took my hand. "I've missed you, Little One." The endearment suggested not so much passion as compassion, and it stirred me.

We sat in the hazy cocktail lounge on the fourteenth floor of the Park Hotel, at a small table away from the dance floor. The orchestra was playing a current favorite, "One Day When We Were Young." We said nothing until the waiter brought our cocktails and we could drink to each other.

"Anna," he said, "I have something very important to tell you. I have come back as I told you I would, and I have come back a free man."

The dancers on the floor looked like a merry-go-round in motion. I wanted to jump on and ride.

"You mean that you and your wife...." I knew what he meant, but had to ask, anyway.

"Divorced," he said. "Legally. But in effect since I first came to China. That was eight years ago, Anna."

He leaned toward me, his eyes glowing earnestly. "Eight years of war. Twelve thousand miles from home. My life is here. Hers is back in Louisiana. I don't blame her. I didn't really blame her for not coming here years ago. We have become strangers, hardly speaking the same language."

I didn't know what to say. He was a stranger to her. He was a foreigner to me. How to work out the equation?

But he really wasn't a foreigner to me. He had spent eight debilitating years trying to save my country. He had recovered my lost sisters. How could I not love him?

"Little One," he said, reaching across the small table to cover both my hands. "I couldn't tell you before, but I feel you must know that I love you and have loved you for a long time."

Inexplicably, a tear landed on my cheek. I freed one hand to wipe it away.

"I want you to marry me," he said. It wasn't a question but a courtly command.

Things were moving too fast for me. The whole restaurant seemed out of control, the waiters, the orchestra, the dance floor. Heart and mind did battle, one saying "Yes," the other "No." I realized I was afraid. I wished I could see more of his face, not just the feline aspect of narrowed eyes and set mouth and chin.

The questions raced through my mind. Parents? Religion? Age? Culture? Society? Mixed marriage?

His eyes softened. "What is troubling you, Little One?"

"I'm afraid we won't be right for each other."

He smiled. "No one is exactly right for anyone. But _ promise we will be nearly right, I for you and you for me."

A current seemed to flow through his hands into mine.

"Give me a little time," I said. "I need to think."

I really needed to think. I also needed to settle some unfinished business with my dearest Dick Ng.

It took me almost two years to make up my mind.

After I had said yes to General Chennault, I called Dick to suggest we have dinner at the Park Hotel the next day. It was Shanghai's best, crowned by a skyroof where we had dined and danced on many a sentimental occasion.

"Any special reason?" Dick was very cautious, even about potential pleasure. "Something I should be very happy about?"

"It's an important evening," I said. "I want us both to remember it."

Actually, it was going to be an excruciating evening.

It was raining hard when he came to pick me up. We drove through a city rejuvenated by postwar riches, manic with night life, neon-lit, and crowded along the wide sidewalks of Nanking Road and Avenue Joffre by throngs of foreigners.

The waiters and the maitre d' made the usual fuss over us. Dick was a regular customer; he was also president of the Central Trust. The combination was fail-safe. They gave us the best table, by a window overlooking Shanghai Bay and its pageantry of twinkling ships.

"Let's have champagne," he said, in a spirit of celebration.

"Let's," I said.

How accustomed I had become to extravagance. Here we were among Shanghai high society, entertained and catered to like royalty, dressed to suit the role, our senses pleasantly teased with riches: sensual music, exquisite food, impeccable service, romantic view, superb champagne. It left very little to be desired.

In Dick's company, it was easy to take luxury for granted. He made me feel it was my due. His chauffeur and car were unfailingly at my disposal, he sent me exorbitant jewelry, he often chose and ordered my clothes. He presented me to his influential friends with a flourish, sent me flowers, introduced me to *haute cuisine*. Under his influence, sinking into excess was as natural as smiling at a compliment.

The champagne came. Dick looked expectantly at me, sensing an announcement, but I stalled. We toasted each other and drank, had dinner, danced, and stared at the ships. His eyes were on me all the time, more steadfast than usual.

In the middle of something I was saying, he broke in suddenly. "You are so young and so beautiful," he said, full of compassion and sadness, as if both qualities were to be pitied.

He was twenty years older, a handsome man in his professional prime, president of the Central Trust Bank, respected and sought after, rich, eligible, kind and decent. But he worried about the implications of keeping company with a twenty-one-year-old woman. He wanted to marry me, and the sooner the better. The motivation was as much propriety as affection. He was uneasy about ambiguity and preferred to keep his affairs—professional and personal—in order, to tie up any untidy ends.

He wanted me to marry him and, in the minds of most people, it was a foregone conclusion that I would.

"Tell me what's on your mind," he said for the third time. "You're being so mysterious." ,

"Please stop asking," I said. "Let's just enjoy our dinner and dance. I'll tell you when I'm ready."

We drank some more. The world seemed to recede. The human figures around me were faceless, the music ebbed and flowed like a remote tide, my limbs were disconnected from my body, my body from my head.

"Let's go," said Dick at last.

"No, not yet." I felt vaguely threatened at the thought of leaving my seat.

"We'll go somewhere else," he said.

"Where?"

"To the Argentine." I knew I had to wake up, and the Argentine, despite the candlelight, was a loud and boisterous nightclub where it was impossible to hear oneself talk or think.

We threaded our way through the crowded room. Before we could find a table, Dick drew me to the dance floor.

He gathered me in his arms. "Please tell me. I can't wait any longer."

I had lost all sensation in my knees, but I drew back a little, trying to stand up straight.

"I'm marrying General Chennault."

"What?" he shouted. The music was deafening.

"I'm marrying General Chennault."

"You're marrying who?"

The band was gearing up for a climax and drowned us out.

"Dick, I am very sorry. I'm marrying General Chennault."

The music came to a crashing stop.

"What?" But this time he had heard me. The band broke out into a new number, a slow fox-trot. Couples were sliding around us, locked in embrace. We stood face to face, not moving, for a long time.

"Repeat that," he said finally, but I couldn't. "You're out of your mind," he said, and steered me toward the door.

We drove home in silence. The numbness I had tried to induce had worn off, leaving only a dryness in my mouth and a tugging in my stomach. My God, I thought, what have I done? All resolve and conviction had left me. Why didn't I want to marry him? I tried to reconstruct the reasons. Then I remembered the hospital, where I had recently spent a week getting treated for a bleeding ulcer, with nothing to do but read and think things through.

I had two men waiting to marry me, and I had to make up my mind. By the time I was discharged, the choice was plain.

They were both solicitous, attentive, and generous, flooding the hospital room with flowers and fruit. They both called regularly to find out how I was, to ask if I needed anything.

The difference was that the General, in addition to his gestures of concern, and regardless of schedule, would visit me each day.

Dick could not always spare the time. The country was approaching the end of a long, drawn-out war; the task of rebuilding the economy was mind-boggling. There could not have been a more demanding time for a man who headed the national bank of China. So it was more than flattering that Dick devoted as much attention to me as he did. The hospital visits should not have meant so much.

But it wasn't just the hospital visits; it was his whole style, lavish but impersonal.

He called one day while I was lying in bed in the hospital, lonely and bored almost to tears. "Did you get the flowers?" he asked.

"Which ones?" I was fed up with the shipments of stylishly arranged bouquets from the florists.

"The ones I just sent," he said.

I began to complain. "Dick, this room is full of flowers. It looks like a funeral parlor. I wish you would come and see me instead of sending me more flowers."

"Darling, now you know. . . ." I knew exactly what he was

going to say. I could recite the admonition word for word: "Darling, now you know I'm a government official. You have to learn that there are times when we must give ourselves to our country. I love you very much, but there are important matters I can't neglect."

This would be followed by my standard question, a petulant "Then I come second?" the response to which I also knew by heart.

"It's different. A man's duty to his country can't be compared to his love for a woman."

"Why not?" I would go on childishly. "You spend more time on your bank and your country, and yet you say you can't compare it."

"Be patient," he would say then. "Some day, you'll understand the difference. You'll see that I love you very much, but that my duty is first to my work."

It is very possible that by marrying him I would have come to understand; wives usually do, if they want peace. But I wasn't yet married to him and my patience, instead of growing, was being severely strained. And I was very young.

And it wasn't just the constant lack of time, but the sudden cancellations and changes even when he did make time for me. He would call a few minutes before we were due to go out to dinner. Something had come up. He was very sorry, he would make it up to me. Then, when he did make it up to me, it turned out he was making it up to others as well. How many times I worked myself up into a state of fevered expectation over a quiet dinner alone with him, only to be told at the last minute that he had invited a couple of friends along. Of course it always ended up being more than a couple. All of a sudden, I would find myself seated at a restaurant with Dick and twelve other people—invariably professional associates of one sort or another—older than Dick and thus much older than I, imprisoned for hours in dull conversation, mostly about high finance.

The General had the sense to avoid similar situations. When

he asked me out, he made it plain that it was because he
wanted to spend the time with me alone, and, if it sometimes
happened that we were joined by others, he put himself out to
include me in the conversation, apologizing tenderly and pro-
fusely later for the intrusion.

The time came, after we were married, when our social obli-
gations were endless. Many of these involved just as deadly and
as seemingly pointless dinners. But these are allowances one
makes in marriage, not desirable features of courtship.

The General knew this very well, and managed things accordingly. He telephoned me each day, and took me everywhere he could. It was clear that he wanted to be with me.
Dick, on the other hand, could never understand why I should
be hurt when he sent his chauffeur to take me for a drive in the
country on weekends instead of coming himself. He lacked, in
short, the personal touch, of which the General was master.

We pulled into Grandfather Liao's house, which was quiet and
tactfully dark. I had told Grandfather that I planned to break
the news to Dick, and, with his usual exquisite manners, he had
retired early, not waiting up for me as he usually did.

"May I come in for a minute?" Dick asked.

"Of course."

Inside, he went straight to the liquor cabinet. "I am going to
help myself," he said with calm defiance, "to your grandfather's
finest brandy."

He knocked down almost half a snifter and stared at the
floor. I could feel his pain from across the room. "It's the war,"
he said finally. "You're not thinking right. You've been through
so much, you've been without a family, you needed someone
like a father to love. I can understand that. But why a foreigner? What sort of future do you see, married to a foreigner?
Chennault is from the southern United States. You don't know
what that means. I do. They'll make life miserable for you.
They'll think you married him only because he is a hero. Think
about that, Anna." He came to sit beside me. "Look," he said.

"I'm not just speaking from jealousy, believe me. You don't have to marry me. But if you're trying to escape, you shouldn't do it this way."

"Dick, I've made up my mind." I was very tired.

"No, you haven't, Anna." He sounded bitter and condescending. "Think about it some more."

"Dick, I have thought about everything there is to think about."

He looked at me as if seeing me for the first time in his life. "You really have made up your mind, haven't you?" He emptied his glass and set it down. "This is good-bye," he said to the carpet. "This is really good-bye."

I saw him one last time before I left Shanghai, but he was no longer the man I had known. He had become a stranger, distant and impenetrably polite.

Years later, in Washington, D.C., when I was appointed president of the Chinese Refugees' Relief by President Kennedy, I came across a case which demanded more of my attention than all the rest. The refugee was the head of a household that had escaped from mainland China and wanted to settle in San Francisco. I gave him all the help I could. It was the least I could do for a brother of Dick Ng. For Dick himself, there was nothing to be done. He had long since died in a concentration camp on the mainland.

24

Everywhere I turned, there was disapproval and warning.

Don't forget, he is an American, you are Chinese.

Such an age difference!

You're so young. Why not wait?

It is only infatuation. The right man will come along.

The words of caution piled up, layer upon layer of pessimism, into a fortification intended to keep us apart.

The blind wall made me pause. I knew it wasn't all imaginary. But in his presence all difficulties seemed almost negligible. He had the knack of inspiring fearlessness, of drawing you into a conspiracy of defiance.

First he hammered away at my resistance. "When are we getting married, when are we getting married, when are we getting married?"

When I cried in confusion and frustration, he comforted me, but pressed on with his mission.

"Darling, don't cry. I know there are problems. Now, unless I'm mistaken, the biggest one is that I'm American and your family isn't going to approve. You're afraid. Am I right or am I wrong?" Another one of his watertight questions.

"Right."

"Then you must tell them," he said. The logic came from the syllogism that fear is challenge and challenge must be confronted. Therefore, fear must be confronted.

"I wanted to sort things out first before I told anybody," I said.

"Nothing to sort out. You love me and I love you. What you need is courage." He made it sound as though I needed some easily available tool, like a monkey wrench.

"Now, whose permission do we get first?" *(Get,* not ask.)

He used to say, of rather more momentous challenges, "Forget about feasibility, it will compromise us soon enough. Let's look at what might be and be invigorated by it." He was talking about severing Japan's sea lanes, clearing the skies of Japanese planes, mobilizing Chinese ground troops to subvert the occupying forces, and protecting the diabolical Hump route to China—all with five hundred combat planes and one hundred transports. He wanted to defend the Hump as Scipio Africanus defended Rome (by striking at Carthage, the enemy's homeland), as Grant took the South by dispossessing Lee of his supply line. He was accustomed to taking on challenges in the heroic mold.

For a man whose business was conquest, this stratagem of

courtship was an easy ascent. He planned it systematically, like any serious campaign.

"Whose permission first?"

"My grandparents."

"All right, ask them. But one at a time. Ask your grandmother first."

"Why grandmother?"

"She's a woman."

"Oh."

"Promise?"

"Well ... yes; but you can't expect them to say anything right away."

"Why not?"

"Because it wouldn't be Chinese. First there'll be tea. Then dinner. Then many visits. It goes on and on."

"Oh, I see," he said, with an air of having grasped a simple principle. "To marry you, I have to court them." He turned it over in his mind. "No problem."

"But not just my grandparents. My father and my stepmother, too."

"And they're in San Francisco." He contemplated the logistics.

But Grandmother had cried when I finally broke the news. "I thought so," she said, shaking her head. The worst suspicion had been confirmed. "I thought so. Why marry a foreigner? What's wrong with Chinese men?"

"But I don't love them, Grandmother. I love General Chennault."

"You are young and you think he is the only man in the world. But he is a foreigner, and he is not young. I hope you will think it over."

I put my arm around her thin, shaking shoulders. "I have thought it over, believe me. Please approve of him."

"I do like him, that makes it more difficult. He is a fine man, but not the best man for you."

"Not the best, Grandmother, the *only* man for me."

Grandfather's reaction was grave, but less emotional.

"No one in our family has married a foreigner. It is not a very good thing." He seemed at a loss for a better expression.

"I love him, Grandfather." I was at a loss myself.

His keen old eyes looked sad. Then he patted my hand. "Ask him to come and play bridge with us."

Victory!

When he showed up with roses, I knew he was serious. "How lovely! My favorite peach roses!" I said.

"Not for you, darling. For your grandmother."

He went through the rituals, step by step: teas, dinners, polite conversation, bridge games with Grandfather Liao who was an irritating overbidder, subtle pressures on my father ("After finding four of your daughters, the least you can do is let me marry one of them"), patient answers to my stepmother's probing questions.

She and Father had flown in from San Francisco, and, having put up as much of a fight as the risk would allow, were submitting to negotiations rather than admitting total defeat.

Bessie, my stepmother, was a physician, and, as such, felt dutybound to determine the General's physical health if nothing else. She took him into the garden for the grilling, forgetting in her diligence to wear a sweater against the autumn chill.

The next day she came down with a nasty cold, losing her voice and the opportunity for further interrogation.

"Good," said the General when I told him, and we laughed so hard we had to hold onto each other.

But there was one last maneuver before victory could be officially claimed. It was the difference between an aggressive checkmate and a graceful, patient end game. From the day the General had first arrived in China, he had entered into a pact of friendship with President and Madame Chiang Kai-shek.

During the tumultuous farewell to the General in Chungking, the Generalissimo had said, "Chennault, you are like a brother to me."

"I owe it to them," he said, "to make the trip to Nanking to tell them of our plans and ask their blessing. Wish me luck."

"I do."

"They may have someone else picked out for me."

"Just let them try."

He came back from Nanking with approval and blessing, but he said, "I'll never propose to another Chinese girl, it's just too much trouble!"

"This is mighty embarrassing," he said one day. "I just announced our engagement to the Board—and you don't even have a ring."

"Well, buy me one, then!"

"Come on," he said, gathering hat, coat, and me. "You're going to have to wear it, so you might as well pick it out."

Arm in arm, we walked down the Bund to Nanking Road.

"Where can I find a good jewelry store?" he asked.

"What would you do without me?"

His grip tightened. "I hope never to do without you."

I knew exactly where to take him. It wasn't for nothing that I'd spent hours in search of the perfect diamond ring. He would have been stunned to know how presumptuous I had been all along.

"That's the one I want," I said, after a decent amount of equivocation. "If you can afford it."

A slow smile of recognition spread across his face. "You've already been in here and picked it out, haven't you?"

I nodded. "What of it?"

"You were way ahead of me after all." He seemed pleased, for once, about being outwitted.

It was a small blue-white diamond set in a slender platinum band.

I felt a little guilty as he hesitated. His pay had been adequate, but the savings from eight years in China had been invested in.CAT. "Maybe it's too expensive?" I whispered.

"How much?"

"Fifteen hundred dollars."

He smiled. "I was afraid you were going to say twenty-five hundred." He hesitated. "It's not too much, but there's just one drawback. You'll have to lend me the money."

The salesman was holding the ring, baffled by our private joke.

"Could you lend me five hundred dollars?"

We laughed again. "And can you get it today?"

I nodded.

He went to the counter and took out his checkbook and fountain pen. "How much in CNC?"

Beaming, the salesman played with a brown, wooden abacus, then wrote a long figure on a slip of paper, turning it around for us to see. Eighteen million dollars in Chinese National Currency!

The General made out the check.

"Someday I can tell our children I paid eighteen million dollars for your ring."

"And that I lent you the money, don't forget."

We were married on a Sunday afternoon, December 21, 1947, at the General's house on Hungjao Road. It was a small civil ceremony, attended by my parents and grandparents, Cynthia (who had flown in from San Francisco "to see the General's knees shake"), and a few of his friends. Anything larger would have been unmanageable. My family had capitulated to the marriage, but not to the extent of underwriting an extravagant wedding, and the General could not afford it.

I wore thirty yards of white brocade handcrafted into an exquisite billowing gown by Madame Greenhouse, who designed my entire trousseau as well. While Cynthia was helping me dress, I kept her amused with accounts of the fitting at Madame's. The litte couturière had cooed and trilled her congratulations as she draped here and tucked there, exclaiming what a lucky woman I was and what a lucky man he was, thinking all the while that I was marrying Dick, who had first introduced me to her. Then, when she saw me to the door, and the chauffeur held open the door not to Dick's car but the General's, she had broken into a funny pantomime of confusion and chagrin.

The ceremony was short and simple. Afterwards, there was a small reception where we cut the towering cake with an ornate Samurai sword once owned by a Japanese general who had fallen in battle.

Then we broke out the champagne, and under a giant bell made out of a thousand white chrysanthemums that hung from the ceiling, we danced by candlelight. The night was ours.

25

Ever since returning to China, the General had thought about an airline: one that would carry relief supplies from coastal ports to the interior, and commercial cargo on the return trip.

The United Nations Relief and Rehabilitation Administration (UNRRA) and its Chinese distribution organization, the Chinese National Relief and Rehabilitation Authority (CNRRA) had been in operation, but these were short-term programs, and the war against Communism was not.

Several months before we were married, Chennault had gone to the United States on a fund raising tour and enlisted the support of two influential Harvard men: Thomas Corcoran, who had been instrumental in winning FDR's approval for the original AVG in 1939, and Whiting Willauer, head of the Far East and Special Territories Branch of the Foreign Economic Administration, both of whom resigned their jobs to take on lobbying for Chennault's proposed airline.

More important, he returned with the blessing of Fiorello La Guardia, who was the Director General of UNRRA, the former mayor of New York, a former employer of Tom Corcoran, and an old airman.

La Guardia promised the General UNRRA money, provided he could get Chinese government approval and an operation charter, which he did, with the help of T.V. Soong, by the end of 1946.

He opened an office at 17 the Bund, Shanghai, and shuttled for months to Hong Kong, Manila, Honolulu, and back, buying planes, mapping new airline routes, and overseeing the airfields, maintenance sheds, and hangars.

Civil Air Transport made its inaugural cargo flight on January 31, 1947, carrying UNRRA-CNRRA supplies from Shanghai to Canton. The airline began as a modest operation: five planes and a small staff made up of veteran pilots from Flying Tiger days and a ground crew recruited from all over the Orient. But by the end of the year, it had grown to eighteen planes and eight hundred twenty-two employees, with a flight log of almost two million miles.

I had taken on part-time work handling publicity for CAT even before we were married (by then I was reporting only occasionally for CNA). We were an overworked staff, headaches were legion, and we did not always get paid on time. But we stuck it out through the usual growing pains while CAT flew through weather and landing conditions reminiscent of the Hump route, eventually setting an unsurpassed safety record despite its reputation of being "the most shot-at airline in the world."

At first the big C-46 and C-47 transports flew into remote areas with tons of food, medicine, clothing, and other relief supplies, dropping rice in double bags where they could not land, and, from 1948 on, bringing back commercial cargoes: wool, cotton, silk, oil, skins and hides, tobacco leaf, tin, and tea.

Then, as the Communists advanced south, the planes flew round-the-clock ferries, landing where they could, airdropping food, guns, and ammunition, and swooping in and out of heavy ground fire to airlift refugees—one hundred six people crammed into a C-46, in one dire case.

Meanwhile, CAT mechanics were putting in sixteen- to eighteen-hour days, for not only did the twenty-five overloaded transport planes have to keep moving, but, with each city that fell to the enemy, the airline had to gather up machinery, equipment, and supplies and retreat to a new base of operations. From a primitive supply line, CAT had taken on a strategic life of its own.

The General was in his element. He knew the geography and climate of China like the back of his hand and directed overall CAT traffic unerringly.

This was his third war, and he was going to fight it like any other. Chiang Kai-shek was an ally, he had always been an ally, and shifting American sentiment was insufficient grounds for an about-face. The original American purpose in 1942—to turn Nationalist China into a "great power" by revamping its military under Stilwell—had been deflected by later events in the war. As one result, there was a growing infatuation among many in the United States with Chiang Kai-shek's rivals, the Chinese Communists. Stilwell, whose frustrated romance with the Chinese Communist Party could only have been quickened by Chou En-lai's flattery,* was not the only captive.

In Washington, the popular concept of Chinese Communism was that it was not "real" Communism but a synthetic product considerably less harmful than the original. Much about Maoism captured the American imagination: the cult of the common folk, with its egalitarian overtones; the messianic zeal of Mao's followers; the spectacle of the Long March and the rough-hewn charisma of the leaders at Yenan; the promise of

---

* In 1938, Chou En-lai is reported to have said to John Davies, Stilwell's political aide, that if Chiang Kai-shek would let him, he would lead the Communist troops to retake Burma and, "*I* would obey General Stilwell's orders."

a new agrarian order. In popular American terminology, the Chinese Communists were "agrarian reformers," "agricultural liberals," and only, in FDR's own phrase, "so-called Communists." Last but far from least of the factors in the Communists' appeal was their growing strength.

When the civil war began in 1946, the Communist forces totaled about one million, the Nationalists about three times as many. By the summer of 1948, the Communists had achieved rough parity in men and weaponry with the Nationalists. The mathematics of this were not surprising. Nationalist forces had kept most of Japan's troops in China occupied and had suffered the lion's share of casualties, while the Communists were consolidating power on a more immediate domestic level, and were stockpiling armaments thanks to Russian dispensation of Japanese Manchurian stocks, and expanding their numbers as a result of Nationalist defections and surrenders.

It was in the American interest to effect a coalition between the Kuomintang (KMT, the Nationalist Army) and the Chinese Communist Party (CCP), originally because the rivalry threatened to undermine the war effort against Japan and invite Russia to side with the Communists against the Nationalists. After the Japanese surrender in August 1945, when the long-forecast civil war began in North China and U.S. forces had already started disbanding, General George C. Marshall, the top American officer in World War II, was sent to Chungking in December to work for a coalition between Communists and Nationalists.

"Crazy, just crazy," General Chennault had said. "They must be crazy in Washington to think it can work. And if it does work, it will only be until the Reds decide it's time for their next move. Chiang Kai-shek has been fighting Communism for twenty-five years. Now that he's down and weak, we want to force him into a coalition that can never last."

He couldn't understand the official blind spot over the futility of coalition. "When will the United States learn," he kept saying, "that the Communist ploy is really very simple? Under strength, they back down; sensing weakness, they take advantage. All this fear of a strong stand causing a big general war is nonsense. Why should the Reds risk destruction when they're doing so well with the tactics they're using?"

A measure of General Chennault's ambition to alter U.S. policy, or at least to try, was that he went to see General Marshall during the latter's visit to China. Marshall was a man of legendary abrasiveness, an example of which Chennault had witnessed while trying to obtain more supplies and equipment for the Fourteenth Air Force and Chinese ground support. Marshall, then Army Chief of Staff, had informed Chennault, in no uncertain terms, that he had picked Stilwell to command the China-Burma-India Theater and had every intention of backing his choice. Whether or not his close personal friendship with Stilwell contributed to such unflagging support, he went on to assure Chennault that "as long as I have anything to say about it, you will never receive another promotion." Coming from a man who had once conceded that Chennault was "a tactical genius," the bias was apparent.

After we were married, the General was away frequently—either closing airfields or opening new ones—and even the letters and phone calls had to be brief. Our first Christmas together, for instance, was spent at the deserted CAT office. But Christmas Eve had more than made up for the sacrifice.

We had stayed up until midnight, huddled on the living room couch, wishing each other a merry Christmas with punctual kisses as twelve o'clock struck.

I handed him his presents, the smallest one a gold cigarette lighter engraved with his initials.

He handed me my present, the only one, an equally small package wrapped in pale yellow silk and tied with a red ribbon. "Jewelry!" I thought. But instead I found a card: "To my darling Little One, with all my love!" and a key with a small tag on which was written "No. 5 Holly Heath." It was the house I had coveted, built of stone, white on the inside and ringed with a garden and high white walls.

"But we don't have the money," I protested.

"I borrowed the money. We'll manage."

On Christmas Day, he had to work.

We walked up seven flights of stairs to the office because the elevator boy was off duty. Through the windows on the landings, we could see the fishing boats in the harbor.

"Are you happy?" I said, wanting him to share my mood.

"Very happy, Little One. I'm sorry we must work on Christmas. It's a hard kind of life to share, I know. Some day I'll retire. We'll go back to the States, I'll teach again, or maybe just hunt and fish and enjoy life a little."

He sounded as if he really meant it, but I knew better.

"You'd never be happy just loafing," I said.

"Well, maybe you're right. There is still so much to do, and so little time."

"Come on," I said, wanting to avert somberness. "Let's not think about work for the rest of today. Let's drive out and look at our new house."

"But we've already looked at it."

"I know. But let's look at it again."

With the house came a household: Wang, the chauffeur, who between wife, daughter, and concubine could never quite make ends meet, mainly because his solution to every domestic crisis was a gift for each; Wang's women, who engaged in constant battle; Wang's daughter, a pretty pigtailed seven-year-old who fixed her stare on the General's chewing-gum- and candy-filled pocket; and of course Joe Dog.

Joe was a dachshund of mellow temperament and high intelligence, a soldier and a faithful follower of the General.

Some of the General's men liked to tell about the time Joe Alsop, the General's Public Relations Officer and later a newspaper columnist, was trying to teach Joe Dog some new tricks. The dog had been doing clever things only a few minutes before under the General's directions, but Alsop wasn't having much luck. The General finally decided to set out the problem.

"Joe," he said to Alsop, "in order to teach a dog tricks, one has to be smarter than a dog." To the men of the Fourteenth who were there at the time, the homily was exactly what Alsop deserved. They thought him a snob, and never really cared for him.

Joe Dog was no snob. He ate everything, followed us through the morning glories, roses, lilacs, and jasmines in the garden, and even sat patiently at our heels on warm evenings, with no better entertainment than the chirring of the cicadas.

He began to worry as soon as he knew I was expecting.

One day in June, as we sat in the garden, he said to me, "How would you like to visit Hong Kong or the States again?"

I had been dreading this. "You're trying to get rid of me," I said accusingly.

"I am."

"Why?"

"For your health."

"What's wrong with my health? I'm as healthy as a horse."

"Not that kind of health, Anna. We have the baby to think about." He wasn't joking. "The war is getting closer."

"Let's leave, then." I wept.

"I have to stay here. You don't," he pointed out.

"But I want to stay with you. I'll take the risk."

"Look, when the Reds start marching into Kiangwan, and CAT has to pick up and move quickly, I don't want to have to worry about you." He was getting impatient.

We quarrelled until the exasperation wore us out. Suddenly, he got up and left the room. I couldn't believe he was giving in at last. But he returned smiling, a revolver in his hand. He set it down on the table, as undramatically as he used to set down his reading glasses or his daily shot glass of Wild Turkey.

"Little One," he said, settling back into his chair, "I hate to be a bully. But either you go, or you face this." He patted the revolver and laughed.

I was aghast at the joke. But he had made his point.

"Let me stay as long as I can," I begged.

"Of course. Just start getting ready so you can leave at a moment's notice."

Seeing I needed comforting, he put his arm around me. "It's for your safety and my peace of mind, darling."

"Where do you think I should go?"

"You have friends in Hong Kong, your father is on assignment in Sarawak, and we have friends in Louisiana," he said. "You choose."

"When the Communists come, where will you be based?"

"Canton, I think."

"Canton, then," I said.

He did let me stay on in Shanghai as long as I could. But one day, when the wild rush of evacuation had begun, I came home from a CNA assignment bruised and badly shaken. The jeep I was riding in had been caught in a mob and set on its side. I felt small twinges in the abdomen—whether of pain or fear I couldn't tell. It was time to leave.

26

"I'm taking you on a trip," he announced a month after Claire Anna was born. She was a frail little thing, and had kept me awake almost every night. Once she had stopped breathing, sending me screaming to Cynthia for help. (Cynthia was visiting from the United States and was helping me keep vigil.) But then the baby had gained strength, and now, for the first time, I could think of leaving her in Cynthia's care.

We went to northwest China on the border of Tibet, stopping

at the ancient cities of Ch'ing-hai, Lingshai, Lanchow, and other CAT bases. When we got back to Canton two weeks later, Claire was doing well and there was an invitation from Washington, D.C., for the General to address the Foreign Relations Committee of the United States Senate.

My first trip to the United States had been a short one in 1948. This trip was even shorter. His testimony was well received. I remember the words of an admirer: "Chennault can convey more to an audience in thirty minutes—and convey it more clearly—than most speakers in two hours." But he was dejected on our way home.

"They listen and they applaud," he said. "They seem to understand and even seem to agree. But there's no action. No change in State Department policy, no encouragement to the Generalissimo's government, no guns, no ammunition, no support."

"Why?" I asked.

"Oh, I know why. Take all those people who heard me speak. Some of them had already made up their minds about me. I'm in business in China, so my motives must be self-serving. Some are really interested, but China is pretty far away. Where's the connection to their daily lives?

"Then there are others who believe I'm sincere, but feel I'm honestly mistaken. I'm wrong and the anti-Chiang boys in the State Department, in the Institute of Pacific Relations, are right. This leaves a few who are with me all the way, but who don't have the time or the energy to do anything about it."

Shanghai fell in May 1949. CAT moved to Canton, and I from my Canton apartment to a house in Kowloon, Hong Kong, grateful that the lonely months were behind me for the time being.

Number twelve Kent Road in Kowloon was nothing like our beloved number five Holly Heath, but a vast improvement over the small apartment in Canton. The setting was peaceful—a residential area surrounded by gardens—and across the street lived Hu Tai, the stunning movie star better known as Butterfly Wu.

The General was indefatigable, despite CAT's steady retreat and a bleak outlook. One day he came home in high spirits. "We bought an LST from the Navy today," he said.

"What's an LST?" I asked.

"A Landing Ship Tank."

"What are you going to do with a Landing Ship Tank, for heaven's sake?"

"We're going to turn it into a floating maintenance base for the planes. This means we won't have to keep dismantling, packing, and unloading every time we have to pull out. We can just float away to wherever it's convenient for us to anchor it." He was all fired up. "We'll dock it near Canton. When the Reds take Canton, we'll move it somewhere else."

"And where will I be?"

"You, Little One," he said, "are staying right here with the baby."

"With both babies," I said.

It was the first time I'd mentioned the second pregnancy, but he was still so distracted that he simply said, "Wonderful. Make it a boy," and, without breaking stride, galloped on with his plans for the LST.

As the Communists moved south from Shanghai, the floating workshop was moved to Hong Kong, while CAT itself shifted its base to Kunming. Then, when Kunming fell, both CAT and the heavily loaded LST moved to Hainan Island. Early in 1950 Hainan, too, succumbed, and the floating workshop made its first move to Kaohsiung, Taiwan. But I had hardly begun to enjoy our life there when it was time to move on again. This time I was to take the two small children, Claire Anna and Cynthia Louise, to visit my father and stepmother in Piedmont, California. The Korean War had begun.

The plan was for me to wait in California until the General could join us, and then the four of us would travel to Monroe, Louisiana, the General's hometown. Afterward, conditions in the Far East permitting, we would all return to Taipei, Taiwan, which we then considered home.

Father had retired from the Chinese Foreign Service after the Sarawak assignment and he and Bessie, now practicing medicine in Oakland, were living in a comfortable two-story house on a hill in Piedmont above San Francisco Bay. Piedmont was pleasant enough, but I was relieved when the General arrived several weeks later to take us to Monroe. I had missed him, and I was eager to see our new place in Louisiana.

On my trip to Louisiana in 1948, we had spent a glorious Indian summer aboard the houseboat of Jimmy Noe, the former Louisiana governer and one of the General's oldest and best friends. Jimmy was a tall, high-spirited outdoorsman, and so infectious was his love for the bayou country that I, too, fell in love with it, as we drifted along the Ouachita River.

About the time that trouble began brewing in Korea, we had given in to Jimmy's urgings and bought a big ranch-style house at 1000 Cole Avenue.

The house was just about ready to move into when the Korean War broke out, and the General was caught in feverish activity in Taiwan all that winter. But by spring of the following year, he had set to work on the new house. He planted a vegetable garden of broccoli, cabbage, peas, peppers, and foot-long turnips; a fruit garden of Calhoun melons and cantaloupes, and a prize-winning flower garden of roses, camellias, chrysanthemums, and dahlias that bloomed the year round.

Before summer ended, he had built Camp Chenanna, a weekend cabin on seventy-three acres of wooded land along the wild Ouachita, and the scene of idyllic weekends of fishing, duck hunting, and my Southern specialties: corn bread, hush puppies, and gumbo.

These Louisiana interludes of one or two months each year were the only respite in the General's increasingly peripatetic life, split among Washington, Monroe, Taipei, and other centers of CAT business.

I worried about him more and more. In addition to the danger of exhaustion, he faced other health hazards. Taiwan's damp island climate was an irritant to his chronic bronchitis. He coughed a lot and often ran a temperature, but kept up the routine of working through to midnight with the help of aspirin and coffee. He was cavalier about doctors' advice, chain-smoking, taking off on trips when he should have been in bed, and denying any infirmity.

"I've had this cough for years," he would say, laughing, "wouldn't know what to do without it. I'm in good shape." I didn't have the heart to tell him how ashen he was beginning to look.

At the end of summer 1951, we returned with the children to Taipei. The General had taken on another war, this time supplying the UN Forces in Korea. Meanwhile, CAT prospered, flying throughout Taiwan as well as along new transoceanic routes to Japan, Bangkok, Hong Kong, Okinawa, Pusan, Saigon, and Manila.

With tourism came increased passenger traffic and new airplanes, soft upholstery in place of the old bucket seats, and uniformed hostesses to serve cocktails and luncheon to our prosperous new clientele.

The CAT build-up continued throughout the Korean War and on through the next Asian war, in Indochina. At Dien Bien Phu, CAT staged another Taiyuan airlift, first delivering and later air-dropping medical supplies, food, and ammunition to the besieged French soldiers.

When the aggression in Indochina escalated, the General began, once again, to plan a volunteer group, this time an international combat force called the International Volunteer Group (IVG). We went on numerous transpacific flights to talk to members of Congress, Air Force friends, and others.

One evening the General came briskly into our suite in the Willard Hotel in Washington. "What would you say to a vacation in Central and South America?"

"A vacation?" I was instantly suspicious.

"Not just a vacation. A top secret mission. I'll be checking out training facilities for the IVG." I had to laugh. He looked like a boy scout on the eve of his first camping trip.

"What are you laughing at?" He looked hurt.

"Just you," I said. "You're nearly sixty years old and instead of retiring, you're going to start another of your private wars—against all the Communists in Asia!"

"So I'm crazy," he said defiantly.

"Crazy but great."

"Then you'll go with me?"

"I'll go anywhere with you."

Like every other business trip we took together, there was time somehow to feed his addiction to lectures and tours of historic sites. A devout sightseer, his mission was to educate and convert me. He had taken me on two separate trips across the United States—from South to North and from East to West—preparing me for the expeditions with route maps, charts, travelogues, and histories.

The passion for history ran in his family. I remember my astonishment when I visited Texas, the home of two of his brothers, for the first time. One brother, William S. Chennault, manager of Western Union in Sweetwater, not only sang about, but grew, the yellow rose of Texas, and could chronicle the Civil War as if it had ended yesterday.

We returned to Washington from Central and South America in high spirits, our memories awash with tropical colors: the orchid gardens in Caracas, jungle-green Bogotá seen from a mountain-top café, blue-green bananas on a San Salvador plantation, the Caribbean's mauve sunset.

But color and spirit faded before long. It was becoming clear that the IVG would never get off the ground. I asked him why.

"Because both sides, Americans and Koreans, are cooling off," he said. "The State Department and the Pentagon are worried that the IVG will make good propaganda material for the Communists. I'm still linked to the U.S. Air Force in people's minds, and the Reds might point a finger at my volunteer group and say it was U.S. military action in disguise."

"And the Koreans?"

"They know that the United States is already committed to strengthening defenses and that a group like the IVG would drain off some of that aid. They prefer direct aid, and they also fear a Red reprisal. They're wrong, of course."

In the end, the CIA would buy out CAT in the mid-1950s and run it as four separate operations: Air America (the Agency's charter airline), Air Asia (aircraft maintenance), Civil Air Transport (commercial), and Southern Air Transport (defense contracts).

From a small relief airline operating on a shoestring, General Chennault had steered CAT, under the pressure of successive retreats from forty provinces on mainland China, to a prosperous ten-thousand-man enterprise. His ambition was to keep it commercial while expanding from the Far East to Europe, South America, and Africa. But in the last years of his life, much against his inclination, his partners Whiting Willauer and James Brennan began negotiating the sale of CAT to the CIA, striking a deal by which Chennault would be relegated to chairman of the board—a kick upstairs to remove him from the daily decision-making process.

In the end, the controversial Air America would be dissolved, and, with the General gone and the government of the Republic of China refusing to renew its license, CAT would die a natural death.

As soon as the General died, the new management lost no time in spelling out my position at CAT. I went to work one morning to find my desk gone, my office almost unrecognizable—classic clues that the axe has fallen. My desk had been removed to an obscure office which I was to share with another.

The CIA transaction had been kept from me for understandable reasons. The Agency's involvement in Indochina was a matter of considerable sensitivity at the time, and I suppose the General saw no point in involving me in office politics at that level.

In later years, when the CIA was busy making a bad name for itself, the question repeatedly put to me was, "How could you not have known your husband was negotiating with the

CIA?" My reply then, as now, is that I had no way of knowing that the General's visits to the CIA headquarters in McLean, Virginia, were anything more than routine briefings or debriefings. The only thing that struck me as odd was his euphemism: He referred to his visits to McLean as "going across the river."

The Book of Sorrow

27

I remember 1956 as the year of the cough. He coughed through the spring, and, when I insisted on his long-delayed and badly needed vacation, he coughed all the way from Taipei to Monroe. There he improved somewhat, but in a few weeks he was restless again and packed the four of us into a car for a motor trip through Canada. From Louisiana to Lake Louise, the coughing continued. I realized how sick he was only when he let me take the wheel on the long ride back. He did not easily relinquish the driver's seat.

Almost as soon as we got home, he left for his annual medical checkup at the Walter Reed Army Hospital in Washington, D.C.

"Phone me!" I pleaded.

But when the call from Washington came several days later, it was a woman's voice. "Mrs. Chennault? One moment please."

Bad news. I knew it at once.

Another voice—a man's—came on. "Mrs. Chennault, this is General Heaton, Commanding General at Walter Reed."

"Is it about General Chennault?" I could hardly breathe.

"Yes. Your husband is all right. But we found a small tumor on the upper part of his left lung. We want to remove it and do a biopsy." Two days later I was in Washington for the surgery.

145

I watched as they trundled him through a white door that swung back and forth violently before closing.

I went back to his room and began rearranging things, straightening his sheet and pillow. He had left an envelope, addressed to me, under his pillow. The letter had been written the day before. August 26, 1956.

Dearest Little One,

If it should happen that I cannot see or be with you in the flesh again, I do want you to know and remember that I shall always be with you and the girls in the spirit. I love you and them as much as anyone can love and I believe love will endure beyond the grave.

The rest of the page swam together in a blur.

Three hours later, Colonel Moncrief, the chief surgeon, came out of the operating room to talk to me, reaching out for my shoulder with the instinct common to those who must frequently deliver bad news. But his words were soothing: "He'll be all right."

They wheeled him out to the recovery room, covered to the chin with a sheet that wasn't much whiter than his still, drawn face. Three days passed before they let me talk to him. The first thing he said was, "Darling, why are you crying? I'll be all right."

"Of course you will," I said. The pretense was necessary.

Then the tests came back and we knew. *Malignant.* The word itself seemed unspeakable, carrying some of the evil that had been spreading inside his chest before the tumor and the surrounding lung tissue were cut out. New tissue would grow, they said. And if no malignancy showed up in twelve months, he might be in the clear. But the conditional "might" remained.

We were back in Taipei in time for Christmas and CAT's

tenth anniversary. He got through the speeches and awards, but couldn't manage the birthday cake.

"You cut it for me," he whispered. "Without you there wouldn't be any CAT."

He used to say that if it hadn't been for me, he would never have come back to China after the war. It was a gracious concession, but I knew better. There would have been a CAT, just in another place, in another guise.

When friends referred to him as the boss, he would say, "I'm the boss only when Anna is not running the show," forgetting for a while that he *was* the show.

Once, after the appearance of my first book (a collection of short stories published in Taiwan), we were at a gathering where several young students came up to us for autographs. The General instantly assumed it was his they wanted, and the look on his face when he discovered his mistake was one of sheer bemusement.

The year went by uneventfully. Back in Monroe, he gardened and fished, gave up cigarettes, and got reacquainted with an old briar pipe. Month after month the hospital tests came back negative. Yet the dark signs played in the back of my mind like sinister shadows.

There were fragments of overheard conversation:

"Anna has more strength than you may realize" (the General's voice); "I'll take care of them, you know you can count on me" (Jimmy Noe's voice); "Is Daddy sick?" (the children's voices).

When the year was almost up, he made an announcement. "Let's take that delayed honeymoon trip. Let's go to Europe."

The surge of enthusiasm buoyed me, but the next minute I was filled with misgiving. How could we go? He wasn't strong enough. "Not yet," I said, suddenly weighed down with despondency. "Not now."

"Yes, *now.*" His urgency startled me. "I don't want to wait."

He was afraid to wait. Oh God, I was afraid too.

We decided to take the children along. But in New York, the coughing turned into spasms. Stealthily, I telephoned the doctors at Walter Reed. Their answer was terrible in its reassurance: Go ahead with the trip, because—the advice implied—nothing can hurt him anymore.

In Paris, he teased me about the notoriety of French men. "They're wicked," he said, "always watch out for them."

I smiled. "Then I should have watched out for you, Monsieur Chennault?"

"Too late now." We laughed, but the sadness in the hidden meaning undid us, and instead of going out to dine and dance, we stopped at a small Catholic church where we knelt side by side and prayed in silence and tears.

In the thirteenth month, just when we thought probation was over and freedom had been won, the death sentence was pronounced with awful finality: A small spot had appeared in the lung cavity.

I began tearing at my chest as though the diseased lung were mine, as though the pain were mine, as though a cold compress were being applied to my heart. It was he who comforted me. "Now, Little One, they only said they found a spot. They didn't say 'You're a goner' or 'There's no hope.' I'm tough, you know; I'll be around a long time."

When I was calm again, I said, "Can't they cut it out again?"

"Yes, but it might do more harm than good."

He was so composed, he could have been saying, "It might rain tomorrow."

We went to Boston for a second opinion and more tests at the Leahey Clinic. He wanted not so much an opinion as a straight answer to the only remaining question. How long?

I shrank from the truth, but he demanded it. "Know your enemy," he always said.

The doctors told him what he wanted to know. He had three to six months left.

He took the news with predictable defiance, driving off with his friend Tom Corcoran for a Boston tour of Revolutionary War landmarks. They argued about Bunker Hill, the *Constitu-*

tion anchored in Boston Harbor, Lexington Green, and the "bridge that arched the flood" at Concord.

It was I who felt in danger of falling apart. My appetite was gone, sleep took so much effort and was so elusive that I woke up exhausted in the mornings, and my skin kept breaking out in hives. I began developing allergies to so many things—chocolate, milk, corn, pineapple, cheese—that I was afraid to eat.

"Look at it this way," he teased me. "At least you aren't allergic to me."

After a month or two trying out different tranquilizers, none of which worked, the doctor prescribed Benadryl, one a night, which at least put me to sleep, though it was habit-forming, and the habit has stayed.

Often I woke up in tears and ne let me rest, trembling, in his arms. "Anna, darling," he said one morning, "listen to me. We've spent every Christmas in Taipei. Let's not miss this one."

And so we made the long Pacific flight, with the children, once again.

On Christmas morning he went to his office, from unbreakable habit, and came home at noon to sip eggnog and open presents with the children. It was only months later that I learned from Dr. Lee, his CAT surgeon, that he had coughed up blood for the first time that morning. There would be many more mornings like that which I wouldn't know about, either.

Before we left Taiwan for the last time, he told me he had called a press conference.

"Why?" I asked.

"Why? Well, because it'll be the last one."

He wound up the press conference with old-soldiers-never-die bravado: "I plan to be around a good many more years."

On January 10, 1958, reporters met us at San Francisco airport. "General Chennault, the report is that you have cancer. Do you?"

His answer cut through the cold January rain. "Afraid I have. That's what the doctors tell me."

"What do you plan to do, General?"

"Do?" Old Leatherface smiled. "Why, I'm going to try to outlive it. If the Lord gives me enough time, I'll beat this one, too. Now let's talk about something important."

One evening in Monroe he got out of bed, hollow-cheeked and flushed with fever, and said, "The doctors won't like it, but I'm going to New York for the CAT board meeting. They're talking about buying a jet transport and I want to get the order placed. We can't delay that.'

His voice grated like sandpaper; the cancer was seizing him by the throat. Yet on January 28, 1958, he cast his vote, as chairman of the board of CAT, for the purchase of airline equipment he knew he would never live to see.

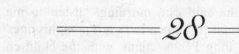

The entries in his diary detail the end: "Radiation ... X-ray: 1,000,000 volts ... bloody mucous ... tubes ... bronchoscopy ... intravenous ... liquid food ... weight 139 lbs. in pajamas." But there were bright passages, too: "March 10, 1958: Started digging gladiola beds at 10:30 and rain started falling at 11:30. Vegetable garden has broccoli, collards, bermuda and hot onions ... peas, mustard, turnips, spinach, beets, and carrots either ready or almost ready to eat. Also cabbages coming on. Flower garden has red buds, jade magnolia, daffodils, jonquils, hyacinth, violets, and pansies blooming."

In May, after he was back at Walter Reed, General Raymond Huft, chief of the Lousiana National Guard, sent his private plane to fly us to the Ochsner Foundation Hospital in New Orleans. Dr. Alton Ochsner was a close friend of the General, and New Orleans was nearer home.

I took a room in Brent House, a hostel adjacent to the hospital for the relatives of patients. There I met Helen, whose husband was dying of stomach cancer across the hall from General

Chennault's room at Ochsner. Helen was a sweet, cheerful Texan whose antidote to despondency was a shopping spree. She was good company on lonely evenings and daytime grocery runs.

About two months into our stay in New Orleans, on July 23, Helen received a visitor, her cousin Edna, a fortune-teller from Texas. By an unhappy coincidence, she happened to arrive on the day that the doctors began preparing Helen for her husband's end. Perhaps, they had gently suggested, she would want to start making the funeral arrangements.

Helen seemed to want my company that day, even though her cousin was arriving that afternoon. "Please stop by this evening," she implored. So when the General had taken supper and medication and was settled in for the evening, I went to knock on her door.

Cousin Edna was a broader version of Helen, but with the same uproarious, earthy humor. She shook my hand and immediately launched into a report of her most recent psychic success. "I've just been telling Helen she'll have her husband around for some time more," she said, as casually as if she were announcing an extra dinner guest.

I looked at Helen, astonished.

Edna smiled with the quiet self-assurance of one who not only tolerates but expects skepticism. "Just you wait and see," she told us.

I had scarcely sat down with the glass of milk Helen brought me when she said, "Anna, let Edna tell your fortune."

I had been expecting this: Ordinarily, the idea would have intrigued me. But I was tired and not in the mood to start any kind of game. I shook my head. "Maybe some other time."

"You can ask me questions if you like," Edna offered. "Ask me any question and I'll give you the answer."

I looked at her and thought for a while. There *was* a question that had been worrying me. I was thinking of returning over the weekend to Monroe where Cynthia and her husband were taking care of the children. I hadn't seen the girls in over a fort-

night and longed to spend a day or two with them. Dr. Ochsner
had encouraged me to go, saying the General was doing as well
as could be expected and would certainly be all right until I got
back. Still, I hesitated.

"Just tell me one thing," I said to Edna. "Tell me if it's all
right for me to leave my husband this weekend."

Edna produced a pack of cards from her handbag and held
out the deck in a fan. "Take one," she said, "but think of the
question while you're taking it. Concentrate."

I pulled out a card and looked at it: the ace of spades. Being
a bridge player, I took it as a good sign. But Edna shook her
head. "Death," she said, with an air of preoccupation. Next she
began placing the cards in alternating face-up and face-down
rows, directing me to remove one here, one there, until she had
her answer.

"You shouldn't go away over the weekend," she said, "because your husband will die in four days."

"Four days? That's Sunday. What nonsense," I said, angrily.

Edna ignored the outburst. "Let me go on and read the other
part of your fortune," she said.

"I don't believe you," I said. I was still thinking about the
four days.

"Just let me finish, please?" Her question had an insistent
ring to it. Without waiting for my permission, she went on:
"After your husband dies, you'll live in a city you hadn't
planned to move to. The first place you'll stay at will have some
connection with the number ten. And two persons will exert a
profound influence on your life. One will cause you a great deal
of sorrow, but you'll be unable to do much about it. The other
will be a source of comfort and happiness. You'll never marry
again, but you'll have lots of men friends who will help and
take care of you."

"Please," I said, "that's enough." I was very upset.

"That's all I'm going to say, anyway," said Edna, a little
miffed by the sudden loss of an audience.

Nothing in his condition seemed to change over the next few days, but I nonetheless cancelled the weekend trip home. He had had a tracheotomy incision and his diminished frame sprouted tubes and pipes. He was very weak, subdued with pain, but was cheered by the daily visits of friends and relatives—especially his grown children.

Letters from well-wishers poured in by the dozens. And one day, a special visitor arrived: Madame Chiang Kai-shek. He had been enchanted by her ever since their first meeting in China so many years ago and had afterward confessed in his diary that "She will always be a princess to me." He had never altered that initial impression, and now his face lit up to see her by his bedside. "Don't try to talk, Colonel," she said, using her old term of affection for him. "This time let me do the talking."

When Sunday came I went to Mass early in the morning and got back to the hospital to find Jimmy Noe and his wife visiting with the General. They stayed a while, then insisted that I lunch with them and another couple at Antoine's in downtown New Orleans, where they had reserved a table.

Sunday lunch was the epitome of elegant tradition in New Orleans, and Antoine's was delightful, yet for some reason the idea held no appeal for me. But the General seemed eager for me to go. He was tired and would only be taking a nap, anyway, he said.

Antoine's was crowded on that Sunday, as on every other Sunday. We lingered over the famous menu, sipped mint juleps, and ordered a multi-course meal that would take the better part of an afternoon to complete.

But suddenly, around 2:30, while we were waiting for dessert to arrive, I began to feel intensely uncomfortable, as if I were being closed in and suffocated. My hair started to stick to my forehead. "What's the matter?" Jimmy said, noticing the sweat.

"I think I'd better be getting back," I said.

Jimmy looked concerned. "Why? What's the hurry? He's taking a nap."

I was feeling worse by the minute. "I'm terribly sorry, I don't feel very well. I think I'll go back to the hospital and rest," I said.

Jimmy jumped up from his seat and took me to his car, where his chauffeur was waiting. "Take Mrs. Chennault to the hospital," he told him. He gave me a kiss through the window. "We'll talk to you later."

When we got to the hospital, I leapt out of the car and rushed up to his room. The nurse was sitting beside him; he was just waking up.

I leaned over him. "I'm back," I said.

He sat up all of a sudden, reached for my hand, and said, "Darling, let's say good-bye." In the next instant he was spewing out blood.

The nurse ran to call the doctor. When she came back with Dr. Ochsner and two other physicians, he was still emptying blood. In less than ten minutes it was over.

Dr. Ochsner looked at his colleagues in puzzlement. "But there was no warning it would be so soon. . . ."

In a sudden great fear I called his name, but he didn't answer me. I knelt by his bed with his blood all over me.

"Cry if you can," said Dr. Ochsner, touching my shoulder.

"I wish to be alone," I told them, and, when they left the room, I covered him with a sheet and went to sit in a chair. I was so very tired, and now alone.

When I try to recall the funeral, I am carried back to the heat and glare of that day in July, to the road through Arlington Cemetery, unfolding before me like a sequence on film. Sealed in the slow, silent, air-conditioned limousine, I felt enclosed in a space as improbable as the inside of a television set—watching an audience of thousands watch me as they slid past in slow and soundless motion.

Even now I can see the parked cars glittering in the still heat, the rude flare of flashbulbs, the black horses with the flag-draped casket in tow, the sweat on the foreheads of the pall-bearers (T.V. Soong, Jimmy Noe, Dr. Alton Ochsner, and Ambassadors Hollington Tong and Whiting Willauer), the mass of famous faces swimming in the dizzy heat waves.

Then I see the flag, removed from the coffin and folded by the hands of ramrod men in uniforms. I see the bronze coffin, burnished by the sun, sinking into the ground. And I hear the dull rumble of drums, ending in a rifle shot that splits the air in a final report.

Edna the fortune-teller must have seen something. The General died within four days; Cousin Helen's husband outlived the doctors' predictions; and I ended up in Washington, D.C., where I had never expected to live.

After the funeral, my sister Cynthia had remained in Washington while I returned to Monroe to set things in order. I had asked her to find me an apartment, one within walking distance of a good parochial school for the girls. She found one almost immediately and called to tell me the good news. "It's a large two-bedroom, in a fourteen-story building," she said, "across the street from Annunciation Church and School. Nothing special, but the location is good."

Something made me ask, "What's the apartment number?"

"Ten twenty-five," she said. "Why?"

But I decided it was no time to go into superstition and fortune-telling.

I decided on Washington largely by default. I could have returned to Taiwan. On the way home from the funeral, Madame Chiang Kai-shek had ridden along with me in the limousine, patting my hand with maternal solicitude and repeating, "You always have a home in Taiwan; please remember that."

But to go back to living in Taiwan without the General was to court sadness in a place that had once meant happiness and hope.

Washington seemed to make sense because it wasn't entirely strange to me, because I had friends there, and because that was where the General's will was probated.

It didn't take me long to find a job absorbing enough to justify the hours, and flexible enough so that I could be home when the girls got back from school in the afternoons.

The job at Georgetown University, in machine translation research, was tailor-made to improve my English, which still gave me hesitation. The Louisiana ladies used to let out peals of laughter at my blunders in usage and idiom. Stung by the ridicule, I would file complaints with the General. "They're always making fun of me. What shall I do?"

"Simple," he would say, with maddening practicality. "Stop making mistakes. Work at it."

"That's much easier to say than to do," I would point out.

"Easier said than done," he corrected me.

"How good is your Chinese, anyway?"

"Terrible," he admitted, cheerfully. "From the very beginning, Madame Chiang Kai-shek told me not to bother struggling with the language. 'Colonel,' she said, 'you'll never learn to speak good Chinese, so concentrate on your job. There will be plenty of people to interpret for you.'"

"And so I end up interpreting for you? I'm supposed to know two languages perfectly, and you get along fine with one."

"But you can't compare the two of us, Anna. You're more talented."

So the early Washington days were circumscribed: language in the mornings, housekeeping in the afternoons, reading and writing and tutoring Chinese in the evenings. The agenda left little time for boredom, or, for that matter, loneliness—especially after I met L.J.

In the mode of urban romances, he lived down the hall from me, a helpful neighbor with whom I exchanged mail and newspapers, shared elevator rides, and chatted in the hallway. I felt comfortable with him from the very beginning, with the way he showed greater interest in my children than in me, looking and smiling at them while talking to me. He was a dark, intense-looking, professorial man, fortyish, with thin hair, thick glasses, and a preoccupation with all matters but the present. But his clothes were stylish, a successful businessman's clothes. Like most people for whom wealth creates insecurities, he was terribly shy. The shyness was infectious, the kind that subverts easy conversation. Strangers usually gave up after the first few unavailing exchanges, but those who got beyond glimpsed a generous man, serious about commitments and loyalties, chronically sad, but with redeeming humor.

His decision to fall in love with me caused him incurable anxiety. He made falling in love an even more complicated business than it already is. At the heart of his turmoil was a conflict of interest. Was it ethical for a friend to promote himself as a lover—or vice versa? As a lover, he was entitled to some selfishness, but, as a friend, his duty was to further my best interests, which included protecting me from the selfishness of demands like his. He wanted me for himself; on the other hand, he didn't want to deprive me of other opportunities. In the abstract, he wished me freedom and independence; in practice, jealousy and curiosity about my every movement consumed him.

Anxiety was his natural state of mind. It was anxiety about automobile defects that led him to acquire a new car every six months. Anxiety, too, over each new car underlay his curious parking habits. On one of our early dates (a concert), he drove me to the theater and let me off at the front entrance. I waited nervously in the lobby for what seemed like an hour before he returned from parking the car.

"What happened?" I asked.

"It took me forever to find a parking space," he apologized.

"But I thought there were parking attendants in the garage."

"Oh, I wouldn't let anyone park my car."

"So you park it on the street instead?"

"Of course." he said. amazed that I should even ask.

I liked his eccentricities. I also liked the way he usually took me seriously while preventing me from taking myself too seriously. Yet he never seemed to take seriously my rejections of his marriage proposals. Others had proposed, some within weeks of the General's death. but had duly retreated after my stock reply: "I'm never going to get married again. I want to be buried next to my husband in Arlington Cemetery."

The intention was sincere—and just morbid enough to put them off. I had paid a high price for the lot in Arlington Memorial. and its value to me was lasting. About a month before the General died. I had begun arranging for a burial with proper honors at Arlington.

This caused the first serious clash between his family and me. Being of proud Louisiana stock. they wanted him buried in Monroe. But I felt he deserved a greater burial than that accorded a local hero. He alone. among the giants of World War II. had been denied. by the military powers that be. the privilege of witnessing the Japanese surrender on the *Missouri*—a meanness he never quite forgave. even though General MacArthur had made a dramatic point of remarking on his absence ("Where is Chennault?" he had asked loudly. "Where is he?").

Reparation was made belatedly. About ten days before he died. President Eisenhower called the hospital to relay to the General. through me. the news that he had been given his third star. "A promotion well deserved." the General had said. adding bitterly. "only it comes ten years too late."

Considering his disappointment. I felt a burial at Arlington was the least that could be done in compensation. His family gave in. but grudgingly. and only after bad blood had flowed.

When L.J. proposed and I delivered my usual line about wanting to be buried at Arlington. he brushed it aside with an impatient *non sequitur*. "Yes. well." he said. "let's cross that bridge when we come to it."

After repeated offers, he blew up in exasperation. "How long are you going to take to get on with life?" By "getting on with life" he meant getting married. "You can't live in the past, you know."

"Why can't we just be very close friends?"

"Ach!" he'd say with total disgust. "There's no such thing between lovers. You're either serious lovers or you're not. You're skirting the issue."

"Well, then, don't bring up the issue."

"Look, let's get away for a couple of days, relax, take things easy, talk it over. Just try me out. You might like me."

So we would go away, and I wouldn't like it. I remember one Christmas in Florida, beginning pleasantly enough, but turning sour as he began harping on commitment again. There were no direct assaults (he'd promised not to bring up marriage and risk ruining the vacation), but the reproach was constant. When I ignored him, he turned to nitpicking and petty faultfinding. I knew there was going to be an explosion, and it came on Christmas morning.

We sat down to breakfast, and right away his mood cast a heavy shadow. The waitress, a young, almost tauntingly cheerful woman, came by with a pot of coffee. "Would you like some coffee now, sir?" she said, standing over his cup.

"Better now than after breakfast," he said, a churlish reference to the fact that coffee had been slow in coming the previous day.

"Sir?" said the girl, confused.

"Never mind, yes, I'd like some coffee." He watched her pour, stiffening as soon as she turned her back. "Just look at that," he said to me, glaring at the cup.

"What's the matter?"

"What do you mean, what's the matter? You can't see what's the matter?"

Small tremors of annoyance were registering at the back of my neck. I closed my eyes. "Just tell me what's the matter, L.J., please?"

"What's the matter is that she poured the cup so full, there's no room for cream, not one lousy drop of cream," he said, banging the creamer down on the table.

The waitress turned around, startled. "You need more cream, sir?"

He smiled at her, the smile of a persecuted saint. "It's not cream I need, miss, it's a cup of coffee with enough room left for some cream, which I have here, but which I cannot use."

The girl flashed him a smile and a wink of bright complicity. "Gotcha!"

She was back in a second, with the same cup minus an inch and a half of coffee.

But as soon as she left, he groaned. I had just taken my first sip of coffee. I set the cup down.

"Now what's wrong?"

"Why, why, why?" he said in a hushed, strangled voice. "Why did she have to spill it into the saucer?" His cup was sitting in a thin film of coffee.

"Here, take mine; we'll switch," I offered, desperate for peace.

"No," he said. He was going to be firm and incorruptible in his annoyance.

"Why don't you let them have a nice Christmas?" I said, the floodgates of anger bursting finally. I pushed back my chair. "Why don't you let me have a nice Christmas?" I marched out of the dining room, went up to our suite, called the airlines for a reservation on a flight back to Washington, and began packing my suitcase.

In less than an hour, I was on the plane, a lone Christmas passenger. It was a luxurious flight, as memorable for the service as for its tranquillity. By the time I got home and the phone rang—he was calling to make amends—the anger had subsided and I could laugh with him. "L.J., I forgive you. But can't you see why we should never get married?"

Still, he kept trying for almost seven years—until he too died of cancer.

L.J. had always teased me about my hypochondria. "You have such a morbid fear of cancer," he'd say.

"Wouldn't you? First Mother, then my husband, then two of my best friends whom you never knew."

"I'm sorry," he said, without really understanding.

The irony was that I had come to expect longevity from him if nothing else. His loyalty seemed indestructible, immortal almost. After he became sick, I went to visit him daily, but it was an unpleasant task, done out of reciprocal loyalty. I hated to watch him fade.

"I'm leaving you all my money," he announced one day.

"L.J., don't be foolish. I don't want your money. Give it to someone else." (He did. He left it to his alma mater in Chicago.)

It wasn't philanthropy so much as superstition. Besides, I felt it was his way of trying to exert a posthumous hold on me.

His mother gripped my hands once, tears in her eyes. "You changed him; you've made him happy."

"If you think he's happy now, he must have been awfully miserable before," I said, intending a joke.

"He was," she said, with simple but stirring gratitude.

Near the end, I had to leave for a few days: an essential out-of-town trip, as I explained. It was a merciful act of the subconscious to avoid the scene of final separation.

He looked at me with unbearable sadness. "Say good-bye?"

"I'll be seeing you," I said.

"You won't be seeing me," he told me, not querulously, but as if gently preparing me for a commonplace letdown, like bad weather.

"Don't talk like that," I said, with a sharpness that surprised us both. "I'll be back in a couple of days."

He just smiled. And when I got back to find him gone, I was more grateful for the memory of that smile than he could have known.

The Autumn Annals

30

I came to Washington equipped with little knowledge about the American political system beyond what I had read in my citizenship primer: basics of the Constitution and American history in a capsule. It was only in 1960, the year I joined the Republican party, that my blooding in politics began.

Whenever I am asked why I joined the Republicans, when General Chennault had been a southern Democrat, I have a simple answer: The Republicans were the first to ask me. I met a woman one day, Sylvia Herman, chairman of the Republican Women's Federation of Maryland. She asked me if I was interested in politics. Yes, I said, as much as a person with my limited knowledge could be. She was organizing minority groups to campaign for Richard Nixon. Would I be interested in working with such a group? I would.

Richard Nixon was not just a chimerical politician. I had met the Vice-President some five years earlier in Taiwan—first at the presidential banquet given in his honor by President and Madame Chiang Kai-shek, then at another reception held for him by the General and me.

After the guests had left, General Chennault turned to me.

"Well," he said, "what do you think?"

"About what?"

"About the Nixons."

163

"I like her. She seems so sweet, so willing to suffer. But the sadness shows in her cheeks."

"Her cheeks?"

"Yes, they're so ... they look as though she's been rubbing her knuckles into them for years."

"Oh, Anna! No, really. But what about him? Don't you think there's something about him? I don't know what it is. I'm not comfortable with the man. Wish I knew why. Bothers the hell out of me."

I had not kept in touch with the Nixons, but when the General died, I remember Nixon's letter as being one of the more thoughtful and sincere messages of condolence. I wrote to thank him, and from then on we communicated periodically, mostly about Asia and Asian Communism, with which he showed a certain fascination.

I mentioned this connection to Sylvia Herman, who was delighted. "Wonderful!" she said. "You're just the kind of person we're looking for."

At that time, unfamiliar with the gushing language of politics, I wondered exactly what that "kind of person" was. But what did it matter? They wanted me.

The minority groups Sylvia meant included Czechs and Hungarians, Germans and Yugoslavs, along with Chinese and Japanese, Filipinos and Koreans, Blacks and Chicanos, among others.

I started out with simple volunteer tasks: writing letters, making phone calls, attending rallies, organizing registration drives, speaking to minority groups. In time, I began to grasp the importance of the precinct, the meaning of grass roots. The reward was a ringside seat at the high points of the great campaign carnival, from the bloody, bone-breaking primaries to the frantic hotel-room hustle of the national conventions.

My first convention, in Miami, evokes memories of earsplitting, eye-opening confusion. H.L. Mencken compared the national convention to a revival or a hanging: "One sits through long sessions wishing heartily that all the delegates and alternates were dead and in hell—and then suddenly there comes a show so gaudy and hilarious, so melodramatic and obscene, so unimaginably exhilarating and preposterous that one lives a gorgeous year in one hour."

Dominating this compelling scene for me was the even more compelling figure of Richard Nixon. For a time I felt that nothing could stand between him and victory: neither hostile crowds nor his own handicaps of poverty and physical plainness; neither the sickening pain of an injured knee nor the highbrow grace and style of his nemesis, John F. Kennedy; not even his own appearance in the cartoon strips as a sewer rat.

After the Nixon-Kennedy television debates, people kept saying I was on the losing team, but I refused to be pessimistic. It would be some time before Nixon's behind-the-scenes TV mishaps would surface: the lack of preparation and advice on the eve of his first debate (he had cut himself off from his media experts); the foul-up of camera lighting and positioning; the luckless injury, on his way to the studio, to his already injured knee; the absence of adequate make-up.

It was my first campaign. We had lost. But the battle had been invigorating, the votes controversially close, so much of the sting was taken out of defeat.

When Democratic friends invited me to the Kennedy Inaugural Ball at the Stadium Armory, I went with almost teenage exuberance, still naïve about the dictates of political loyalty. With the event came one of the worst snowstorms ever to hit Washington. The streets were flanked with high hedges of ice that ruined my seventy-five dollar gold sandals. But it was worth it for the sheer exclusivity of the event, the engaging picture of Jack and Jackie, the nightlong dancing, the euphoric singing.

Afterwards, a group of us went for a nightcap at the Gaslight Club (of which I was later to become the first female member), where we dissected the ball and I was berated for having found a flaw in Jackie Kennedy. Her white gown was stunning, I said, but her feet were so big, I wondered what size she wore. But no one had noticed. How peculiar of me to focus on such a detail! How Chinese! A few months later, some of those same women had cause to find fault with more than the size of Jackie Kennedy's feet. At a luncheon for her, given by the wives of congressional leaders, the First Lady failed to show up. In her stead came Jack, apologizing for her absence (she was not feeling well, he explained) and charming us all. The incident might have had a happy ending—except for the discovery that Jackie had not been in bed, but in New York, shopping.

My first White House appointment, announced by President Kennedy in the Rose Garden, was to head the Chinese Refugees' Relief Organization.

The exodus from mainland China was reaching serious proportions as thousands of refugees fled famine, drought, and Red Army conscriptions to farm labor, swimming by the droves across the Pearl River to Hong Kong and Macao. A considerable number were finding their way into the United States.

Ex-presidents Hoover, Truman, and Eisenhower were advisory members of the organization, as well as Richard Nixon. Jack Anderson was its secretary.

"Who's Jack Anderson?" I asked. Drew Pearson's assistant, I was told. Pearson was writing his *Washington-Merry-Go-Round* column at the time and Anderson was collaborating on the column part-time and also serving as chief of the Washington bureau for *Parade* magazine. Jack and I hit it off well from the start.

Years later, in 1968 and 1969, Anderson would often check with me before writing any Vietnam-related stories. Jack and I have our political and ideological differences, but we nonetheless remain friends.

The third angle in the organizational triangle of the Chinese Refugees' Relief Organization was the treasurer, David Lee. David later went into the restaurant business with Mrs. Trudie

Ball, a joint venture that produced the Empress Restaurants, of which Jack and I became minor shareholders.

In Washington, where politics and entertaining are as indivisible as two sides of the same coin, it was not surprising that I, who delighted in entertaining, should take on the role of political hostess. The progression was simple. I was considered sociable and well-connected, and was single, thus free to seek out and cultivate whomever I pleased, able to bring people out and put them at their ease. I had an interesting apartment, filled with family heirlooms and antiques. I was an enthusiastic cook. And, I came with a certain exotic Asian aura. Invitations to my dinner parties became a coveted item. Politicians are forever eager to caucus and convene, and the more comfortable the locale the better.

My penthouse apartment at 4201 Cathedral Avenue had become a popular watering hole for ranking Republicans by the time Senator Barry Goldwater decided to run for President. It was there, in the living room, that some of the early strategy and program meetings took place, manned in those embryonic stages by Senator John Tower of Texas and Peter O'Donnell, the energetic chairman of the Texas Republican Party. Over beers which, no matter how cold, never seemed cold enough for Peter, they planned the campaign that would be one of the most disastrous in the history of Republican politics.

Caught up as I was in my campaign activities—of which the serving of beer was only a very small part—I did not realize that I was engaged in a losing battle, nor that I was getting one of the most important lessons in American Presidential politics: that the courage of conviction, no matter how incandescent, cannot on its own capture the Presidency.

If ever there was a candidate of clear-cut conviction, it was Barry Goldwater. Even his physical features confirmed this: the tall, square frame; the features chiselled, it seemed, by some precision instrument; the voice as crisp as kindling.

His tastes, too, ran to the tangible and the well-defined: machines and engines; stories with beginnings, middles, and ends; sharp and clear landscapes like the terrain of his native Arizona.

In particular, he loved the technology of airplanes, having flown one of the early C-47s over the Hump as a major-general in the USAF reserve. His curiosity about General Chennault was boundless.

He believed in morality and patriotism and defended those unfashionable concepts with a sincerity and fervor rare in the compromise of politics. His misfortune was the failure to make a simple political adjustment: the alignment of ideology with reality.

Solutions and prescriptions poured out of him unsifted by caution. He said whatever was on his mind, the press be damned, the liberals be damned, the world be damned. His unrestrained metaphors branded him as hawkish, trigger-happy, irresponsible. The Bomb. The Nuclear Test Ban Treaty. Social Security. These were the issues that damaged him. It didn't matter that he was completely honest, completely honorable; that he refused to exploit the race issue when he could have; that he refrained from making political hay out of the personal affairs of opponents. His proposals for war and peace were undiluted, too strong for some Americans to swallow. He ran perhaps ten years too soon. His defeat did, however, pave the way for Richard Nixon's reemergence in 1968.

31

I met Nixon again in 1965, while on business in Taipei. He himself was there on semi-official business, trying to promote Pepsi-Cola for Don Kendall, chairman of Pepsico and a client of Nixon, Mudge, Rose, Guthrie, Alexander and Mitchell, the Wall Street establishment at twenty Broad Street to which

Nixon, in his new incarnation as a New York lawyer, belonged. He had bowed out of his last political debacle, the California gubernatorial campaign of 1962, with his famous assurance to the press that they would not have him to kick around anymore, and was now in what ex-politicians call the private sector, traveling without fanfare.

Rumor had it that the Chinese government was under some pressure from the State Department not to give Nixon the royal treatment. (Even with his new persona, Nixon could create uneasiness.) Accordingly, neither the United States Ambassador nor the Chinese Foreign Minister was at the airport to greet him. Later, the U.S. Embassy sent a junior officer along with the chief of protocol from the Chinese Foreign Ministry to pay him an ostensibly casual visit, though they did arrange, for the next day, an audience with President Chiang Kai-shek. As an unacknowledged visitor, Nixon stayed not at the U.S. Ambassador's residence but at the famous Grand Hotel facing the Tan Sui River.

I heard through the grapevine that Nixon was in town and, feeling somewhat sorry for his reduced political circumstances, decided to call him on the day he was leaving to offer him a ride to the airport. He seemed overjoyed to hear a friendly voice and accepted my offer with celerity.

When I arrived at the Grand Hotel to pick him up, it occurred to me that Nixon was somewhat agitated at the prospect of leaving Taipei without a send-off of any sort. But, at the last minute, Ambassador Konsin Shah, the Chinese chief of protocol, arrived, shook hands all around, and it was time to leave.

Then it happened. As Nixon followed me into my car, he cracked his forehead on the door. It was a hard, resounding blow that left no doubt about the pain. He bit his lip hard, not uttering a sound, and turned pale. Blood was oozing out of his forehead, spilling in a thin trickle across the bridge of his nose.

I reached into my purse for a handkerchief and pressed it to his forehead, against the gash. He cupped it hastily in his hands, muttering, "I'm all right, I'm all right." He seemed frantic with embarrassment, looking back every once in a while, handkerchief still pressed to brow, at Ambassador Shah's car, which was following ours, as if in terror of having him discover the accident.

He mumbled apologies about my dress, which was white and, by now, conspicuously spattered with drops of blood. At the airport, he thanked me repeatedly for seeing him off and promised to be in touch.

In the spring of 1967, while on a lecture tour of Asia, I received a cable from Nixon requesting that we meet in New York as soon as possible. A few days later, at his Fifth Avenue residence, in a building shared with his rival, Nelson Rockefeller, Nixon told me that he was definitely preparing to seek the Presidential nomination. For this, he said, he needed my help. He had a feeling that Vietnam would be a hotly debated issue among the candidates. Would I serve as an advisor on Southeast Asian affairs? He became disarmingly conspiratorial. He would never get all the information he needed on Southeast Asia from the State Department. Nor could he even count on friends in Washington. He had to rely on people like myself, well-informed, trustworthy, and with solid connections to the Vietnamese leaders, to supply him with reliable information.

I would be happy to help, I told him, flattered by the request.

I asked him what he planned to do, in the event of his election to the Presidency, about the war in Vietnam.

He thought for a while and said, "If I am nominated, which I hope I will be, I want to end this war with victory."

I wasn't sure what he meant, so I said, "How will you do that?"

"I need to know more about the real situation," he said with discouraging vagueness. "As you know, I can't get all the information from the Johnson administration or from the State Department. This is where you come in. As a lecturer on Asian affairs, you can be of great help to me. I'd like to look at this situation with your help and then try to do what I can."

I asked him then whether he would be willing to go to Vietnam to meet President Thieu.

His response was quick and eager. "Oh, yes, I really need to talk to him personally. I've never met him."

Perhaps, I suggested, he should send a select group of Congressional and other leaders to Vietnam on an advance mission. Then he himself could plan to meet later with Thieu. That would allow him time to do some homework. There was a lot to be learned, I reminded him, beyond the standard TV and press coverage of the war.

He thought this was a good idea, a very good idea indeed. Who did I think should head the Congressional group?

I recommended two Republicans, Senator Tower, and former Ambassador Robert Hill of New Hampshire. Excellent, said Nixon. Excellent choice.

The discussion appeared to be over for the time being. He asked me when I was leaving on my next trip to the Orient. I said I was scheduling one at that very moment. Good, he said. Could we talk again when I got back? He held out his hand, smiling with boyish gratitude. "I'm so glad you've agreed to help me."

I realized I had some of my own homework to do and, as my first assignment, decided to fly down to Monroe to visit an old friend, Governor Noe. I knew of no one else who could answer the questions I had with more insight and candor. He was a devout politician, a true southern Democrat, weaned on Louisiana State politics as it evolved after the assassination of Governor Huey Long. Governor Noe, or James A., as all his friends called him, now owned television and radio stations in Louisiana and his son, James A. Noe, Jr., in New Orleans, had already formed the Democrats for Nixon.

After a superb dinner, which one could safely expect as a guest at his home, James A. and I settled down before a crackling fire to talk about Nixon. He began with the Checkers speech.

With verbatim mimicry, he said: " 'One other thing I probably should tell you, because if I don't they will probably be saying this about me too. We did get something—a gift—after the election. A man down in Texas heard Pat on the radio mention the fact that our two youngsters would like to have a dog. And believe it or not, the day before we left on this campaign trip we got a message from Union Station in Baltimore saying that he had a package for us. We went down to get it. You know what it was?' " The Governor's face broke out in a perfect Nixonian smile. " 'It was a little cocker spaniel dog in a crate that was sent all the way from Texas. Black-and-white and spotted, and our little girl, Tricia, then six years old, named it Checkers. And you know, the kids love that dog and I just wanted to say this right now that regardless of what they say about it we are going to keep it.' "

It was an amazing impersonation. "Great speech," said James A. "What a great performance! A milestone in Nixon's political career."

"With that one speech he converted himself from political liability to Eisenhower's apolitical asset."

"Tell me more about it," I said.

"Well, Nixon knew that the Checkers episode could really hurt him, undo him politically. So he decided to capitalize on it. You see, in 1952, the Eastern Establishment had picked him to run with Eisenhower on the Republican ticket. Do you remember Governor Dewey, Governor Tom Dewey of New York? He was the man who recommended Nixon, but later, because of the Nixon Fund scandal, dropped him like a hot potato. But back in those days, Dewey was a kingmaker and he had nominated Nixon.

"The 1952 presidential campaign was a watershed in many ways," said James A., warming to the subject. "Nixon irritated some of California Governor Earl Warren's supporters by coming out for Ike. During the campaign, some of Nixon's enemies slyly suggested to the press an investigation of a special fund collected for Nixon by some of his California friends. Naturally, the story broke during the campaign and Nixon was in trouble."

"Why? Was it illegal to have special funds at that time?" I asked.

"No. In fact, the Democratic nominee, Adlai Stevenson, had a special fund, too. I know because I contributed to it. The difference was that Adlai Stevenson had full support of the Democrats, while Nixon couldn't even get Ike to lift a finger to help.

"You see," he said scoldingly, "the trouble with you Republicans is that you never stand up for your man when he is in trouble.

"Nixon's going to need help," he continued. "As it is, the Vice-Presidency doesn't carry much weight. When the press asked Eisenhower what decisions Vice-President Nixon was responsible for, Ike said, 'If you give me one week, I might think of one. I don't remember. . . .' "

Several months later, when I was chairman of the National Women's Advisory Committee for Nixon, I was reminded once more of this condescension toward Nixon. When I asked Mrs. Mamie Eisenhower to serve as honorary chairman, she accepted, but with a patronizing smile. She said loftily, "My husband trained him well."

32

From the beginning it was clear that John Mitchell was commander-in-chief of the campaign. He was a difficult man to fathom—a personality of crosscurrents flowing hot and cold by whim—and despite close collaboration with him on two successive campaigns, I never felt I knew him.

In 1968 I found some of his procedural quirks interesting, if not odd. He had a private number where he could be reached at all times. But so acute was his concern about wiretapping that he would change the number every few days or so. This precaution seemed to me to border on paranoia, until, several months later, I realized that I might do well to take a page out of his book.

At the height of the campaign, I was on the phone with Mitchell at least once a day, much of the conversation consisting of messages I had been asked to relay to him by various people both within and outside the campaign.

Mitchell was attending fewer and fewer meetings by then— Tom Evans, his deputy and an attorney of the Mitchell law firm usually stood in for him—but his presence was very much felt, his approval sought on all major decisions.

As Mitchell grew busier and more inaccessible, this close contact I maintained with him generated considerable discontent in the ranks of the frustrated.

What business did I have getting through to him on his private number? What exactly was my function?

But my communication with Mitchell was only a small fraction of the sum of my political involvement. I served, for example, on a foreign policy task force chaired by Senator John Tower, of whom I had spoken so highly to Nixon. The committee was made up of a number of powerful Republican leaders: Governor John Volpe of Massachusetts (later Secretary of Transportation); Rogers C. B. Morton of Maryland (later Secretary of Commerce); Congressman Melvin Laird of Wisconsin (later Secretary of Defense); Senator Charles Goodell of New York; Ambassador Robert Hill of New Hampshire; Bryce Harlow (who had worked for Eisenhower), now vice-president of government relations for Procter & Gamble; and others. Not on the committee, but a frequent participant at our weekly meetings at the Capitol Hill Club, was Senate Minority Leader Everett Dirksen. It was with these personalities, as much as with the campaign committee, that I was involved.

I cannot now remember whether it was Nixon or Mitchell

who first suggested the meeting with Bui Diem, the South Vietnamese Ambassador to Washington and Minister of Foreign
Affairs in Air Marshall Nguyen Cao Ky's cabinet. A native of
North Vietnam, French-educated but equally fluent in English
and French, Bui Diem came from a distinguished and literate
family, owners of the *Saigon Post*. I had known him and his
wife in Marshall Ky's heyday, long before their assignment to
Washington.

I relayed to him the message that Nixon was eager to meet
him, a request that didn't seem to surprise him in the least.

The Democrats, he said, had already contacted him with a
similar request. "Suddenly," he told me, "I have become very
interesting. They tap my phone, they intercept my mail, they
monitor messages I exchange with Saigon."

I wasn't sure if he was being serious. "Why don't you complain?" I asked.

"I have," he said, "to the State Department. It's gotten me
nowhere."

Bui Diem and I took a shuttle flight from Washington to
New York on a snowy Sunday morning. We arrived at Nixon's
apartment on time, but Nixon was out meeting the former governor of New York, Thomas Dewey. Mitchell was there to greet
and entertain us until he returned.

Mitchell received us warmly, reminding me that he had met
me before, with my late husband, whom he admired. He hoped
we would be working very closely together in the future.

About half an hour later, Nixon arrived, full of apologies,
acknowledging Bui Diem with great warmth when I introduced
them. Then he turned to me. "Anna is my good friend," he
said. "She knows all about Asia. I know you also consider her a
friend, so please rely on her from now on as the only contact
between myself and your government. If you have any message
for me, please give it to Anna and she will relay it to me and I
will do the same in the future. We know Anna is a good American and a dedicated Republican. We can all rely on her loyalty." Almost in the same breath, he said, "If I should be

elected the next President, you can rest assured I will have a meeting with your leader and find a solution to winning this war." It was quite a speech. John Mitchell sat nodding in somber concurrence with every sentence Nixon completed, like a schoolteacher pleased by a pupil's performance.

After half an hour of discussion, Nixon, Mitchell, and Bui Diem went into Nixon's study for another conference.

An hour later, they emerged from their conference for more talk about Vietnam. The two main themes that Nixon kept coming back to were that I would be the sole representative between the Vietnamese government and the Nixon campaign headquarters, and that he would, if elected, follow my suggestions of sending a study team to Vietnam, leading eventually to Nixon himself meeting with President Thieu to talk about ending the war. I remember his parting words as he rode down in the elevator with us. "Anna is a very dear friend," he repeated to Bui Diem. "We count on her for information on Asia. She brings me up to date."

Not long after the meeting with Nixon in New York, Bui Diem met me one day to complain that politicians and campaign workers from both parties had been to his office to scavenge for morsels of information from him and he found it all very disturbing. His telephone, moreover, was tapped—he was sure of it—and he had learned that his messages to Saigon were being read. Could I do anything about it? I said I was hardly in a position to influence the Democratic campaign workers, but that I certainly would try to talk sense to the Republicans. Bui Diem seemed inordinately grateful. He was loath to offend anyone, he said. But in view of my special liaison status, he thought it would be best to register his complaint with me.

I got in touch with Mitchell, reaching him at one of his updated numbers, and set up a meeting with him. "Look," I said, "Bui Diem is getting fed up. Everybody's bugging him. The least we can do is to leave him alone."

A look of vast annoyance came over Mitchell's face. "I think I know who's responsible," he said. "I'll talk to them, make sure they stop bothering him. They aren't supposed to go anywhere near the Vietnamese Embassy. Tell Bui Diem it won't happen again—not from us."

If Mitchell made good his promise—and I have no reason to believe otherwise—the slap on the wrist of whoever was responsible cannot have earned me much popularity. I occupied an ambiguous position. Once, when Mitchell, Ambassador Robert Hill, and I were on a conference call, Mitchell at one point said the conference was over and asked Hill to get off the line. Actually, it wasn't. But the message was clear: He wanted to talk to me alone. Later, Hill teased me about my preferential treatment. We were good friends, and I knew the teasing was good-natured, but he did say, "You know, Anna, a lot of people at campaign headquarters are jealous of your intimacy with the top brass."

But I was really too busy to worry about jealousy and envy. In the spring, I took over as chairman of the Women for Nixon National Advisory Committee. It was a dynamic mix of female talent: Claire Booth Luce, Shirley Temple Black, and hard-working wives of Republican Congressional leaders: Betty Ford, Louella Dirksen, and Lou Tower, among others.

The Miami convention, coming as it did in a year of bitterness and violence—a year of riots and assassinations, bloodshed and hatred, arson and demonstrations—was as bland and subdued as any national convention could be.

The Nixon command, headquartered in two hundred rooms at the Hilton-Plaza Hotel, was a model of advanced planning and smooth engineering, wired and crosswired with radios, telephones, and switchboards by communications experts who had reconnoitered the Hilton-Plaza almost a year in advance. In the hallways and up and down the elevators through the top four floors that served as command headquarters, Nixon operatives moved about with swift efficiency, their individual ranks and ratings on the coded blue badges they wore.

At Miami Auditorium, the convention hall, the atmosphere seemed somewhat more in keeping with the reality of the times: State troopers milled about, nuzzling their walkie-talkies; helicopters circled and droned overhead; and anti-war demonstrators chanted their programmed protests. Inside, however, the delegates mingled amiably, the Wyomians in their cowboy hats, the Hawaiians with their flowers, the red-and-white Ohioans, and the orange-and-yellow Californians.

A delegate from Washington, D.C., I was one of two Chinese-Americans, the other being Dr. Bill Chin Lee, who was running for the City Council. In a district that is overpoweringly Democratic and Black, Bill, a Republican Chinese, seemed to me deserving of every bit of help he could get. So when the roll call for the state delegates began, I persuaded Carl Shipley, the Washington, D.C., chairman, to yield his roll call to Bill, since the network coverage would be valuable to him. Just before the roll call began, I whispered a sudden thought to Bill. He followed the suggestion—and created quite a stir. When it was his turn to be recognized, he faced the television cameras trained on him and answered first in Cantonese, then in Mandarin, and only then in English. The audience did not realize what he was doing until he had completed the rote. But by then we had received almost thirty seconds of exposure, where he normally would have had one or two.

Later the Spanish-speaking delegates caught on to the idea and tried to follow suit, but the secretary quickly put a damper on any further gimmicks by prohibiting the use of foreign languages.

The predictable nitpicking business of conventions followed: hours and hours of bickering over resolutions, and sitting through committee meetings that dragged on till one and two in the morning.

Then came the night of the nomination—the night Nixon gave the best speech of his career. I knew, through Mitchell, that he had agonized over it for days beforehand, and it showed. It had coherence and poignancy, fetching cheers and tears, as it moved from the picture of the luckless child ("He sleeps the sleep of a child, and he dreams the dreams of a child.

And yet, when he awakens, he awakens to a living nightmare of poverty, neglect, and despair. . . .") to the child that would be the next President of the United States.

But back in his hotel suite, just after his selection of Spiro Agnew as his running mate, Nixon was his old spontaneous self again. He had called a number of us into his quarters to inform us about his choice before announcing it to the press.

It had been a difficult process of selection, he told us. Groping for a metaphor, he explained it this way: "It's like . . . like going into a department store and looking for a new suit. There's just so much to choose from." If Agnew was offended by the sartorial simile, he didn't show it.

Although I had worked closely with Mitchell throughout the 1968 campaign, I did not meet Martha until after they had moved into Watergate, for Mitchell was a staunch believer in keeping home clearly separated from work, at least in the beginning. But soon after the elections, he came to enlist my help with an apartment. He and his wife already owned a house in Rye, New York, he said, so they were looking to buy a large apartment in Washington for themselves and their daughter Marty. Mitchell had been to my penthouse on several occasions and liked the building, so I put him in touch with the management. Within a few weeks he had bought a duplex at Watergate East, six floors below mine in the same building.

I was introduced to Martha for the first time only after we became neighbors and found ourselves in the same elevator one day on our way to the President's reception.

"Martha, this is Anna Chennault; you've heard me talk about her," said Mitchell.

Martha looked me over in the most blatantly curious way,

with a mischievous smile. "Well, well," she said, "if I had only known what a beautiful woman my husband's been working with, I would have been so jealous." She was so uninhibited about the rivalry, so honestly competitive, that I liked her instantly.

As neighbors, we began to see a great deal of one another. Mitchell would call frequently in the evening and ask if he could come up to talk to me about an issue or problem he had on his mind, or Martha would call and invite me down to have a drink with them, or a game of bridge. Since we often went to the same parties and functions, we would ride together and, upon returning home, would stop at either their apartment or mine for a nightcap. Often we went together to the weekly White House Sunday worship, a ritual introduced by the Nixons.

We used to have a standing joke about Mitchell's use of possessive pronouns as applied to people of questionable loyalty. For example, so long as things were going smoothly between the Nixon administration and the South Vietnamese government, he would refer to the latter as "our" friends; if on the other hand he felt that Thieu or any of his associates in Saigon were being in the slightest way contrary, they would immediately become "your" friends. Then, one day, in relating a problem he was having with Thieu, he began, "Your friend is making the situation very difficult."

For some reason, the joke ceased to be funny anymore, and I snapped, "Let's stop this 'my friend' and 'your friend' business. They are our friends, our allies, like it or not, so why be divisive, even in jest?"

Mitchell seemed a bit startled, but before he could respond, Martha said, "Anna is right," with a defiant and emphatic nod.

"Now, wait a minute," said Mitchell, "just wait a minute. I can handle one woman at a time; but if you both start attacking me, I'm going to leave this room." And he kept up the pretense of indignation even when we continued to tease him.

It was all in good fun, but it could easily have turned into a sudden spat between the two of them—as it did one evening after dinner at my place. The rest of the guests had left, but the Mitchells had lingered behind and the three of us were dissecting the evening in a lazy, disjointed sort of way when the two of them began arguing about some triviality or other. I was only half-listening to their all too familiar exchange when Martha suddenly threatened to throw her shoe across the room at her husband. "Just you try," was Mitchell's tired response. With one swift motion, Martha reached down, pulled one spike-heeled sling-back shoe off her foot, and hurled it at Mitchell who, either from frequent practice or excellent reflexes, neatly ducked the flying object.

But war had been declared, and Mitchell rose from his chair, shoe in hand, hovering over his wife, and said, "It's time to go home."

Martha looked down at her other shoe and began to rub it. "I don't want to go home," she said, in a flat sort of voice, but it was not a serious challenge, and after a few seconds she got up to leave.

When I first knew Martha, she seemed to take on everything with fun-loving, high-spirited energy, whether an argument about politics or a game of bridge. When she sat down to play the piano, it was no sedate parlor performance but a sudden outburst of song and sentiment as she riffled the keys and wagged her head with unrepressed gusto.

In a generation of politicians' wives reared to hold their tongues, Martha was a misfit, accustomed to speaking her mind and making it up without prior consultation. As long as she was the attorney general's wife, however, she enjoyed a certain license to be herself. She organized needlepoint classes for the wives of administration officials, an obligation for which few had any enthusiasm. Yet such is the hypocrisy of protocol that some of the women attending the class complained to each other behind her back and ridiculed the exercise, but contracted out their needlepoint assignments rather than cross Martha Mitchell.

Most unfounded rumors circulating about politicians (or their wives) can be traced to malice of one sort or another, but the rumor of Martha Mitchell's alcoholism was simply a case of misinterpretation. It was not that she drank too much, but that people simply couldn't believe how she could say some of the things she did without being drunk. She took perverse delight in speaking out of turn, in pricking the balloons of the pompous and, on many an occasion, simply making a scene. But in all the years I knew her, I never once saw her drunk, not even during the long bridge games we (Martha, Kathleen Stans, Mrs. Khadduri—the wife of a leading Middle East expert—and I) would have once a month, when she never consumed more than two highballs over an entire evening.

The label of alcoholic was a convenient one for a high government official's wife who expressed unpredictable opinions. But Martha wasn't drunk, for example, on the night she became emotional about Vietnam. It was just after General Lew Walt, the distinguished commander of the Third Marine Amphibious Force, had returned from Saigon. I had invited him and a small group of White House and Pentagon officials to dinner, which was proceeding smoothly until, halfway through the evening, Lew began describing to us the situation as he saw it in Vietnam.

I no longer remember the particulars of his informal briefing; it seemed to contain nothing new or startling—until Martha suddenly burst out crying, saying how sad the whole thing was and how we had no business being in Vietnam.

A pained and embarrassed hush fell over the dinner table, broken only by the awkward sounds of another guest who was sitting next to Martha trying to soothe her. Then Mitchell came to the rescue and took charge, much as a long-suffering parent comes to claim a troublesome child. "She's had a long day," he offered in explanation, and shepherded her down to the seventh floor.

A better explanation for Martha's outburst would have been the reminder that her son was serving in Vietnam. As it was, she created the impression more of a petulant child than of a grieving parent.

By the time I came to know Martha well, my relationship with Mitchell had gone through several stages, from close cooperation throughout the campaign, to disappointment after the election (when he was too worried about his confirmation as attorney general to stand up for me when his help could have counted), and back to a kind of wary association as neighbors in Watergate. But I found myself liking Martha despite her erratic ways, and when they left Washington to return to New York in the wake of the Watergate investigations, I missed her company.

The last time I saw her was in New York City, after I received a troubled call from her asking if we could meet in my apartment. I knew by then that she was quite ill, yet couldn't help feeling a slight chill when she informed me, with an air of grave confidentiality, that people were always listening in on her conversations or watching her. We had had these conversations before, when she would telephone me from time to time— along with her other confidants whom she telephoned compulsively—to fret about her safety and her life, about the reporters who always seemed to surround her apartment, about violent strangers in crowds who would suddenly lunge and tear at her clothes or pull at her hair, about the people surrounding her husband who were trying to separate the two of them, about still others conspiring to take her daughter away from her . . . until I, like all her other confidants, felt drained by her delusions.

But the last time I saw her, she seemed even more tormented than usual. She began calling UPI's Helen Thomas, she explained, when Herb Kalmbach, Nixon's lawyer and vice chairman of the Finance Committee, tried to get her committed to an institution, once even locking her in her room, for fear she would speak out of turn during a sensitive period in the Watergate hearings.

She must have sensed my uneasiness, for she suddenly broke

off in the middle of her tirade and pushed up her sleeve to expose her forearm. "Look," she said, "this is how they treat me. Manhandled by a security guard. See? All black-and-blue."

Shortly after that last meeting, she became ill with the bone cancer from which she would die within the year. When I read about her death in the papers, it was not the cancer that I kept thinking about, but her fierce gesture of pushing up her sleeve as she struggled to prove to me the validity of her fears. And whatever their origin, I could not dispel from my mind the angry black-and-blue marks across the poor confused woman's arm.

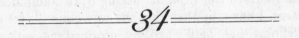

Long before the convention, Mitchell had told me that while the other Republican candidates were bound to come out hawkish and hard-hitting on Vietnam, Nixon's own stance would be on the conciliatory side—a posture then officially assumed at Montauk Point, Long Island, where Nixon was catching his breath just before the convention. Reached by telephone from the Rockefeller camp already bivouacked in Miami for the convention, Nixon surprised everyone by agreeing to build a Vietnam peace plank into the Republican platform, one that would lean toward negotiation. His own prescriptions for peace, however, continued to be vague. He could not elaborate until a thorough study of the situation had been made.

Privately, I continued to travel to Vietnam as a weekly columnist for a leading Chinese daily, while continuing to keep Nixon and Mitchell informed about South Vietnamese attitudes vis-à-vis the peace talks. These attitudes, confirmed in my many encounters with President Thieu, remained intransigent.

I had first met Thieu a year earlier, in 1967, in Saigon, where

I lectured frequently and also did promotional work as an airline representative. The meeting with Thieu was intended as an informal presentation of credentials. I was delivering a message from Nixon requesting that I be recognized as the conduit for any information that might flow between the two.

Thieu had just been elected President, and he was in his first flush of power and triumph, full of ebullience and optimism. At the Presidential Palace, where I was a guest, President and Madame Thieu and I spent a long evening together. The visit was unremarkable, but memorable for the lighthearted affection that seemed to flow between Thieu and his wife, a lovely, attentive woman with equal proportions of shyness and sparkle who seemed to thrive on her husband's teasing. ("I may be Commander-in-Chief," he would say, "but she is Controller of the Commander-in-Chief"—to which she would respond with playful reproaches in alternating Vietnamese and French.)

One other memory persists about that evening: Thieu's account of a recent summit meeting he had attended in the Philippines, and the photograph he handed me of the leaders there—President Ferdinand Marcos of the Philippines; President Park Chung Hee of South Korea; Thanom Kittikachorn, the former Prime Minister of Thailand; President Thieu of Vietnam; Vice-President Ky of Vietnam; Harold Holt, the Prime Minister of Australia; Sir Keith Holyoake, the Prime Minister of New Zealand; and, towering above them all, Lyndon Johnson, as recognizable and distinctive as a Texas oil rig.

The post-convention campaign trail involved, for me, the inevitable shuttling back and forth between Washington D.C. and New York. In Washington were the assorted committees (Citizens for Nixon and Agnew, the Republican Issues Committee, and others, like the Women for Nixon-Agnew, and the National Republican Women's Finance Committee, which I chaired). In New York were Nixon's offices and the Finance Committee, co-chaired with Maurice Stans. It was there, in the course of raising money for the bottomless campaign coffers, that I learned the wisdom of accepting the one dollar donation as readily as the thousand dollar offer. It is a precept of fund raising that the one dollar contributions represent more than the arithmetic of small amounts adding up. They represent commitment, for anyone who parts with a dollar for a cause can probably be counted on for a vote. On the other hand, I also know not to ask too little of those who can afford large contributions. In such cases, if I ask for ten dollars and they turn me down, I am embarrassed. But if I ask for one thousand dollars and they turn me down, *they* are embarrassed.

As the campaign neared its climax, the great burning political issue, Vietnam, began sending heat waves back to its source in Saigon. Whenever I saw President Thieu, I had to listen to his complaints about the steady pressure brought to bear on him by the Democrats to attend the Paris Peace Talks. "Why should I go?" he would say. "Why should I walk into a smoke screen? There is no real agenda, no one is ready." Then he would let out a sigh of resignation.

"We Vietnamese are so dependent on American aid. We're at the mercy of your President.

"But, there comes a point when we have to stand up even to our benefactors, and be ourselves. We are elected leaders after all, and, because of this responsibility, because I represent the interests of our people, I would much prefer to have the peace talks after your elections. I think it would be good for both America and Vietnam."

After hearing him out, I would ask him, to make sure, "Is this a message to my party?" and, invariably, he would say, "Yes, if I may ask you to convey this message to your candidate."

My next visit to Saigon, in the spring of 1968, was marked by something of a welcome at Tan Son Nhut Airport. Madame Khiem, the wife of the Prime Minister, was there along with Dr. Nguyen Tao Duc, Thieu's special assistant on foreign affairs; Ambassador Chen of the Chinese Embassy; an aide from General William Westmoreland's office; and several U.S. Embassy types. Standing in a separate cluster were representatives of the Flying Tigers Airline, of which I had been Vice President of International Affairs since the beginning of 1965.

I was to stay with my sister, Connie and her husband, James Fong, the chief of commercial affairs of the Chinese Embassy in Vietnam. Their house was adjacent to the U.S. Ambassador's residence at twenty Ly Van Han, and, from my bedroom, facing the Ambassador's backyard, I could hear and watch His Excellency's comings and goings by helicopter.

Dr. Duc picked me up at my sister's the next morning for informal conversations with President Thieu. In the evening the Prime Minister and Madame Khiem put on a huge dinner for my benefit. It was an act of friendship more than a political gesture, for I had known Khiem since his days as ambassador to Taipei, and subsequently, from 1962 to 1965, in Washington.

In the course of the evening, we discovered that Khiem and I were born in the same year, and thus shared the same horoscope.

"Oh, the year of the Ox!" sighed his wife knowingly. "Work, work, work."

We joked about the characteristics of oxen.

"Tenacious, methodical," said Khiem.

"Down to earth, helpful, hardworking," I added.

"Yes, we are plodders," Khiem went on. "We can also be stubborn. But we are strong."

"Or we pretend to be strong," I said. "Ox women put on a tough front, pretending to be self-assured. But it isn't all facade. Ox women really are bored with sentimentality. They like independence."

"We have to be independent," Khiem said. "We're leaders, after all. Loners. We have to be confidence-inspiring."

"Oxen are great storytellers," Mrs. Khiem intervened with deadpan observation.

"Great leaders, you mean," her husband corrected. "Look at all the famous oxen: Napoleon, Camus, Hitler."

"Stubborn," Madame Khiem continued relentlessly, "authoritarian. Bad losers. Rigid. Jealous. . . ."

Khiem and I were suddenly eager to change the subject.

Later on, Madame Khiem passed on a prediction she had heard, that 1968 would be a very difficult year. Khiem said, no longer teasing, "Can you think of a year which has not been difficult?"

He was answered by the screams of the curfew siren, one short and two long blasts. I went home to Connie's, listening in bed to the uneasy hush of the city, pulled out of sleep at one point by the noisy chopping of the Ambassador's helicopter delivering him to his enclave.

35

Back in Washington, toward the end of October, peace (to paraphrase Bertolt Brecht) threatened to break out. On October 11, a "breakthrough" in the ongoing negotiations with the North Vietnamese in Paris appeared in the form of a feeler from that contingent. If the North Vietnamese agreed to South Vietnamese participation in the peace talks, would the Americans agree to an "unconditional" bombing halt?

By October 15, Thieu was said to have agreed to a bombing halt, provided his government were included in the negotiation and settlement process. By October 27, ten days before the U.S. Presidential elections, news of the tacit agreement had begun to leak out. Both Vietnams would participate in future negotiations; the United States would stop bombing North Vietnam; but reconnaissance flights might continue over the North; and retaliation could be expected in the event of any attack on the South Vietnamese.

On Thursday, October 31, Lyndon Johnson went on television to announce the cease-fire and to express serious hope for the Paris peace talks. But the next day, Friday, brought Thieu's contradicting statement: "The Government of South Vietnam deeply regrets not to be able to participate in the present exploratory talks."

The confusion that followed was enormous, punctuated with despairing questions. How could that be? How could Saigon have agreed and then reneged? Or was it Thieu who had given his agreement without his cabinet's approval, and if so why? Had he blundered, then retracted his offer? Or had he given no assurance in the first place? Worse, was Johnson playing politics at Vietnam's expense?

The night of Johnson's State of the Union address, I remember being at Perle Mesta's at the Sheraton Park Hotel. Perle had gone through several moves since her Spring Valley days, when I had first known her. She had sold her house there to Vice President and Mrs. Johnson, and moved to twin apartments at Watson Place, near Massachusetts Avenue, to give those up eventually for the suite at the Sheraton Park. Each move was to a smaller place, her need for physical space dwindling with the accretion of fame and age until, reduced further by illness, she quietly moved away from Washington, D.C., to Oklahoma, to the confinement of her family.

I had first met Perle just after General Chennault's death, at a dinner party given by Maryland McCormick. Maryland's husband, the Colonel, was publisher of the *Chicago Tribune* and a Republican of ultra-conservative ilk, with a record of having endorsed Robert Taft for President against Eisenhower in 1952, finding the latter too "liberal."

But Maryland was one of those breathtakingly straight-talking individuals who show that it is possible to live and breathe politics without wadding one's opinions in cotton wool. "Richard Nixon!" she would say with unconcealed disgust, "what a choice!" Then, in defense of her disapproval, she would add, "You can't trust the fellow!" as if choices in politics were that simple and straightforward.

Maryland introduced me to Perle Mesta, herself no mincer of words. Perle did a quick scan of me with her ultraviolet vision and said, "So what's a Chinese woman going to do in Washington?"

Before I could answer—not that I had a comeback to so blunt an inquiry—she said, "You're young and charming, my dear.

Now's the time. If you want to get married again, go someplace else. This isn't the town for marital bliss. But if you want to set the world on fire, this is the place. Very flammable, Washington."

At her Sheraton Park suite the evening of the State of the Union speech, we were just finishing dessert when I was called to the telephone. It was Mitchell, needing to talk to me with some urgency. As usual, he wanted me to call him back from another more "anonymous" number. I jotted down his number: (914) WO7-0909, and went to find Tom Corcoran, my escort for the evening, to see if he was ready to leave. By then, most of the guests had gone on to see a film and Tom suggested we take our leave and go to his brother David's apartment, which happened to be another suite in the same hotel.

David Corcoran was away at the time, so the minute I got to his place, I picked up the phone and dialled Mitchell, after asking Tom to get on the bedroom extension. I had a sense of needing moral support, or a witness, or both.

Mitchell picked up on the first ring. "Anna," he said, "I'm speaking on behalf of Mr. Nixon. It's very important that our Vietnamese friends understand our Republican position and I hope you have made that clear to them."

I was accustomed to Mitchell's vagueness, attributing it to his excessive caution, but I detected this time a specific request behind the non-specific tone. However, it was late, I was tired, and I wasn't sure quite what it was I was to make clear to the South Vietnamese. All I knew was that the instructions seemed to have changed from the ones I had been given, simply to keep Nixon informed of South Vietnamese intentions. So I said, "Look, John, all I've done is relay messages. If you're talking about direct influence, I have to tell you it isn't wise for us to try to influence the South Vietnamese. Their actions have to follow their own national interests, and I'm sure that is what will dictate Thieu's decisions. I don't think either we or the Democrats can force them to act one way or another. They have their own politics, you know."

But Mitchell sounded nervous. "Do you think they really have decided not to go to Paris?"

"I don't think they'll go. Thieu has told me over and over again that going to Paris would be walking into a smoke screen that has nothing to do with reality."

"Oh, all right," Mitchell sighed at last, with lingering anxiousness. "But be sure to call me if you get any more news."

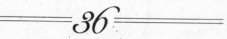

Tuesday, November 5, 1968, was overcast and, for that time of year, cold. I cast my vote early in the morning in Washington, D.C., and flew to New York to join Mitchell, Stans, and other Nixon faithfuls at the Waldorf-Astoria for the election-night wait.

After checking into the Waldorf-Astoria, I went over to election headquarters to report to Mitchell. A number of people were waiting to see him, but he skillfully placated them as he came out to ask me into his private office. "You look confident," I told him.

"I am," he agreed. "He's going to win." Then he put on his somber banker's face, the one he wore whenever something personal needed to be said. "The whole campaign has emphasized Vietnam," he began, "and you've done a great deal to help Mr. Nixon. You've done a great job. We'll never forget that. I'm sure Mr. Nixon will want to see you after the election, so let's keep in touch the rest of the day."

We chatted a while longer, then he escorted me out of his office, through the small crowd still waiting to see him, telling them he was going to get a haircut, and walked out of the building with me.

The afternoon sped by in a jumble of meetings: with Tom Evans, the lawyer at Nixon's old law firm; with Herb Klein, the man in charge of the press; with Maurice Stans, the Finance Committee chairman; with longtime Nixon retainer Murray Chotiner; and with Eleanor Williams, who took care of handling the big contributors to the Finance Committee.

Then came the interminable night watch, each one keeping vigil at his own observation post: Nixon in his bedroom in Suite 35H; his inner circle—Dwight Chapin, John Erlichman, Bob Haldeman, and Laurence Higby (Haldeman's assistant)—in the TV monitoring suite next door; Robert Finch of California (Nixon's campaign director in the 1960s and his closest friend and confidant), Klein, Chotiner, and Mitchell in the operations room next door, where they were plugged into Republican organizations throughout the country; Nixon's family in another suite; and, in 25A, the literati: William Safire, Pat Buchanan, Raymond Price (Nixon's speechwriter), and Leonard Garment (in charge of media).

Accredited with the gold-and-blue ribbon that provided access to the inner sanctums, I paced nervously from outpost to outpost, checking in with Stans and Mitchell for the latest returns and exchanging information with campaign workers. The hours and the returns ticked by until, around 4:30 in the morning (about an hour and a half after Nixon decided it was time to go downstairs and claim victory as the new President of the United States), Mitchell brought me the news that Nixon wanted to see me immediately after his victory announcement in the Gold Room.

But such was the chaos caused by the long delay in the California and Illinois returns that by the time the President-elect could go on television in the crowded Waldorf-Astoria ballroom, at 12:30 P.M., he was already packed and ready for his trip to Key Biscayne. Word finally arrived from Mitchell saying that my meeting would have to be postponed to the following week, and then it would take place either in Florida or Washington, D.C. I was too exhausted to care at that point.

It wasn't until the following Monday that I received a call from Mitchell's office, asking me to meet him in New York

City. In the meantime, Thieu had sent me a copy of his congratulatory telegram to Nixon, along with a reminder to fulfill his campaign promise to visit Vietnam. Thieu's message had been sent through the State Department, but, complained Ambassador Bui Diem, Nixon had not responded. I had then tried calling Key Biscayne to talk to Mitchell, but without success—until Monday's call.

On Wednesday, November 13, I flew to New York City to see Maurice Stans in the morning and Mitchell in the afternoon. Mitchell was quick to get to the point. Nixon, he said, had agreed with Johnson to come out with a joint statement announcing a Vietnam policy. And so, "We need to do something about our friends in Saigon."

"Do what about our friends in Saigon?" I asked, not yet understanding.

"Well, persuade them to go to Paris," he said.

"You must be joking," I said, flabbergasted. "Two weeks ago, Nixon and you were worried that they might succumb to pressure to go to Paris. What makes you change your mind all of a sudden?"

Mitchell just shook his head. "Anna, you're no newcomer to politics. This, whether you like it or not, is politics."

I gathered up my coat. "I don't play that kind of politics. You go and tell them yourself," I said, and left in a rage.

Later that evening, in my room at the Waldorf-Astoria, I received a call from Herb Klein. "Anna," he said, "I'm not going to beat around the bush." (Suddenly, bluntness seemed to be the order of the day.) "You must promise to say to the press that our friend does not know about our arrangement with President Thieu." (The friend in this case was Nixon. How I was beginning to hate their use and concept of that word.)

"What arrangement are you talking about?" I said. "I know of no arrangement; I never made any arrangement."

As though he hadn't heard me, Klein said, "We know you're a good soldier; we just want to be sure our friend is protected."

"Why should your friend," I said, talking like them despite

myself, "need protection?" I couldn't understand why they were behaving as though they feared their own shadows.

No sooner had I hung up than the telephone rang again. This time it was Tom Evans. He wanted to know if I could stay over to meet with Mitchell again the next day.

"What for?" I snapped, still furious.

"We want you to deliver a message," he said, with impressive audacity, "to the Vietnamese ambassador urging President Thieu to send a delegate to the Paris Peace Talks, and also to tell him that Nixon won't have time to visit Vietnam just yet."

"Look," I said, "you don't seem to understand." I found myself talking through bared teeth. "I'm on my way back to Washington. Give the assignment to someone else."

Nausea was beginning to jar my system. I went into the bathroom and turned on the shower for distraction: first the hot water, then the cold. Before the right temperature had been mixed, I could taste the salt running down my face in painful tears.

The next day, back in Washington, I got a call from Senator Dirksen. He had to see me, he said. Please, please don't delay. The leader of the Republican Party and the man with the silver tongue was doing one of his famous numbers on me. I recognized it, but was powerless to resist.

It turned out to be a short meeting. Since I had refused to carry out the mission to see the Vietnamese ambassador, he said, Nixon had asked him to do the honors. He had just wanted to keep me informed; and to make sure that I would not let anger get the better of me by talking to the press.

"I don't know what's going on," I said coldly, "much less what to say. Their game's beyond me."

"Don't be angry with me," said Dirksen. "I'm just doing my duty."

The last time I saw Dirksen was by his hospital bed as he lay dying at Walter Reed Army Hospital. We had a brief but good conversation, at the end of which I said, "Senator, I'm not angry anymore at what happened, but I'm going to tell the story someday." "You go ahead and do that," he said. I suppose restraint, along with most other things, had ceased to matter to him by then.

After Nixon had resurfaced from Key Biscayne and issued his joint statement with Johnson promoting the Paris Peace Talks, I continued to be plagued by calls from Nixon's lieutenants on the one hand, and by the press on the other. Meanwhile, I was caught up in preparations for the Inauguration. This irony came about because Nixon had asked me to serve on the Inaugural Committee—a pat on the back after the kick in the head—and I was helping J. Willard Marriott, the committee chairman, and General George Olmsted, his vice chairman for the governors' reception.

Typical of the annoyances of the time was an interview I gave to a *St. Louis Post-Dispatch* reporter. I assumed when he first called that he wanted to talk about the Inauguration, and referred him to the man in charge of publicity. But the reporter insisted on seeing me personally.

He came to my office in the Investment Building in downtown Washington, D.C., and showed me a story he had just written, the thrust of which was that some Democrats alleged that Hubert H. Humphrey's defeat could be attributed to the South Vietnamese government's refusal, ten days before the U.S. Presidential elections, to join the Paris Peace Talks—an act of sabotage traceable to Republican skulduggery.

The reporter studied me carefully as I read the piece. Afterwards, he said, "I've been told that it was you who carried out the assignment to influence the Vietnamese leaders, that President Nixon sent you to Saigon a month before the elections. Do you have any comment?"

"Yes, I have a comment," I said, handing him his story with the secret impulse to fling it in his face. "Your story is rubbish. Where did you hear these reports—from the Democrats or the Republicans?"

At this he laughed, as if he had caught me setting a trap which he had long since anticipated. "Oh, from both sides," he said.

If his story appeared, he didn't send me a copy.

The anxiety over news leakage kept festering. Senator John Tower and Ambassador Robert Hill both kept coming to me with their respective hopes and fears. Tower was being as helpful to me as he could. He called Mitchell and Klein on several occasions to protest the treatment I had been given and was even confident at one point that he had extracted a promise from Klein to correct some of the bad publicity, but of course he was mistaken.

Hill was waiting for confirmation of a coveted assignment as ambassador to Spain, and was concerned lest rumor thwart his appointment. "I can't understand what they're trying to do," he kept repeating fretfully, about Nixon's post-election Vietnam policy.

"Why don't you find out?" I asked him. "You've been friends with Nixon for over twenty years."

"Friends with Nixon?" he asked, as if to say, "What a preposterous idea!"

Early in December 1968, another ambassadorial type, Robert Murphy, was appointed to head the transition team. Murphy, a seasoned diplomat, was former Undersecretary of State and now chairman of the Corning Glass Company. He was sent by Nixon to see me soon after his appointment, arriving with snow boots and umbrella and looking uncannily like Chamberlain: tall, bony, weathered, and every angular inch a diplomat. He took off his snow boots, still sparkling with fresh snow, while I made him a cup of tea and unceremoniously prodded him to state his business. I was becoming impatient with the endless emissaries. Murphy, still holding his teacup with a crooked finger, cleared his throat and said, "Mr. Nixon asked me to come by and see you in order to let you know how much he has appreciated everything you've done for him."

"He certainly has strange ways," I said, "of showing it." The poor man looked down into his tea leaves and, shaking his bowed head, accepted the slight in silence.

Suddenly he said, "This Clark Clifford—can you understand why he's behaving like a madman, why he's attacking the South Vietnamese?" This was just idle chatter. We both knew that Murphy was beating around the bush, trying to placate me by making it seem as if my views and opinions mattered.

"I don't know him that well," I said, "so I don't know what's going on in his head. I suppose he's mad at the Vietnamese because they've refused to take orders from him."

"Well, I've known Clifford for over twenty-five years," Murphy declared, "and I've never seen him behave like this." Then, ever the gentleman, he offered the benefit of doubt. "Maybe he's tired beyond belief and needs a rest."

We shifted to news about Bui Diem, who had just returned from Saigon. Had I seen him since his return? Murphy wanted to know. Yes, I said, and he had been full of sympathy and commiseration.

Murphy cleared his throat again, the introduction to another awkwardness. Would I be interested in any political assignment?

No, I said. The election had been a bitter lesson, leaving me with no desire to serve in the new administration.

But I shouldn't feel that way, said Murphy. With my expertise in Asian affairs I should continue to make myself available. My experiences and skills would be invaluable.

Oh, I would certainly do that, I said, because I did still want to serve my country.

This seemed to reassure Murphy somewhat, as if he had just been exonerated from a personal misunderstanding. He left an hour after he had arrived, struggling with his snow boots, assignment accomplished. By that time we were both speechless with exhaustion. It had been a long year.

But the ultimate handshake came months later, at a White House function, when Nixon took me aside and, with intense gratitude, began thanking me for my help in the election.

"I've certainly paid dearly for it," I pointed out.

"Yes, I appreciate that," he murmured, suddenly uncomfortable. "I know you are a good soldier."

That summer, when my name once again made the rounds in connection with Vietnam, I went to see Congressman Clement Zablocki (D–Wisconsin), who has since become chairman of the House Foreign Affairs Committee. I had met Zablocki through Warren Knowles, the former governor of Wisconsin, whom I had dated for a while back in 1968. I approached Zablocki, a Democrat, because enlisting the help of a Republican member of Congress might smack of political favoritism. Zablocki was sympathetic, but in the end advised me against trying to take any kind of action. "There's no need for an investigation, Anna," he insisted. "You've done nothing wrong. Just try to forget the whole thing."

I tried, but it wasn't easy.

I met Henry Kissinger while the transition to the Nixon administration was taking place, in the days when he was still a dowdy, professorial type, as far removed from his later image of flamboyant global strongman as one could imagine. But his brand of personalized diplomacy was there from the start.

Whenever we met, usually to discuss Vietnam, he seemed always to prefer to conduct business off-hours, to meet on weekends. He was not a man who believed in leaving his work at the office.

I remember being asked, at a black-tie dinner soon after I first met him, what I thought of him. I didn't know him well enough to make a judgment, I said.

But what was my immediate impression of him?

"Well," I said, seizing on the first impression that came to mind, "he needs to do something about his socks."

"Socks?"

"Yes, socks. I can't stand men who wear socks too short to measure the distance between trouser cuff and shoe."

I believe at that moment eight pairs of eyes were lowered to check out corresponding socks.

Actually, it wasn't the socks that bothered me so much as his compulsion to impress. Once, at a small sit-down dinner I gave at my Watergate apartment, we were interrupted by several telephone calls from the White House. It was the President wanting to speak to several of the guests there (John Mitchell, John Erlichman, H. R. Haldeman, among others) by turn. As each one got up to take his call, I could see Kissinger becoming increasingly nervous, wondering, I suppose, if and when his turn would come.

When dinner was over and the phone calls had died down, Kissinger turned to me and with forced humor said, "Well, I didn't get any calls from the White House, but the next time I come to dinner at your place I'll make arrangements with the White House operator to call me so that I won't feel left out." The absurdity of his ego reminded me of a strange little vignette described by Kafka, of some self-important bureaucrat who has in his employ a man whose sole duty is to lend the bureaucrat a certain stature by telephoning him periodically wherever he is, at meetings or in restaurants.

Several years later, at another dinner—this time a Chinese banquet—at my place, the opportunity arose to have a bit of fun with the famous ego. After exclaiming how he loved Chinese food, Kissinger wanted to know why it was I hadn't named a dish after him. I had done it for other special guests, why not for him? "But I have, Dr. Kissinger," I told him. "The soup tonight is named in your honor."

"Really? What are you calling it?" Kissinger asked, beaming.

"Well," I said, "I concocted a very special dish right after the war which I called Bombing Tokyo. Then, after that, there was another dish, called Bombing Moscow. Now I have this wonderful soup which will make you famous." I paused while Kissinger began to show signs of discomfort.

"Well, what is it?" he insisted, prepared for the worst.

"Negotiator's Soup," I told him. Kissinger chuckled—with relief.

He continued to call on me over the years, usually on Vietnam-related matters, until 1972, when he went on television to announce that "peace is at hand." I told Nixon afterwards that Kissinger ought to refrain from such definitive statements during the campaign, for peace was not in fact at hand, and empty promises could cost Nixon the Presidency.

When Kissinger heard that I had voiced dissent, he stopped consulting me altogether; however, we continued to see each other socially.

He derived especial pleasure and triumph from wooing "the enemy" (like Mao Tse-tung and Le Duc Tho), seeing perhaps in the feat a kind of muscular victory. Friends and allies, on the other hand, were there to be used or abused. There were countries like India and South Vietnam, which he called "feminine" states. The Japanese, who remained untouched and unimpressed by his power games, were "little Sony salesmen."

But in the case of South Vietnam, the lack of respect was mutual. In 1969, I remember having tea with Minister of Foreign Affairs Tram Van Lam, who had just returned from the so-called Paris Peace Talks.

"Kissinger?" he said. "Arrogant, especially toward Asians. He's going to sell us down the river. Also, his ambition is so large, it'll claim more than one victim. Not just the United States, but Vietnam as well."

Three years later, President Thieu could not have held too different an opinion about Kissinger. As he later recounted the negotiations to me, Kissinger arrived in Saigon on October 18, 1972, to present his draft to Thieu. The peace agreement, allowing as it did the North Vietnamese to remain in their position while United States troops withdrew, was of course tantamount

to a surrender. But Kissinger by all accounts was fully determined not to take no for an answer.

The forces assembled the next day at the Independence Pal-
ace. On the American side, Kissinger; General Creighton
Abrams, Army Chief of Staff and former United States com-
mander in Vietnam; Philip Habib, U.S. Ambassador to South
Korea and later political advisor to the U.S. delegation to the
Paris Peace Talks; and Admiral Noel Gaylor, Commander-in-
Chief of U.S. forces in the Pacific. The South Vietnamese in-
cluded President Thieu; Tran Van Huong, Speaker of the
House and former Prime Minister; Prime Minister Khiem;
Foreign Minister Tran Van Lam; Deputy Foreign Minister
Nguyen Phu Doc; Tran Kim Phuong, the last South Viet-
namese ambassador to the United States; Ambassador Pham
Dang Lam, chief of the South Vietnamese delegation in Paris;
and Thieu's cousin and special advisor, Dr. Hoang Duc Nha.

Kissinger's first offense (apart from giving North Vietnamese
chief negotiator Le Duc Tho preference over Thieu) was to
present Thieu with only the French version of the treaty. Thieu
naturally asked to see the Vietnamese translation, whereupon
Kissinger insisted that this was not necessary since the two ver-
sions were the same. At this, Thieu pointed out that while he
was a French-speaking Vietnamese, he was still Vietnamese
and preferred to see the original document if only to compare
the translation.

After much needless stalling, he was finally given the Vietnamese version, in which he found inconsistencies in more than
twenty points.

These discrepancies sparked off another round of arguments,
alternating between Kissinger's impatient demands to hurry up
and sign, and then Thieu's stubborn delays. The haggling went
on over a series of phone calls. When next the two parties met
in person, Thieu had become monosyllabic, refusing to speak
English except through his interpreter, Dr. Nha.

Dr. Nha, perhaps Thieu's most trusted aide, had the unenvi-
able task of dealing with Kissinger while Thieu played for time,

which meant turning down repeated requests from Kissinger to meet with Thieu. Driven to distraction by the prospect of not getting his way, Kissinger felt the time had come to remind Nha who he was. "I'm an envoy of the United States," he stormed, "not an errand boy. I *insist* on seeing your President!"

Dr. Nha hastened to assure Kissinger that he wouldn't dream of considering him an errand boy, but he still could not see Thieu that night.

"Why is it," Thieu asked me rhetorically, "that Kissinger hates Nha so much?" The question came just after I had seen Ambassador Ellsworth Bunker, who sought to pass on through me the message to Thieu that perhaps Dr. Nha should be relieved of his duties in the palace in return for some ambassadorial post. The same message was repeated a few months later by the new American ambassador, Graham Martin.

Miraculously, Nha was able to hang on till the end of 1974.

But back in October 1972, the whole situation was so hopeless that it seemed the parties were not above invoking Divine Intervention. Tran Van Lam told me that on October 20, at the official residence of the Ministry of Foreign Affairs, the meeting was opened with a prayer: *May God bless this meeting between the Republic of South Vietnam and Dr. Kissinger.* Those were the supplicants: not South Vietnam and the United States, but South Vietnam and Dr. Kissinger.

But by October 22, benediction was still out of sight. Thieu told Kissinger that the agreement, as it stood, spelled surrender, and, as such, he could not approve it.

Kissinger flew into one of his legendary rages. "If you choose not to sign," he said, "I can sign a separate agreement with Hanoi."

Then, in a petulant aside so characteristic of the immature and threatened ego, "As for myself, I will never set foot in Saigon again. *Never* again. This will be the worst failure of my diplomatic career."

Thieu is said to have made sympathetic noises throughout this foot-stamping, punctuating the tantrum with gentle reminders that while he felt for Kissinger's career, he had a country to defend.

It was in fact Kissinger's last trip to Vietnam. The Paris Peace Agreement, unchanged in substance from the draft, was signed on January 27, 1973. Rather than the worst failure of his diplomatic career, the Agreement was a tribute to his grandstand tactics of threat (the bombing of Hanoi and the mining of Haiphong being as much an attempt to strong-arm the South Vietnamese into accepting the American solution to the war as to break the North Vietnamese spirit).

With this method, he emerged a hero and winner of the Nobel Peace Prize.

In early April 1975, I made my last trip to Saigon, a city that had grown on me over a ten-year relationship. It was only a few weeks before the city would fall to the Communists, and the government would have to flee—along with the remaining Americans and the stampeding refugees. But none of this was glaringly evident on the surface of things. Life went on; the city teemed; the war was somewhere else.

Schoolgirls hurried to school, black hair and white *ao dai* flapping in the wind. Lissome young women in pale silks and chiffons and satins fluttered like pastel butterflies along the dappled tree-lined streets. Toothless old women and black-toothed mountain women hobbled along to the market with their baskets and carrying poles. This was the noon rush hour, and the traffic jam was at full throttle: the bicycles and Bluebirds, the pedicabs and pedestrians, the baby Renaults and the Deux-Chevaux all trying to squeeze and drown each other out.

The scene was familiar, unchanged in the details. But there was a difference this time. The difference was not in the setting or the props or the characters, but in the lighting. All of a sudden, Saigon appeared in a different light, as if a naked light bulb had been switched on somewhere.

In China, I had been weaned on war, and left with a peculiar sensitivity to its sights, sounds, and smells. What I could see now was not the suffering alone—this was the city's lasting legacy—but the terrible futility of the suffering, as though every death and maiming and loss had been uselessly sacrificed, for a cause betrayed and lost. In every old woman I passed on the street, I saw a wife without a husband, a mother robbed of her children, a woman with a future every bit as bleak as her past. I heard, in the early hours of the morning, the song of schoolchildren, plaintive and painfully reminiscent of the song we as schoolchildren had sung in China: *"Vietnam will not surrender—Vietnam will not fall."* It was a prayer for a miracle, but the prayer was unanswered.

After the fall of Saigon, I was sent by the White House to see President Thieu in Taipei, Taiwan, where he, Prime Minister Khiem, and their families had flown from Saigon on April 30. I sent separate messages to both of them to tell them I was on my way.

The separate messages were necessary for reasons of protocol and personal sensibilities, for Thieu and Khiem, once the best of friends, had been turned into adversaries by politics and war.

Then there were also the delicate relations between Thieu and Ky. Ever since the election in May 1967 that had placed Thieu as President and Ky, the most powerful man in South Vietnam for the last three years, as Vice President, the rivalry between the two had intensified, the conflicts sharpened by the assorted aides and advisors who jockeyed for power from both sides.

When President Thieu appointed his trusted friend, General Khiem, Prime Minister, Khiem naturally inherited the enmity against Ky. The division was understandable for other reasons.

Thieu and Khiem were Army, Ky was an Air Force man.

For years, whenever I visited Saigon, Thieu, Khiem, and I would meet for lunch, often on long Sunday afternoons at Thieu's summer home in Wan Tou. But things changed after Thieu's re-election for the second term in 1973. The good-natured camaraderie was gone. The wives had almost stopped speaking to each other.

Rumors, accusations, and counteraccusations began flying about. Thieu was trying to isolate himself; he had turned a deaf ear to his ablest advisors. Madame Thieu and Madame Khiem had perpetrated this or that act of hostility against each other. Prime Minister Khiem wanted to be President. And so on, through endless permutations.

Of the three principals, I suppose I was closest to Prime Minister Khiem, whom I had known since the early 1960s, when he was serving as Vietnamese ambassador to Washington, D.C. Marshall Ky was then in power, and Khiem more or less in exile in the United States. It was only after Thieu's election to the Presidency that he was recalled to serve as Prime Minister.

In the winter of 1969, I had flown to Saigon for the wedding of Khiem's only daughter, Jackie, to Trung, whose father was the president of Air Vietnam. After the Buddhist ceremony, at which I was the only non-Vietnamese, a lavish wedding dinner followed in the garden of the Prime Minister's residence. The stars were all out that night, shining in full wattage on the young, touchingly handsome couple. (The next year, Trung's youngest son was wedded to Thieu's only daughter, Mai, turning into sisters-in-law the daughters of the two most powerful men in Vietnam.)

Before leaving Washington, D.C., I had been asked by President Gerald Ford and Kissinger, principally through General Brent Scowcroft, deputy director of the National Security Council, and through Robert Hartmann, chief counsel to the President, to carry certain messages to Thieu. They were mainly concerned with inquiring about his future plans, and with impressing upon him the inadvisability of visiting the United States at that particular time (the kind of "courtesy" most recently extended to the Shah of Iran).

I had been to Taiwan barely a month earlier on another sad occasion: to attend the funeral of President Chiang Kai-shek. But there was one redeeming outcome for which I can claim partial responsibility. When news of Chiang's death reached the White House, I received a call from Robert Hartmann, saying that the President wanted me to be one of the seven delegates to attend the funeral. I thanked him for the honor, feeling genuinely flattered that it was the second one extended to me by the Ford administration, the first being the offer to appoint me United States Treasurer. It was an offer I could and did refuse, after deciding that the staff of two hundred to three hundred people and the job of signing dollar bills and promoting United States bonds were not exactly commensurate with my abilities or ambition. Besides, presidential appointments being as transitory as they are, I felt it wasn't worth the risk of placing my own business (in international consulting) on hold.

I then asked Hartmann who had been appointed to head the delegation, and he told me it was Secretary of Agriculture Earl Butz. This struck me as inappropriate, for as I said to Hartmann, "We surely can't have forgotten this soon what Chiang Kai-shek has meant to most of our generation. Even leaving aside the Cairo Conference and his equal status with Roosevelt and Churchill at that stage of World War II, he *has* been our greatest ally. Do you really think it proper that the Secretary of Agriculture be asked to represent the United States? Shouldn't it be the Vice President, at the very least?"

He thought about this for a moment, then said, "I guess you're right, but we can't get Rockefeller to go at this time."

"Why not?" I asked.

"Well, for one thing he's too busy, and for another, he just got back from representing the President at another funeral. Remember, he's just been to Saudi Arabia for King Faisal's funeral. He's not going to have the time."

"Bob, I'd like to suggest that you do your best to persuade him he should try to find the time," I said.

He said he would do what he could. The next day, he called me back with the news that he had broached the subject to Rockefeller, who had agreed to go. "But now we have another problem," he said. "Meanwhile, Senator Goldwater, who is also a member of the delegation, has decided to go to Taiwan on his own. He was pretty peeved that the President wasn't sending anyone higher than Earl Butz and wanted to dissociate himself from the 'insult' by traveling apart from the official delegation."

"Well, just tell him the plans have changed and he'll come along when he hears Rocky is going," I said.

"But that's just the problem," said Hartmann. "He's gone off to the West Coast, it's a weekend, and I don't know where to find him. When Rockefeller finds out that Goldwater is acting this way, *he's* going to get upset. You know how the two of them have been since Goldwater ran for President and didn't get Rockefeller's support."

"Let me take care of it," I told Hartmann. I began to make one phone call after another. No one seemed to know how to get in touch with Goldwater until, at last, I managed to reach Judy Eisenhower (Goldwater's secretary and Ike's niece) at home. I explained the dilemma to her and she responded with her usual quick intelligence.

Within a short time she had reached Goldwater on the West Coast and conveyed to him the message that the Vice-President would be leading the delegation and that Goldwater should accordingly be prepared to be picked up in Honolulu by Airforce Two on our way to the East.

The trip not only went without a hitch, but I shall always recall with some pride the picture on the flight back of Rocky and Barry laughing and joking and teasing each other like the oldest of friends.

It was eight o'clock in the morning, but an amazing number of friends were there to meet me upon my arrival in Taiwan:

General Cliff Louie, the president of China Airlines, and his wife Pearl, who welcomed me with a bouquet of roses; my brother-in-law, James Fong, chief of the Commercial Mission of the Republic of China for almost nine years, and my sister, both of whom had escaped from Saigon on the last plane; Colonel Chiu, special assistant to Prime Minister Khiem, and the man who had welcomed me time and again at Ton Son Nhut Airport in Saigon. Chiu was pale and drawn, but managed his warm, reassuring smile, as if nothing had happened. The Prime Minister and Madame Khiem had asked to visit with me that afternoon.

There were more familiar faces waiting inside the terminal: Cynthia Lee, my other sister, and with her, Madame Kieu, the wife of the Vietnamese ambassador to Taiwan, and sister-in-law to President Thieu. Madame Kieu, in her gentle, discreet way, let me know that President and Madame Thieu were expecting me for lunch at Ambassador Kieu's residence. This was wonderfully worked out. I had been concerned about how to arrange to see both Thieu and Khiem; now it was settled. I would see President Thieu first and after having lunch with him would visit with Prime Minister Khiem.

By noon I was at Ambassador Kieu's residence in Tienmou, an unpretentious bungalow on the outskirts of Taipei. It was not my first time there. Ever since his appointment as ambassador to the Republic of China, we had become friends, and our friendship had strengthened over the years. We had much in common, since he had spent many years in China during World War II. He had escaped from Vietnam when it was overrun by the Japanese, and had joined the Chinese Army against the Japanese in the southern part of China. His Mandarin and Cantonese were, as a result, equally good.

Arriving at the Kieus' bungalow, I entered through the side door. Kieu came out to the courtyard to meet me, grasping my hand but saying little as he escorted me to the living room. Thieu was already sitting there, with his back to the door.

It was strange and somehow unseemly to come upon him this

way. I was used to meeting him either at his weekend home (once the Emperor Bao Dai's), on the beautiful beaches on Won Ton, or at the Independence Palace in Saigon, where the entrance to his office was guarded by a pair of ivory tusks that must have belonged to the world's largest elephant.

A sense of poignancy flooded me as I walked the few steps to greet him. He stood up at that moment and turned to face me. We shook hands and embraced in silence. When I finally looked into his face, I saw tears in his eyes.

Kieu broke the silence and said, with forced joviality, "Aren't you people going to sit down so I can offer you some tea?"

At last Thieu said to me, "Are you all right?" His solicitude was impressive. I was the one sent to comfort him, yet he was concerned for me. I gave him the messages from Ford and Kissinger. They seemed flat statements, holding no surprises, or consolation, or even much relevance.

My reunion with Thieu's chief rival, General Ky, took place two months later, when he and his wife, Mai, came to dinner at my place with former ambassador Bui Diem. Bui Diem and Ky had been close friends for many years, serving as the Foreign Minister and Prime Minister respectively in the same cabinet, and sharing common origins as North Vietnamese from Hanoi.

The Kys had just rented a house in Fairfax, Virginia, having arrived in the United States a month before by way of Camp Pendleton, the refugee camp in California. Ky was in a bitter frame of mind, which he had conveyed to the press. He blamed on Thieu much of the loss of South Vietnam, and had nothing good to say about Camp Pendleton, either. But he wanted to put all this behind him and find a job, preferably in farming. He was also determined to do whatever he could to help fellow refugees resettle in the United States.

I had not seen Ky and Mai since their escape from Vietnam and was struck by how different they looked. Ky was wearing a well-cut business suit, but there was none of the air of dashing playboy and daredevil pilot of the old days. His boyishness had been replaced with a careworn sobriety. Mai was even more

altered in appearance. She wore a simple skirt and blouse, subdued and almost severe by comparison with her stunning *ao
dai;* her hair was cut short; and her face seemed vulnerable
without any make-up on. But the total effect of her presence
was still striking and her figure was as lithe and supple as ever.

She talked about Camp Pendleton and about relocation with
obvious distress. So many Vietnamese had come to them for
help, she said. But there was only so much one could do when
one was already crowded into a house with fourteen other people. "My husband," she said, touching Ky's arm, "has such a
big heart. He wants to help *everyone.* But we need help
ourselves."

I could sense the strain in her voice. She was, after all, taking
care of her mother, Ky's mother, his five children by his previous marriage to a French woman, and her own eight-year-old
daughter by Ky. She was also the only one in the family with a
driver's license and was constantly on the road, driving one
member of the family or another around.

I couldn't help thinking of the vast contrast between her new
life and the one she had led as wife of the Prime Minister of
South Vietnam. The image of past splendor that came to mind
was a trip I had made with Mai and Ky from the Philippines
back to Saigon. We had just attended the inauguration of President Marcos, and, hearing that I was flying back to Saigon, Ky
invited me along on his private plane. They were newly married at the time, and I remember Mai's extraordinary radiance
as she stepped into the plane, the interior of which was the
color of orchids, her favorite.

One of Mai's delightful qualities was the way she remained
unspoiled by all this attention and opulence. I remember one
lunch party in Saigon, after which she came up to me and said
impulsively, "Oh, don't let them drive you back to your hotel,
let me drive you." Her eyes were dancing like a prankish
child's. But the next moment she looked downcast and sighed.
"Maybe I'd better not, my husband would be very angry with
me."

She once confided in me that she really didn't enjoy the life of a prime minister's wife. So I asked her what kind of a life she would lead, given the choice.

"A quiet one," she answered, without hesitation. "With my husband. Maybe on a farm, maybe in a small town. In a small house of our own, raising our children and just being happy."

In 1969, when Mai and Ky (then Vice President) came to the United States as guests of Nixon, who had just taken office, Mai surprised and charmed the press with her utter lack of guile. When reporters asked her what she wanted most to do in Washington, she said it was to go to a department store and buy a few toys to take back to her children. One of the reporters said, incredulously, "That's all you want to do?" "No," she replied, "but even going to the department store to buy a few things might not be possible, because we have no private life and my husband has told me not to go shopping because then we will be criticized."

On that same trip, I gave a reception at my Watergate penthouse in Mai's honor, to which I had invited all the Cabinet wives and the wives of the Senate and House leaders, as well as a few ambassadors' wives, and some community leaders.

They swarmed over Mai like locusts, exclaiming, "Oh, what a figure!" and clamoring to know her waist measurement. "It can't be more than nineteen inches," said someone. Mai, in her charmingly simple way, said, "Oh yes, it's twenty inches." And she stood in the midst of all that vulgar interest with perfect poise, beautiful and willowy, the only expression in her fluttering hands, and a faint smile on her lovely face that so resembled a cautious gazelle's.

Ky himself was not having such an easy time, either. I took him to California to meet Governor Ronald Reagan, who was fresh from a trip to the Orient and eager to talk about Asia and Vietnam.

From Washington, D.C., we flew to Sacramento on an Air Force plane sent by the Governor, to attend a dinner at his private home. (The down-to-earth Reagans had decided from the start that the Governor's Mansion was a firetrap and had elected to remain in their own house.) There, we were still on our cocktails when the demonstrators gathered in front of the house, waving placards and chanting abuse: "General Ky Go Home!" "Down with Vietnam!" and so on, and becoming noisier by the minute. Ronald and his wife Nancy, both visibly embarrassed, took turns apologizing to Ky for the disturbances, then said nothing more about the whole business, which was the best they could do under the circumstances.

After dinner, when Nancy and I went upstairs to her room, I saw once more the kind of price often exacted by the harsh agenda of a public life. The room was crowded with exercise machines of every imaginable sort, all to keep her bad back in check. The problem was chronic and the chance of improvement slight, considering the kind of schedule she was required to keep. She told me about the pain, how it was there all the time, varying only in degree—an amazing confession, coming as it did from a woman who projected health, beauty, and boundless energy. But Nancy was and is an amazing person, capable of remaining true to her gracious and courageous self under the most difficult of circumstances.

The demonstrators were still going strong as the party broke up, and the Kys were forced to leave by the back door, like thieves in the night rather than official guests of the President of the United States.

Fate continued its strange games. The July 7, 1977 issue of the Washington *Evening Star* ran a picture of the Kys. The headline over the United Press International photograph read: *Nguyen Cao Ky—Grocer*. The story traced the obvious ironies: Nguyen Cao Ky, the diminutive jet ace who rose to be Prime Minister and Vice President of South Vietnam, operates the cash register at a liquor store and delicatessen in Norwalk, California, a suburb of Los Angeles, while his wife, Dang Guyet Mai, packages orders.

But there were other ironies absent from the story, not the least of which was that Mai at last had the kind of life she had dreamed of in her more conspicuous existence: anonymity, a modest standard of living, plenty of time with her husband. But what a price to have paid!

Settled on the other side of the country, in Springfield, Virginia, are former Prime Minister Khiem, my astrological twin, and his wife, leading lives not unlike the Thieus'. When last I saw Khiem two years ago, he was "adjusting his life," as he put it, and enjoying the innocuous pleasures of cooking and gardening. I had the Khiems over for dinner and it was a melancholy sort of occasion, filled with reminders of changed fortunes, broken lives, and the startling passage of time. The Khiems' two children, Jackie and Kenneth, had gone to school in Washington, D.C., and I had known them well as children. Now Jackie was the mother of two, living with her banker husband, Trung, in Paris. And Kenneth, just graduated from UCLA, was a handsome, serious young man, full of unanswered and perhaps unanswerable questions about the war they had survived. "I was too young," he confided to me, "when we surrendered, and never understood exactly what was happening. I wish I could find out more. But my father won't tell me. He never tells me anything. He won't talk about the war."

I remembered my own adolescence through the war in China, confusing enough, despite being so much better defined and thus more easily confronted than the Vietnam War. I understood his struggle to make sense out of a senseless, inconclusive story.

"Kenneth," I said, "you must be patient. It's probably too painful for your father to talk about it right now, but I'm sure some day he will. It won't be too long."

Mrs. Khiem had wrenching stories to tell about relatives left behind in Vietnam to who knew what miseries? Prison camps and retraining centers, if they were lucky. Thousands had believed in deliverance, only to be betrayed by a confused set of policy decisions in Washington which left until the very last moment—four days before the final collapse of Saigon—the evacuation of fifty thousand refugees. In the end, those who had been promised help did not get any, while others who might have remained behind with less risk bought their way out of the country with the age-old currency of connections and bribery. It was a tragic exodus, made more tragic by those who had survived it only to die within the year: Khiem's mother, Mrs. Khiem's mother, and Thieu's mother, who had expired in Rome.

In Vietnam, life had been deformed by war and hardship. But it was still their home, their country, their fight for freedom. The war was over now; a new life had begun in the United States. But the leaders of Vietnam now were middle-aged refugees, jobless, dispirited, and carrying with them the onerous reminder of a tragedy that Americans would just as soon forget.

Many of them would open restaurants that recreate a macabre nostalgia, providing for the generation of Americans who had done their time in Vietnam the flavors and smells they had grown to savor despite the unsavory conditions of war.

It was in one of these restaurants, in Georgetown, that I encountered the last of my old Vietnamese friends, Colonel Chiu. He was waiting on tables, obviously working himself to the bone. But when he saw me his face lit up, the way it used to whenever I arrived at Tan Son Nhut Airport in the old days. He was a little harried but as cheerful as ever, unashamed by his diminished station in life. I asked him how he was doing.

"I have a wife and six children to support," he said simply, "and this is as good a way as any of doing so."

The Book of Odes

39

I have often wondered what sort of gyroscopic variations my life would have followed over the last decade or so, had I lived in some place other than Watergate. For Watergate has meant for me not just a way of life but a frame of reference in my continuing political education.

In 1966, when I bought my penthouse at the Watergate, the strange riverfront structure with its toothy balconies already bore the stamp of elitism. It was the first of its kind in Washington: a seventy-million-dollar complex of luxury cooperative apartments enhanced by swimming pools, specialty shops, a view of the Potomac, and proximity to the White House. But it was only after the installation of the new Nixon administration that Watergate came into its own as the residential seat of power, becoming to the Nixon era what Georgetown had been in the Kennedy years.

Little by little, the influx of Nixonites began until it seemed that everybody who was somebody in the administration lived at Watergate: White House Chief of Protocol Emil Mosbacher and his wife Patricia; Attorney General John Mitchell and Martha; Finance Committee Chairman Maurice Stans and his wife Kathleen; Secretary of Transportation John Volpe and his wife Jeanne; Chairman of the Federal Reserve Board Arthur Burns and his wife Helen; Senator and Mrs. Robert Dole of Kansas; Senator Ed Brooke of Massachusetts; White House speechwriter Patrick Buchanan and his wife Shirley; and Nixon's personal secretary, Rose Mary Woods.

The Democrats were not without representation, however. We had Senator Russell B. Long of Louisiana and his charming wife Carolyn; Senator Alan Cranston of California; and, as if anyone could forget, the Democratic National Committee headquarters on the sixth floor of the Watergate office building.

Yet, for all its social airs, Watergate had its shortcomings and those of us on the inside carried the usual tenant grievances and grudges around with us, airing them at every opportunity in hallways and elevators. Martha Mitchell's pet complaint was the noise. The balconies, she thought, were so close together that even whispers carried. Her neighbors in turn complained about Martha's vocal sound system, especially when it was amplified to address the maids. Kathleen Stans complained about the trapezoidal and triangular rooms that "zigged and zagged" and made her dizzy. And Jeanne Volpe joked about the laundry line on the terrace. (Once she had hung out some unwieldy white curtains on the terrace to dry, and, as coincidence would have it, her husband, the Secretary of Transportation, just happened to be flying overhead in a helicopter with the President of the United States. In pointing out his apartment, he drew attention to the sheets. The story got around and, as stories have a way of doing, grew way out of proportion.) We all complained about the roar of jets landing at the National Airport, about the river stench that wafted up to the balconies on hot summer days, and about the petty nuisances of maintenance that plague all tenants.

But none of these problems was as disturbing as the problem of security. Despite the closed-circuit TV cameras and round-the-clock monitors at the front desks, an alarming number of thefts and burglaries had occurred.

So on Monday, June 19, 1972, when I first read about the break-in at the Democratic National Committee on the sixth floor of the Watergate office, I figured it was only the latest in a series of burglaries, and thought nothing more of it until the following Monday at the Republican National Committee Headquarters in northeast Washington. There, during a small committee meeting, I remember overhearing a snatch of conversation that went something like this:

"Hey, this Gordon Liddy ... did you read about him?"
"Who's he?"
"His name's familiar; wasn't he working at Headquarters?"
"Well, he's got himself in trouble ... mixed up with the break-in at the DNC office at Watergate."

It was the last I heard on the subject until about two weeks later, when, once again at the White House, we were being briefed in preparation for the upcoming GOP Miami convention. At the end of the briefing, John Ehrlichman stood up and asked if there were any questions.

I raised my hand. "John," I said, "I wondered if you could tell me any more about the break-in at Watergate? I live there, so I'm interested in knowing what it's all about."

Laughter rippled through the room. I heard someone say, "Nothing like starting with the really important questions."

Another voice said, "Who cares about Watergate?"

I remember Ehrlichman's reassuring smile as he delivered his answer. "Anna," he said, "by the time we get to Miami for the convention, this will all be water under the bridge. All of this will be cleared up. So don't worry about it."

I wasn't sure what to make of this. But Ehrlichman had dismissed my question in such an offhand way that there was obviously no cause for concern. I felt a little foolish for having brought the matter up. Well, whatever it is, I thought, it couldn't be worse than the burglary that had taken place in Rose Mary Woods' apartment: According to news reports, she had lost seven thousand dollars' worth of jewelry.

It was at Watergate that I began entertaining in earnest, though entertaining as the Merriweather Post generation had known it was on the decline—a casualty of recession. But my parties were in any case never very large. With rare exception, they were limited to three tables of twelve each, and the emphasis was on detail rather than extravagance.

Over the years, I have found that my formula for successful parties remains much the same: to follow my instincts, to trust the natural rather than the contrived. For example, I have never been a slavish adherent to the principle of pairing. When I find my guest list to have a disproportionate male-female ratio, I never try to even it out for form's sake. And instead of numbering the tables for seating purposes I set them apart by motifs, usually through flower arrangements: chrysanthemums on one table; irises on the next; camellias on the third, and so forth. The food I serve (and often cook myself) is almost always Chinese, and based on the three sound precepts of Chinese gastronomy: A dish must be pleasing to the eye, fragrant to the nose, and appealing to the palate.

After dinner, I usually provide music and dancing or some other form of entertainment, such as parlor games, or dancing lessons given by an instructor hired for the evening.

But one rule I have consistently observed is to limit the cocktail hour to exactly that, a practice that seems both fair and sensible, fair because guests who arrive punctually shouldn't be penalized for the sake of those arriving one or two hours late, and sensible because it minimizes premature drunkenness.

Shen Chungying, a seventeenth-century *bon vivant,* wrote a number of treatises offering hints on food and drink to hosts and guests. The guidelines, for all their quaintness, make eminently good sense even today. On games involving alcohol, for example, Shen Chungying warns: "Sometimes a guest is fined to drink, but cannot take it. He begs to be allowed to drink the next time, which is a good idea for both host and guest. Sometimes the officer of the game insists on his drinking until the man throws up. This is very silly." Clearly a man of moderation, Shen Chungying also cautions that "one should drink within one's limits when on an excursion to dangerous high places; when on a voyage; when the ground is full of thistles;

when something important has to be attended to on the morrow; when traveling alone without servants; and when recently recovered from an illness."

But restraint, as everyone knows, can be carried too far, and so, "if a host cannot drink himself, he should ask some of the guests who can to take his place at dinner to prevent the dinner from getting too dull. There is not much fun in sitting down to a sumptuous dinner in a freezing atmosphere."

In order to avoid this kind of freezing atmosphere, I usually ask each guest, at the start of dinner, to stand up and say a few words about himself: who he is and what he does. It is amazing what a simple request like that produces (vivid proof, if nothing else, that it is easier to be long-winded than brief), and I am always forced to remind the guests that what I want is a few words, not a speech.

Once dinner is underway, I firmly believe that the key to enjoyment is light conversation, because, as I once said to a reporter interviewing me, nothing kills the appetite like discussions about rheumatism, backaches, and death. Anyway, I have always had a low tolerance for lengthy conversations about bad news of any sort. One should try to maintain a sense of what is appropriate at the dinner table, or, as Shen Chungying would have put it: "At a dinner with new relatives or children, one should not talk of poetry and history, which will embarrass those who cannot follow."

Along with a sense of propriety should be a sense of ceremony: Few things are as important as the presentation of a meal. It can make a world of difference—at least one thousand dollars' worth of difference, as I once discovered. I was setting up a fund raising dinner at one thousand dollars a plate, and on my list was the president of Hill and Knowlton, Bob Hill. He turned me down with a perfectly legitimate excuse: "I can't pay a thousand dollars for a meal which serves meat," he said, "when I'm on a diet and can only eat cottage cheese."

"That's no problem," I told him. "If cottage cheese is all you can eat, I'll see that you get served cottage cheese."

Hill found this an amusing idea, but one that could hardly be executed at a fancy fund raiser. So I struck a deal with him: If he came, I would see that he got his cottage cheese.

I then telephoned Senator Everett Dirksen. "For a thousand dollars," I said, "would you be willing to help me serve a dish of cottage cheese?" Dirksen thought this was a small service to perform for the price and agreed to the scheme.

On the night of the dinner, I took an ornate sterling silver plate, surrounded it with fresh roses, and scooped onto the middle a mound of snowy cottage cheese. The plate was then carried to the table and ostentatiously served to Hill by none other than Senator Dirksen in apron and chef's hat.

Hill was overjoyed. "That's worth more than a thousand dollars!" he kept exclaiming with delight.

"Of course it is," I agreed. "Your picture will be all over the papers. You can't buy that kind of publicity for a million dollars." His picture was indeed splashed across the papers.

The idea of donning a costume and playing a bit part seems to have unfailing appeal at parties. I have noticed that most guests will serve as bartender or butler at the drop of a hat. At a dinner I once gave in honor of Robert Prescott, president of the Flying Tigers Line (and my then boss), I had a minor crisis on my hands. A heavy snowstorm had come down, and by late afternoon it was clear that none of the help I was counting on would show up. In desperation, I dropped everything I was doing a few hours before the guests arrived and I made up an apron and cap for the bartender, another for the maid.

When Prescott arrived, I handed him an apron, pushed him toward the table of drinks, and asked him to get to work. Another friend of mine, a woman, was given the maid's uniform and told to do the same; a third friend acted as doorman and took care of the coats. The amateurs performed eagerly and admirably, making the evening an unqualified success. The players had not only revelled in their parts, but the maid (who in real life employed three of her own) pronounced herself vastly more appreciative of the profession, the doorman said it was amazing what concentration it took to match people with their coats, and the president of the Flying Tigers had carried out his duties with such aplomb that he wondered if he hadn't missed his calling.

It was one of those unplanned victories, ending on just the right note with the guests' timely departure. For, as Shen Chungying would say, "Guests should leave when it is just right. Some guests overstay their welcome, causing great inconvenience to the host and his servants. This is especially hard in extreme cold or hot weather." And as I said, it was a cold, snowy evening.

It was also during my early Watergate years that I came to know Tongsun Park. I had met him in the early sixties, at the home of then Korean ambassador Dr. Chang Yang, a Hawaiian-Korean physician who had known General Chennault and been a close friend of the late president Syngman Rhee.

Chang Yang introduced me to a young man with a chubby baby-face wearing oversized glasses and an expensive suit. "Meet an able young Korean," said Chang Yang. "He is anxious to do something for our country."

Tongsun Park and I found we had much in common. He had studied at Georgetown University, where I had produced a Chinese-English research dictionary. I had been to his country several times, both before and after the Korean War, with my husband, where we were house guests of President Rhee.

It was a particularly bitter winter, and Rhee was in a matching frame of mind. The Americans had cut off the electric heating in the Blue House (the Korean Government's White House)—a gesture of spite, Rhee was convinced, following the disagreement between the Koreans and Americans about the exchange rate between U.S. dollars and Korean yen. I remembered his words: "No country should depend upon another for survival."

Tongsun Park seemed to find all this fascinating; at least he listened very attentively as I went on to mention other connections to Korea. The successor to Chang Yang, who was ending his ambassadorial term in Washington, D.C., was Chung Il Kwan, another good friend of mine and, as it turned out, a family friend of Tongsun Park's.

"When the new ambassador arrives," said Park, "we must all get together." We did, and from then on Park called on me frequently, and for reasons neither of us had any illusions about: He wanted entrée into the higher political and social circles.

He was a personable young man, and I was quite happy to introduce him to those among my friends who wielded power of one sort or another. They all found him impressive. He was obviously very smart, very ambitious, in possession of all the tools necessary to realize his ambitions: cultured, socially alert, and utterly charming.

He also had a fine knack for turning awkward situations to advantage. When Maryland McCormack bought the old Japanese Embassy at the corner of Massachusetts Avenue and R Street, she threw a housewarming party where my escort, Tongsun Park, was the only male to arrive in a dark blue suit.

Park took one look at all the black ties as he shook hands with Maryland, and said evenly, "I didn't wear my black tie because I thought it would detract from my embroidered underwear."

It would have been a joke of questionable taste, except that the delivery was perfect. Tongsun Park sounded like a man as renowned for his underwear as Gucci is for his shoes—and everyone burst out laughing.

Years later, I reminded Park about his embroidered underwear when he was discoursing on the appalling lack of security around CIA headquarters in McLean, Virginia. We were having dinner at my place—Park, CIA Chief Vice-Admiral William F. Raborn, and I—and Park was going on about how most security measures around top-security areas were sadly inadequate.

"But in McLean of all places? How can you say that?" I asked.

Park thought for a while, obviously weighing in his mind whether to tell a story or not. "I'll tell you how I can say that," he said finally. "I was held up there."

"Where? At the CIA?"

"Right behind the CIA headquarters, on a little road. I had a flat tire suddenly and stopped to change it. All of a sudden, two men came out of nowhere. They pulled a gun on me, took my money, my jacket and trousers, my shirt, my identification, credit cards, everything. I had to change tires in my socks and underwear, and drive home that way."

When Vice-Admiral Raborn and I had recovered from our laughter, I asked Park whether he had at least been wearing his embroidered underwear.

"I don't think it's so funny," he grumbled. "All that nonsense about the whole area within ten miles of the CIA being safe and protected. . . ."

One of Park's obvious talents was his ability to penetrate certain political and social spheres ordinarily closed to outsiders. His password at first was culture. He was known to overwhelm people with his gifts of Korean curiosities and objets d'art. He entertained elegantly at restaurants and in his tastefully appointed townhouse at the corner of Twenty-second and R Streets. He sponsored cross-cultural gatherings and ethnic entertainments, like the "Little Angels," a beguiling choir of Korean children.

His generosity seemed authentic, directed as much toward his own family as toward potentially valuable contacts. When his brother Ken Park came to Washington, for example, Tongsun Park presented him with the most expensive set of golf clubs available on the market.

Ken Park was the only Gulf Oil representative in Seoul, a

wealthy entrepreneur who had inherited their father's tanker ship business. Tongsun Park told me that he represented his brother's interests in the United States, but had reached a point where he wanted to branch out on his own, to "promote Korean culture and to foster cultural and economic ties between the United States and Korea."

It all sounded very wholesome and harmless, and, when he told me of his plan to start a private club at the corner of Wisconsin Avenue and P Street in Georgetown, I assumed this was part of the scheme to set a cultural exchange in motion. He had engaged an interior decorator to do the whole building, he said, with materials imported from England and Spain, and handcarved woodwork imported from Korea.

The club was an instant success, becoming a favorite watering hole for the movers and shakers of the nation's capital.

Later, when news of the Korean influence-buying scandal broke and Tongsun Park was indicted, I wasn't terribly surprised, for it did not seem inconsistent with his freewheeling generosity. But it did surprise me that he had covered so much ground within so short a time.

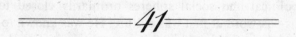

41

If I had to characterize the Carter administration with a single metaphor, I would point to the *Sequioa* incident. The *Sequoia* was the old presidential yacht on which every American president since Herbert Hoover had lounged and entertained. I had been on her several times, the last in 1976, when Barry Goldwater and his wife, Peggy, were celebrating their fortieth wedding anniversary on board. The *Sequoia* was a magnificent, wood-paneled vessel, about fifty years old, and royally equipped. She slept twelve, carried a hundred and fifty comfortably, and cost almost eight hundred thousand dollars a year to operate. She was the ultimate status symbol, and a natural target, like the limousines for White House staffers, for elimination in the new budget-conscious Carter administration.

So the *Sequoia* was auctioned off and sold to the ninth bidder, a Florida real estate tycoon named Thomas Aquinas Malloy, for the sum of two hundred eighty-six thousand dollars. But, when the new owner took possession of the boat, great was his surprise and indignation to discover that the *Sequoia* had been virtually stripped of all her historic fittings. Complaining bitterly, he demanded that the government "put all the darn stuff back where it belonged.

"I didn't know there were pickpockets on board," fumed Thomas Aquinas, who said he regretted not having specified exactly what the government was entitled to remove. "They bring us back the dining room table but take the chairs, they give us back the bed in the President's stateroom and then take the two small chairs and side tables.

"The Harry Truman piano is probably in someone's apartment right now," added Malloy, as a painful afterthought.

This story seemed to me to reflect the peculiar style of the Carter Administration. Make the grand gesture that will leave people with the impression that you are in favor of tight budgets and low spending, but secretly hang onto the trimmings.

Perhaps I am only disgruntled because I myself have felt the pinch. Time was when I could pick up the phone and call the White House for any number of favors: permission to dine at the White House mess hall, to arrange a special tour for friends, or to reserve the Presidential Box at the Kennedy Center—if it was not being used—for a group of friends.

The Presidential Box was a perquisite to be cherished: twelve perfectly positioned red velvet seats, the bonus of a separate sitting room to relax in during intermission, champagne and soft drinks in the refrigerator, and the envy of curious commoners in the galleries below.

Such special privileges are the rewards of power. And who can honestly deny that they are eminently satisfying? The truth is that equal opportunity is good, but special privilege even better.

====== *42* ======

This is the winter of 1978, the winter of Father's death. San Francisco is foggy, as always, and colder than usual. From the airport, where Cynthia has just met me, we take a limousine toward the Bay Bridge, toward Oakland and the hills beyond, toward the suburb of Piedmont, where Father lived and died and now waits to be buried.

As we cross the bridge, the fog closes in, so thick that it blocks out the Bay, that it hides even the bright orange antirust paint on the bridge girders. But now and then it lifts to expose, briefly, a color postcard that could be London or Rio or Hong Kong. Then the fog comes down again, and the picture is erased, opens once more, closes and opens, again and again, showing us, bit by bit, the vast distances below, beyond, and behind. The slate gray winter waters, Alcatraz Island sitting abandoned, the gardens of Sausalito, Oakland's ugly dun buildings, the shipyards of a huge naval base. . . .

Cynthia and I look out our windows, saying very little. We are both preoccupied, I with Father's death, and she, if I know her at all, with the same. We were together for Mother's death, too, sunk in silence then as now.

Forty years and ten thousand miles separate the deaths of our parents.

Suddenly, I am back in China, in the wartime capital of Kunming, seeing my sisters off at the airport. They have survived a war and now are filled with excitement, San Francisco-bound. Only one thing mars the moment: I am not going along.

They have pleaded with me time and again to change my mind, and now, just before the plane takes off, they remind me there is still time. But I am resolute. Mother's death is still fresh in my mind, and I have not forgiven Father. My sisters know this and have tried to argue away the anger. They assume my decision is a vengeful act, an act of bitter protest.

But it is more than mere anger that keeps me in Kunming, it is another, more powerful instinct: the instinct of curiosity. I want to see what lies in store for me alone in China, with all the risks and challenges. I want to question, learn, and experience *on my own.*

All my life I have been inquisitive, a trait that has led me into improbable, difficult, often dangerous situations. I am thinking now of Indonesia in the autumn of 1965. It is the year of the abortive Communist coup attempt, and the streets of Djakarta are stained with Chinese blood. The Chinese community, long resident on the archipelago, is blamed for the coup, and Moslem mobs are running amok in a frenzy of reprisal.

The newspapers are full of horror stories. Rampaging students are burning Chinese stores and throwing proprietors, and their families, alive onto bonfires. Across the islands of Indonesia, villagers wielding *parangs* and *kris* are beheading Chinese schoolgirls and their mothers. The slaughter claims hundreds of thousands and the muddy waters of the River Solo turn from beige to reddish brown as the bloated bodies are swept down to the sea.

As I step off the plane in Djakarta, the carnage is in full ferment. My host leads me to a waiting car and the driver takes us to the towering Hotel Indonesia, which stands like a misplaced model among the uncompleted skyscrapers that crowd the dusty city. In my glass-walled suite high above the strangely unfinished capital, my host warns me of the riots taking place only blocks away. Djakarta, he says, is a charnel house, and he beseeches me not to leave the hotel without his personal escort.

I am aware of the danger, I assure him. He need not worry. But after he leaves, promising to return later, I know I cannot simply sit there. I have come to Java on business, as an airline representative, as a lecturer on Asian affairs, and as a journalist contributing to the *Voice of America* and to newspapers in Taiwan. And what reporter can resist the dual temptation of good copy and a first-person narrative?

I make my way downstairs through the air-conditioned lobby, redolent of clove-flavored tobacco smoke. Women in earth-colored batik caftans and *sarong kebaya* and men in black fez caps are bustling about.

Outside, I find my driver sitting behind the wheel of the car my host has arranged for me. At first he refuses to go anywhere. He has his orders. It takes the persuasion of *pugli,* the local equivalent of tea money, to change his mind. Reluctantly, he turns down the curving driveway out of the flowering hotel grounds, along sunbaked boulevards lined with spreading flame trees . . . toward the scene of the latest rioting.

The narrow streets of the Chinese quarter are choked with students who have deposited the gruesome debris from their bonfires along the stinking cement-walled canals left by the Dutch. We pull up before a tidal wave of rioters, and as I open the door to get out of the car, the outraged slogans and shouts of protest are almost deafening.

The driver pulls me back roughly into the car, and I see in his face the kind of anger provoked by a sudden fear for one's life.

Afterwards, when my host discovers that I have flouted his orders, he is even angrier. Am I crazy? What am I trying to do? Deliberately taunt a mob? I, an American Chinese with no outward markings to set me apart from a local? Do I know how foolish and naïve my behavior has been?

I am contrite. I promise to behave.

But the truth is that I do know. I know the risks I am taking, the fate I am tempting. Yet I am simply following that inquisitive instinct, a calling that makes me appear to defy logic, reason, and common sense.

I think of another incident earlier in the same year. I have come to Saigon in the wake of the Buddhist uprising against the government of the generals. Saigon is still beautiful, like the face of a woman showing the wear and tear of prolonged misery, yet bearing in its lines a faded refinement. The core of the old French colonial city, with its orange tiled roofs and white walls blossoming with bougainvillea, wisteria, and other gaudy flowers of the tropics, is still enchanting.

In the heart of town, several Buddhist monks have recently immolated themselves for the TV cameramen that crowd the city in search of air time. I want to meet the man masterminding these dramatic acts of protest. Thich Tri Quang is one of the two leaders of the Buddhist uprising, the younger, more threatening figure whose headquarters and ever-changing whereabouts remain shrouded in secrecy.

Through an intermediary I send word to him that I would be grateful for a private interview. Thich Tri Quang surprises me with his reply: I can have my interview, but on his terms. The meeting is to take place in secret at his headquarters. And I must go alone, without escort or interpreter.

I agree readily, and the next day he sends a man to fetch me. On the cramped outskirts of the sprawling city, we come to a labyrinthine complex of one of the great Mahayana Buddhist pagoda systems. The guide leads me through a rabbit warren of tiny pathways sentried with small shrines and *stupas,* and littered here and there with fallen bricks.

Through roofed alleys, we enter one paved courtyard after another—watched, I feel sure, by invisible eyes that blink behind the countless dark corners and shadowy windows.

It is a no-man's land of sinister religion and violence, where even heavily armed government troops fear to tread—a doubly inhospitable world for a woman.

At last we come to Thich Tri Quang's austere quarters, buried deep in that bewildering maze. Thich Tri Quang is a small, slight man and it would be hard to imagine that he will one day survive a sixty-seven-day hunger strike. The interview lasts three hours. We talk and argue, about politics, about religion, and about other matters of life and death.

Afterwards, he informs me that I am the first woman he has allowed into his quarters. He never says why I am the exception.

The next day, I see Air Marshall Nguyen Cao Ky and tell him of my three-hour conversation with his archenemy. Ky looks incredulous. "You're doing much better than I," he says. Then he shakes his head, struck by another oddity: Not only have I managed to interview his inaccessible enemy, but I have the nerve to come and tell him about it.

Curiosity and nerve. These two qualities used to cause General Chennault to shake his head. "Anna," he would say, "we pilots have to do the most lunatic daring things, but you take the cake." It was a backhanded compliment of the highest order.

He would have been proud and pleased, I think, by this book—the way he was when my first book appeared in Taiwan so many years ago.

But it is not to mourn him that I have written this book. Nor is it to mourn Grandfather Liao, in some ways the most important man in my life. It is not even to mourn Mother, or Fong Tan, or, even now, my father, whom I can weep for at last.

I have written this book to fulfill a promise to a very dear friend. We have been close since first we met, though we knew from the beginning there would never be marriage. Perhaps this is what has made the stolen moments over the years so precious, the moments when it is enough to be alone with each other, just to say, "I miss you."

Fame has not changed him in the ten years I have known him. When I see him on television, hear him on the radio, or read about him in the papers, he is true to my memory of him, to the man who captured my imagination ten years ago and who does so now, when he flies ten or fifteen thousand miles just to spend a day with me.

In all this time, he has asked only one thing of me. "Please write your book," he says each time we meet.

For years I have put it off, saying, "Someday . . . I'll write about all that I've learned; about my education. Someday there'll be a book."

This is the book I meant—and it is for him that I have written it.

Epilogue: Normalization

The first suspicions dawned on me on Friday afternoon, December 15, 1978, during a Republican Eagle Committee meeting at the Madison Hotel. The two million dollars in private donations earmarked each year to support ongoing Party activities had been raised from each of the two hundred members; the newly elected Republican Senators and Congressmen had been introduced; Republican National Committee Chairman Bill Brock had spoken, followed by ex-President and Mrs. Ford; and on came Senate Minority Leader Howard Baker to announce a slight change in the afternoon schedule, due to a summons from the White House.

The meeting broke for lunch, and as we were leaving the room, there was some discussion about what the summons meant.

"I bet you," I said, "that it's not SALT, not the Middle East, not Iran. I bet you it's China."

This was not a wild premonition but a half-educated guess. For since the beginning of December, rumors had been rife of an impending rapprochement with Communist China.

"Do you think it's going to be about normalization?" someone asked.

"I wouldn't be surprised," I had to admit. "By now everyone's more or less expecting it. But when they begin to talk about normalization, they should go slow."

I was assuming at that point that the process of discussion and analysis that would normally take place on such a momentous issue had just begun, and didn't realize that my worst suspicions had been not only confirmed but surpassed by then.

Meanwhile, another curious thing had happened. Gerald and Betty Ford, who had flown in from Florida for a few days, left before lunch, though we had been expecting them to stay. It was only later, when Carter had made his announcement and Ford had come out in favor of the decision, that I understood the sudden departure. Ford had been to the White House two days before, on Wednesday; the President had asked him if he would publicly endorse the decision; Ford had agreed. But he knew he would have to give his endorsement as a private citizen, since approval of normalization could hardly be the official position of the Republican Party. This meant that he had to leave the meeting before the news was announced that afternoon.

Anyway, at 2:30 P.M., I talked to Baker on the telephone and was told that the President had asked him and the other leaders of both Senate and House to return to the White House at 6:00 P.M., when he would give them some important news.

By 4:00 or 5:00 in the afternoon, I was beginning to get calls from the press, who had been informed of a press conference at 9:00 P.M., asking if I knew what it was the President was supposed to announce that evening.

"You have more news than I do," I told them.

Then, at 5:00 P.M., I talked to Minister S. K. Hu—Ambassador James Shen was in Arizona—of the Chinese Embassy. He had been asked, he said, to meet with Warren Christopher, Deputy Secretary of State, after the President's press conference. I realized then that the impending news was probably more disturbing than I had imagined.

By 7:30 P.M., the Eagle Committee members had left the Madison Hotel for dinner at the Metropolitan Club and it was there that Baker finally broke the news. Carter was going to announce at 9:00 P.M. that the United States was to assume full diplomatic ties with Communist China and sever diplomatic relations with the Nationalist Chinese government in Taipei.

The news left me in a state of numbness, though I had been preparing myself for something like it. Almost automatically I asked Baker, "What about the Mutual Defense Treaty?"

"Apparently, Teng Hsao-ping [Vice-Premier of the People's Republic of China] has agreed that it won't have to be abrogated until one year after normalization," said Baker.

"And then what?" I asked.

Baker shrugged. "It seems we'll keep economic and cultural ties, and continue to supply Taipei with defense weapons."

Stunned though I was by these developments, I felt something tugging at the threads of memory, some parallel situation in the past, until all of a sudden a day in 1972 came back to me. It was early January and Nixon had asked if I would come to the White House to talk to him about China. He asked me the usual questions about what I thought of the future of Chinese Communism in Asia, and I gave him my usual answer: The Communists had consistently sought to stir up unrest and revolution throughout the Asian continent since taking power in 1949—and that the casualties were spread throughout almost every country. Korea remembers, I said. India remembers. The Philippines remember. And Indonesia has never forgotten that Peking almost won control of their country by duplicity, infiltration, and rebellion during Sukarno's regime.

"People in the Free World," I said, "entertain the vague hope that the Chinese Communists will somehow reform themselves. This is because they misunderstand the difference between Soviet and Chinese Communism. The hard-and-fast ambition of the Soviets is to communize the world by imposing their political system on every state, and, acting as a police state, to enslave the world. Keeping in mind this ambition, they can and have revised tactics, so long as the strategy remains unchanged.

"But in the case of the Chinese Communists, there is no question of tactical revision or reform, for any such changes endanger the survival of Communism in China. The traditional Chinese political philosophy based on the Confucian Three Principles of the People—the philosophy of solving social and economic problems in a benevolent way—is still the cultural soil in which Communism grows. If the Communists try to revise and reform, therefore—to shake the soil up even briefly—they are risking the uprooting of Communism which, after all, is not that deeply and firmly embedded in the ground."

Nixon listened carefully, then, as if he had absorbed nothing of my warning, asked me what I thought the Nationalist Chinese position would be if the United States were to approach the Mao Tse-tung regime in a spirit of friendship.

"Mr. President," I said, "if you decide to abandon Taiwan, it will be tantamount to the United States telling the Free World that it can no longer depend on it for support. You will be telling your erstwhile allies they can either make peace on the best terms possible with the Communist world, or prepare to die if they still believe freedom is worth the price.

"In the case of the Nationalist Government," I went on, "it is impossible to predict what measures she will take to protect herself, but they could include the development of nuclear weapons or even some military or political arrangement with the Soviet Union against the common Communist Chinese threat.

"Please move cautiously," I entreated him. "If we give the impression that we are softening, it could badly hurt our position in the Pacific. If the United States withdraws from Northeast and Southeast Asia, it would be as serious and dangerous a step as pulling out of Northwest and Southwest Europe. Taiwan is the pivot joining Northeast and Southeast Asia, and its strategic significance is crucial. It is smack in the center of the chain of islands and peninsulas along the coast of East Asia from Japan to Singapore. It is the western front line of defense for the Americas, it is the key to Japan's western strategic flank, and it is the critical point on the rim of the Far East facing the most likely route of aggression to Southeast Asia.

"Abandoning Taiwan," I said in conclusion, "would shake the confidence and trust of our other allies in Asia and, most immediately, would prolong the Vietnam War because the Communists, both Russians and Chinese, would consider it an admission of weakness."

At the end of our discussion, Nixon thanked me for my views and said, "I'd like to have Dr. Kissinger come and join us for a while. Would you mind?"

In came Kissinger for a very brief visit, the main purpose of which seemed to be a group photograph of the three of us, taken by Ollie Atkins, the White House photographer. Nixon was smiling, Kissinger was smiling, and I, little realizing what they were smiling about, felt obliged to do the same.

Ten days later, Nixon, to the surprise of everyone, including myself, announced his historic trip to mainland China—the trip that would produce the Shanghai Communiqué.

Friends of mine began to regard me with some suspicion. "You knew all along?" they asked, accusingly. I swore I didn't. "But you talked to them just a few days ago. They must have said something."

"Yes, we did discuss both Nationalist and Communist China," I told them. "But there was no hint that this would happen."

However, when I saw the photograph of my meeting with Nixon and Kissinger, I realized I would have a tough time claiming innocence. We were all three smiling in a most joyous and incriminating way.

To return to the evening of December 15, 1978, however, at exactly 9:01 P.M. President Carter, sitting before his highly polished wooden desk in the Oval Office, appeared on television to deliver the "good news" that the United States and Communist China had secretly come to an agreement. Assurances followed that the agreement would not "jeopardize the well-being of the people of Taiwan," though "there is but one China, and Taiwan is part of China," with Peking the "sole legal government of China."

The accomplishment was a masterpiece of secret wheeling and dealing, the culmination, as the public later learned, of months of clandestine meetings between National Security Advisor Zbigniew Brzezinski and Communist Chinese envoys Han Tse and Ch'ai Tse-min, in Washington, D.C. So well kept was the secret that when Carter phoned Secretary of State Cyrus Vance in the Mideast to summon him home, he referred to the agreement that had just come through as "the matter that only the five of us know about."

Suddenly I understood why it was that the Nationalist Government had been told only seven hours before (when President Chiang Ching-kuo was shaken out of his sleep in the middle of the night), and why it was even later that U.S. Congressional leaders were informed. What better way for the President to avoid confrontation with voices of dissent? By so doing, he had defied a unanimous Senate resolution calling on him to consult with Congress before breaking this very treaty with Taiwan, and he would not have to wait for Congress to reconvene in January to secure its approval. In effect, he had arrogated to himself the authority to sever a treaty with another nation.

The mutual defense treaty had originally been ratified by a two-thirds vote of the Senate, and Senator Barry Goldwater was the first to challenge the President, filing suit with twenty-five others to prevent the abrogation of that treaty without Senate approval. As Goldwater put it, "It touches every one of our nation's treaty commitments. If the President can break the treaty with Taiwan on his own authority, then he can withdraw from NATO or pull out of any other treaty without consulting Congress or getting its consent." By extension, it would follow that the next President of the United States could abandon the Panama Canal Treaties at his discretion.

But what of precedents—other treaties that have been terminated in the past without Senate approval? As Goldwater points out, those were not bilateral defense treaties with military allies, but were in effect less important bilateral agreements rather than treaties.

Whatever the outcome of the court decision on this constitutional question, the fact is that normalization was achieved through high-handed secrecy and unnecessary haste, by a President who had campaigned so vigorously against secrecy in government—in particular against secret diplomacy as practiced by past Republican administrations.

The haste is even less understandable, given the paltry gains of such precipitate action. For under this sudden arrangement, it is clear that we gave away far more than we received, and among our many losses is the loss of respect—no insignificant matter in any intercourse with the Chinese. In the business of diplomacy alone, Americans have done more courting, conceding, and compromising than the Chinese—a political kowtowing that reached full expression in the way Henry Kissinger, to the amusement of Chinese editorial writers, went from table to table at an official Peking banquet in his honor, toasting his hosts instead of being toasted.

In hard terms, the Communist Chinese have conceded nothing through normalization. Their only apparent concession lies in their grandiose position of "not objecting to" Carter's assurances that Taiwan need not fear invasion from the mainland and that the United States will continue to supply Taiwan with defensive weapons.

By comparison, the sacrifices we have made are disproportionate and harmful in economic, strategic, and political terms. The hope that normalization will make for increased United States economic opportunities, for example, is meaningless considering that two-way trade between the United States and Taiwan in 1978 totalled eight billion dollars or almost seven times as much as two-way trade concluded between the United States and the People's Republic of China.

Even if normalization were to lead to increased trade with the PRC, it would not necessarily be comparable to the increases seen by other countries, like Canada, who have also normalized relations with Communist China. In fact, since most American business overtures to China have been made mostly in cooperation with the experienced and market-wise Japanese, it is safe to assume that the Japanese will use the leverage to their own advantage, keeping for themselves most of the benefits of such transactions.

Nor is normalization a guarantee, as the optimists would claim, of beneficial grain sales by the United States on the scale of those made by Canada and Australia after normalization with the PRC in her bad grain years. For Peking could just as easily conduct a "great grain robbery" in the manner of the Soviets in 1972, a commercial stunt that would ultimately hurt the United States economy. The PRC is in fact unlikely to provide a predictable grain demand. The Chinese Communist economy, because of its relatively undeveloped financial system, is not equipped to handle extensive credit dealings—a handicap that can only inhibit trade with the United States in the long run, especially since American companies are disinclined to do barter trade.

Where imports from the Communist Chinese are concerned, they have few industrial goods useful to us, and the chief commodities they would prefer to export are labor-intensive products, like textiles, which they can arbitrarily price and dump. Operating as they do in a controlled economy, they can manipulate prices to keep their own people employed, at the expense of ours.

Of equally questionable benefit is the recently negotiated claims settlement. The claims and counterclaims from assets frozen in both countries since the Revolution have been balanced off at the expense of United States claimants. For in the settlement, the one hundred ninety-seven million dollars' worth of United States claims in the PRC was held equivalent to the eighty million dollars of PRC assets frozen in the United States. As a result, an American investor with a claim on assets in China will recover only forty percent of that claim.

The losses to the United States through normalization are even more considerable from a strategic standpoint, given Taiwan's military installations and, because of its location, potential monitoring capabilities in the context of SALT or other strategic questions involving both the PRC and the USSR.

The dissolution of our security treaty with the Nationalist government can only shake the confidence of Japan, Korea, and other Asian countries with whom we share commitments. Japan, for example, has obviously seen our acquiesence on normalization as a signal to augment her military capabilities—a step that will necessarily change her attitude toward us.

But beyond these signals of unreliability toward our allies is the somewhat less discussed issue of morality. In a *Washington Post* editorial on the moral dimensions of normalization, former intelligence officer Ray Cline (now with the Georgetown Center for Strategic and International Studies) points out that "there is an open, pluralist society in Taiwan, and the goal toward which Taiwan is consciously and steadily moving in accordance with the Constitution of the Republic of China is representative government with firm guarantees of human rights. To consign a U.S.-oriented, pluralist Chinese society with a free-enterprise trading economy to dictatorial Communist Party control from Peking is not merely amoral—it is immoral."

It is the kind of immorality that men like my late husband, General Claire Lee Chennault, were confronting—men who had the conviction and the imagination to oppose Communism even when it was unfashionable to do so.

Until the day he died, Chennault tried to tell Americans the truth about Asia. He was not playing the role of prophet without honor; he was not trying to be Lawrence of China; he was simply bent on warning both the public and the politicians that Chinese Communism was not a sham product, but a real and deadly poison that could, if allowed to go unchecked, enter the bloodstream of all Asia.

Yet twenty years after his death, the President of the United States, in a supreme irony, is saving Communism in mainland China just when it is failing. With our technology and our credit, we have embarked on a rescue mission to save the leaders of the PRC from having to admit to their own people, for the first time, that Communism and Maoism have kept their country backward, their peasants in abject want, and their proletariat stifled.

We are protecting Peking from a confession it would have had to make: that the eighteen million Chinese on a small island off the Asian mainland shore are enjoying a far more prosperous and rewarding life, with a standard of living three times higher than that of the nine hundred million under Peking's totalitarian rule.

This is the practical conclusion about normalization most have failed to draw: that worse than the betrayal of a loyal ally, it is, simply, wrongheaded. And, if this seems fundamental and simplistic, it is no more so than the lives of men like Chennault, who may have seemed to be tilting at windmills when in fact they were, as Thucydides said of Zeus, "causing our ill wind to change."